IMPROVING PUBLIC MANAGEMENT

IMPROVING PUBLIC MANAGEMENT

Les Metcalfe and Sue Richards

European Institute of Public Administration

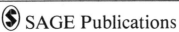 SAGE Publications

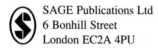

SAGE Publications Ltd
6 Bonhill Street
London EC2A 4PU

SAGE Publications Inc
2455 Teller Road
Newbury Park, California 91320

SAGE Publications India Pvt Ltd
32, M-Block Market
Greater Kailash – I
New Delhi 110 048

British Library Cataloguing in Publication Data
Metcalfe, Les
  Improving public management. — 2nd ed
  1. Great Britain — Politics and
  government — 1964-
  I. Title   II. Richards, Sue
  354.4107   JN425

ISBN 0-8039-8400-6

Printed in Great Britain by
Billing & Sons Ltd, Worcester

Contents

Preface

This book examines the current process of management reform in British central government. Reform has been a continuing theme of Margaret Thatcher's tenure of office as Prime Minister since the Conservative victory in the 1979 general election. It is becoming clear that the changes introduced mark a watershed in the evolution of British government. First, the political impetus behind reform has been sustained long beyond the time when many, inside and outside Whitehall and Westminster, had expected it to fade. Second, the central place accorded to the concept of management in diagnosing the weaknesses of British government and prescribing remedies has set a new direction and instigated changes in the culture of Whitehall which will be difficult if not impossible to reverse. The higher civil service has had to revise its preconceptions and working assumptions about its role and responsibilities. Top civil servants, as well as their subordinates, have had to come to terms with an array of management techniques, policies and principles which in the past they perceived as peripheral to their main functions of advising on policy and protecting ministers. The direction of change has been firmly established. The task in the future will be improving public management.

Within this broad perspective there is a substantial range of choice about how to proceed. Many challenging problems have to be resolved at both the conceptual and the practical levels. There has been a substantial evolution and a process of building on experience since 1979. In this book we consider what has been done and assess the appropriateness and adequacy of the new management philosophies and practices which are being introduced. Improving public management can be facilitated by a deliberate effort to learn from experience. Much has already been done and there is no shortage of examples to stimulate further development. For instance, there is now a good deal of experience in the use of budgets and management information systems as management tools. There is also a much increased understanding of the complexity of managing change in governmental contexts where the delivery of services involves several or many different organizations. The selection and discussion of particular cases is intended to add to understanding of general themes.

In discussing what has been done we use 'Efficiency Strategy' as an umbrella term to characterize the various initiatives that sprang from the programme begun by Sir Derek (now Lord) Rayner. This term is likely to prove too restrictive to reflect adequately the full range of developments in public management which are now on the horizon. But it captures the spirit of most of what has been done so far. Priority has been given to increasing cost-consciousness and selecting management tools and techniques which will economize on resources and promote greater efficiency in their use. As we point out, these are not the only relevant issues in the public management field. There are questions of effectiveness and flexibility in the face of change which cannot be dealt with simply by reducing resource inputs. But it is impossible to deny the relevance of economy and efficiency in a period of economic austerity which seems likely to continue with the expected decline of North Sea oil revenues.

Discussion of management cannot escape being prescriptive by inference if not by intent. Hence it is important to keep close to empirical realities. Prescription should not be separated from description. In assessing the Efficiency Strategy it is necessary to look at what it has actually attempted to do. We have included therefore a good deal of empirical material, some available from published sources — more perhaps than people recognize — and some obtained from unpublished documentary evidence and from interviews with those involved. Descriptive material is important not only to give substance to major themes and illustrate the great diversity of projects that have been undertaken but also to dispel misconceptions about how changes have been made — about methods of managing change.

If the Efficiency Strategy were merely a one-off cost-cutting exercise such questions about methods of managing change would be academic in the traditional civil service sense of irrelevant. But for a continuing process of public management improvement there are important practical lessons which are highly relevant to the future. One of the key methodological features of the Efficiency Strategy is the machinery created to give effect to political intentions, notably the Efficiency Unit established within the Prime Minister's Office and the Financial Management Unit (and later the Joint Management Unit) an offshoot of the Treasury and the Management and Personnel Office. Another important feature of the method by which the Efficiency Strategy has worked is the extent to which departments have been given responsibility for managing change rather than having preconceived reform proposals thrust upon them. Many previous reform efforts have failed precisely because they did not secure the commitment of those directly involved in their implementation. As the objectives of change become more ambitious so, the capabilities and commitment needed to implement them will progressively increase.

Public management is not a self-explanatory, fully-developed concept. Part of the task of this book, therefore, is to consider what management means in government — in effect to build a concept of public management by reflecting on the development of the Efficiency

Strategy. There are, of course, marked differences of view about how public management relates to more familiar management concepts. It is all too common for critics of the performance of public organizations to jump to the unwarranted conclusion that there are ready-made private sector solutions available. Or, alternatively, to seek remedies in prescriptions drawn from general management and ostensibly applicable to all organizations. Both of these sources of ideas are worth investigating. Applying them depends, however, on criteria drawn from a concept of public management.

As the Efficiency Strategy has unfolded it has become clear that there are distinctive public management problems for which new solutions must be found. Improving public management is frontier territory — an area of genuine innovation where civil servants will have to develop and apply new concepts to fit the tasks and political constraints of government. In the past the obstacles to significant and lasting gains in efficiency and effectiveness have often been regarded as insuperable. Now, some of the cultural and institutional sources of resistance to change have been overcome. The challenges are considerable but it is possible to envisage a broadening process of innovation which pushes back the frontier of management thinking. Government might again take on a leadership role in the management field as it has done occasionally in the past.

How far and how fast this process of innovation will actually proceed is difficult to say. But in developing an analytical perspective on public management we seek to provide concepts and criteria to assess the progress that has been made as well as a basis for guiding future action. Our own view is that increasingly what will be needed is more organizational flexibility to adapt to change and cope with new problems in a rapidly changing environment. Government is now approaching the point where it is becoming clear that public management is a creative function of guiding change and not only a constraining function of tightening up cost control systems.

Importantly, this means that improving public management cannot stop short of requiring changes in the constitutional and political environment. The traditional concerns of public accountability cannot be simply swept aside in the supposed interests of greater efficiency. But neither can existing institutions of accountability be regarded as immutable or incapable of improvement. Existing forms of constitutional myth and ritual should be exposed to the same kind of scrutiny and evaluation as more workaday areas of government. Where necessary they should be replaced by more appropriate and effective ways of regulating the exercise of public power. It is in this area, where concerns with performance and accountability meet, that some of the distinctive concerns of public management emerge.

We began the research on which this book is based at the Civil Service College. Some of the material was originally developed for training courses involving civil servants concerned with the implementation of the Efficiency Strategy. We were fortunate in having good access to papers and to people actively involved in moving the Efficiency Strategy forward. This is an opportunity to acknowledge the extensive cooperation and help we have received from within the civil service. It is also the occasion for acknowledging the special help of a number of people in particular. At the beginning of the research the encouragement and support of Brian Gilmore, then Principal of the Civil Service College and David Lewis, Director of Public Administration and Social Policy, was vital. The College's support for the project continued when Noel Moore became Principal. We also had the advantage of the willing cooperation and incisive observations of Clive Priestley, the first head of the Efficiency Unit and his successors, Ian Beesley and Kate Jenkins. We were fortunate in being closer to the action than researchers often are, not only by being inside the system at the Civil Service College but also because of the time we spent working in the Efficiency Unit (Metcalfe) and at the Treasury (Richards). The final phases of the work were completed at the European Institute of Public Administration and the London Business School whose support we also wish to acknowledge. For helping to inform our thinking on specific topics we would like to thank David Bradley, Peter Hennessy, Bob Hewes, Christopher Joubert and William Plowden.

Final responsibility for the book is ours, but its completion would not have been possible without the care and efficiency of the secretarial assistance provided at the Civil Service College by Maureen Barratt and Annette Meramo, at EIPA by Nicolette Brouwers, Margo Tangelder and her staff, with particular thanks to Denise Grew, and at LBS by Anitra Hume-Wright.

Second Edition
This second edition includes an additional final chapter describing the developments of the late 1980s and early 1990s, particularly the creation of agencies for operational management within the civil service, and the establishment of a new framework for the relationship between strategic policy setters and the management of operations.

1
Thatcherism and Raynerism

Force of circumstance and political ideology have combined to push many governments towards administrative reform and modernization in recent years. In the United States and Canada, and in several European countries including Denmark, France, the Netherlands and the United Kingdom, initiatives are well under way, while the Belgian government and the European Commission have embarked on modernization programmes more recently. The strategies and detailed objectives of these reform efforts vary from country to country. But they spring from a common background of adverse economic conditions and governmental overload. Governments are under pressure to be less profligate in their demands on national resources and more efficient and effective in managing the limited resources available.

There is a new emphasis on public management as an important function of senior civil servants and even of ministers (Gunn, 1985). The stress on improving public management is partly an acknowledgement of the increasing impact of new information technologies in government and is partly, in one form or another, associated with privatization, since much of the impetus has come from the right of the political spectrum. In Britain, with which this book is primarily concerned, the changes date from the assumption of office by a new Conservative government in 1979. When Margaret Thatcher led the Conservative Party to victory in the 1979 general election, few civil servants anticipated the major changes that were to affect them directly. The Conservatives' election manifesto had propounded the new government's philosophy and spelled out its plans. Monetarist policies, the dominant theme of what has since become known internationally as 'Thatcherism', had major implications for the scope of government and the size of the civil service. 'Rolling back the frontiers of the state' was a colourful expression of the belief that government should get off the backs of its citizens and taxpayers and that every effort should be made to give incentives to private sector wealth creation as against public sector wealth consumption.

Thatcherism included a clear political commitment to reduce the size of the civil service and increase the efficiency of government. A smaller and more efficient civil service was a clear objective. But past experience and their well-developed sense of *déjà vu* (Plowden, 1981) misled senior civil servants into discounting electoral commitments to administrative reform and spending cuts. The sparse achievements of

the earlier attempts at administrative 'revolution' in Whitehall had led
to disillusionment with administrative reform by the mid-1970s (Fry,
1981). Results in other countries were equally uninspiring as the
following comment on a long succession of attempts to reform US
government shows:

> ...those efforts apparently account for an insignificant share of the total
> administrative changes that occur, are seldom followed by systematic
> efforts to assess their effects, seem to be a source of frustration and
> ridicule, become regular and unlamented casualties of experience with
> trying to achieve significant reform and yet are persistently resurrected by
> the political system. (March and Olsen, 1983: 282)

Moreover, civil servants were more used to the critique of the radical
left than the radical right. Indeed, in the early months of Mrs
Thatcher's government, much of the running in public discussion of
the civil service was made by members of the outgoing Labour
government, anxious to analyze and justify their role in an
administration that had been firmly rejected by the electorate.
Perhaps this distracted attention from the radicals now occupying
positions of power, or perhaps senior civil servants assumed that the
Conservative government, like its predecessors, would be pulled into
the centre. Castigating waste in the civil service provided a useful
electoral slogan, but the realities of office would modify extremes and
moderate the new government's views.

Instead, it was top civil servants who had to come to terms with new
and uncomfortable realities. The announcement of a programme to
improve management and efficiency in government was not in itself
an event of dramatic novelty but, to the surprise of most civil
servants, words led to deeds. An Efficiency Strategy was
inaugurated, initially under the guidance of Sir Derek (now Lord)
Rayner. As a result, the term 'Raynerism' rapidly came into common
currency as a personalized way of referring to this campaign. With
prime ministerial backing, its momentum has been maintained. A
powerful combination of careful planning and ideological
commitment provided the driving force behind this component of
Thatcherism. The populist appeal of animosity to public servants lent
emotional reinforcement to the goals of reducing the role of the state
and reversing the trend of rising public spending.

For many civil servants, the impact of Thatcherism on morale,
career prospects and pay are negative. Early in the life of the Thatcher
government a target of 100,000 civil service job cuts was announced.
By the target date of April 1984 the number of civil servants had been
cut from over 730,000 to less than 630,000. This is not as steep as the
cuts many manufacturing businesses have had to make, but it is substantial. Furthermore, the effort to achieve a leaner and fitter civil

service has been accompanied by important changes in expectations. Senior officials, who formerly saw their roles principally as policy advisers, are now expected to give a higher priority to managing resources and improving departmental performance. The Prime Minister herself has maintained a firm commitment to improving management in government departments and changing the attitudes and behaviour of the civil servants involved in running them. Ministers have not been immune from this determined campaign. They too are expected to play roles in managing their departments — a task that some do not contemplate with relish. Politicians as much as civil servants are having to come to terms with new and unfamiliar ways of thinking about their roles and responsibilities.

Thus the evolution of the Efficiency Strategy is forcing a re-examination of basic assumptions about the organization and management of the business of government. Traditional concepts of public administration are being called into question, and there is widening interest in the application of management concepts to government. This does not sweep away the traditional concerns of public administration but it does demand new answers to old questions. In addition because current initiatives are bringing new questions to the fore the limitations of civil service thinking about management have been laid bare.

The Efficiency Strategy is a response to long-standing problems. The need to improve public management and the scope for improvement are rarely challenged. Government is big business. The progressive acquisition of functions by government and the enlargement of the public sector as a whole during this century have created concomitant management problems. Although there is ample evidence that conventional forms of public organization are ill-equipped to deal with the problems facing them, innovation in public administration has not kept pace with the increasing scale, scope and complexity of modern government. The chronic problem of poor administrative performance became a cause of acute concern about overload and ungovernability in the 1970s.

The Efficiency Strategy has broken through the barriers that previous initiatives have failed to surmount because circumstances were created that gave top management in government departments no alternative but to act and provided them with a methodology for doing so. Politically imposed reductions in manpower made departmental responses obligatory. But they also created the risk that Raynerism might be stereotyped as nothing more than an exercise in short-term cuts. The scrutiny programme that Rayner inaugurated, which is explained later in this chapter, provided not only a tool for investigating selected areas of departmental work with an eye to demonstrating the inadequacies of previous management and making savings, but also provided guidelines and models for improving public management. The long-term success of the Efficiency Strategy depends on how effectively it balances these short-term and long-term concerns.

The Efficiency Strategy

The purpose of this book is to examine the development of the Efficiency Strategy thus far and consider what lies ahead. It is worth observing at the outset that our task is an unusual one. There is progress to report. Improving efficiency is certainly not a new idea, but it is not a field of conspicuous success. Administrative reform is a political commitment honoured more in the breach than the observance. In Britain and elsewhere, the record is a disheartening one. Grand schemes have rarely survived the initial phases of implementation. A few years after the start of a reform or reorganization it has often been possible to tell the complete story: generally it has been a post mortem rather than a progress report.

By contrast, the efforts currently underway show signs of taking root and bearing fruit. The Efficiency Strategy started by Sir Derek Rayner in 1979 has continued under Sir Robin Ibbs who succeeded Rayner as the Prime Minister's Special Adviser on Efficiency after the 1983 general election. Mrs Thatcher's enthusiasm for reform shows little sign of flagging and this gives us the opportunity to investigate, evaluate and learn from a significant and continuing development in public management. It also provides the occasion for considering, in wider terms, some of the basic issues of public management: how managerial improvements impinge on policy-making processes and the constitutional implications of giving management a higher profile.

The next section of this chapter investigates the origins of the Efficiency Strategy, particularly the lessons learned from earlier attempts at reform. The focus then moves on to the contribution of Sir Derek Rayner and role of the Efficiency Unit in developing that strategy. Rayner is best known for the efficiency 'scrutiny', examples of which are discussed in detail later in this book. The following section outlines the main features of the scrutiny process and further developments from it. The penultimate section deals with what Rayner called 'lasting reforms', or 'changing the culture of Whitehall'. The final section is a summary to guide the reader through the book.

The Pre-history of Raynerism

Raynerism has to be seen in the context of previous attempts at institutional reform. In the two preceding decades there were several major efforts to reform the organization and management of central government. The civil service has been the centre of reforming attention throughout its existence but the pace accelerated from the Plowden Report onwards. The 1961 Plowden Report on the public expenditure process which led to the setting up of the Public Expenditure Survey aimed to alter fundamentally the nature of planning in government. The Fulton Report on the civil service followed in 1968, with major recommendations for change. A third round came in the early 1970s with Edward Heath's radical proposals for enhancing the strategic decision-making capacity of the Cabinet, through 'super departments' and 'hiving off', through the Central Policy Review Staff, and also through the creation of the Programme Analysis and Review system. Concurrently, major, ill-fated changes in structure and management were taking place in local government and the National Health Service.

Despite the efforts and resources that had gone into these reforms, there was widespread disillusion with each of them. The Public Expenditure Survey system, set up after Plowden, had been blown off course many times and had proved inadequate to the turbulent economic environment of the 1970s. Some of Fulton's proposals had been put into effect — for instance, the setting up of the Civil Service College — but many had not. There is a widely-held view that Fulton was deliberately undermined by senior civil servants unwilling to countenance change (Kellner and Crowther-Hunt, 1980). By the end of the 1970s, 'hiving off' had proved politically impractical since ministers felt compelled to intervene in politically sensitive matters, even when 'hived-off' organizations were constitutionally separate; Programme Analysis and Review had all but disappeared; and the Central Policy Review Staff had been forced into the margins of the policy process by Labour governments whose concern was short-term survival rather than long-term thinking.

Before the 1979 Election it was by no means certain what, if anything, a Conservative government might do. The Rayner approach was not the only possible line of attack on the civil service that was being considered by the Conservative Party. During the 1979 election campaign, Mrs Thatcher was advised on the efficiency of the civil service by Leslie Chapman, a former official at the Property Services Agency whose recently published book, *Your Disobedient Servant* (Chapman, 1978), told how he had fought in vain to cut costs, but was undermined by his superiors in the department who did not take efficiency seriously. He proposed that a strong task force of efficiency experts be appointed to compel departments to cut costs. No doubt, as poacher turned gamekeeper, he would have been a candidate for this task force. This is not what happened. Useful as a whistle-blowing civil servant was in the election campaign, someone of greater standing with a proven track record of business management success was required when the task was not just to criticize but to develop a positive strategy for improvement. The economic philosophy of the new government called for a shake-up of the comfortable worlds of protected management in the public and private sectors. The cold winds of international competition were blowing and an adviser was needed who knew how organizations could survive and prosper in that environment. The mantle fell upon Sir Derek Rayner who, as well as continuing to be a joint managing director of Marks and Spencer, became the Prime Minister's special adviser on efficiency and head of the newly created Efficiency Unit within the Prime Minister's Office.

Rayner — the Man and the Myth
Anyone who relied solely on press reports for information about the early work of Sir Derek Rayner in setting up the Efficiency Strategy would gain a distorted view of the process. With a few honourable exceptions, the newspapers presented a picture of the Prime Minister's champion, bringing with him the good news from the private sector, carrying her colours into the heartland of the enemy, the civil service, and there single-handedly belabouring the inefficient and the wasteful. Exciting as this image was, it owed more to the journalistic need to personalize the process than it did to reality, which is altogether more complex, subtle and sophisticated. The picture of Derek Rayner as a giant among men may have been misleading but it is none the less important, because, for many thousands of middle- and junior-ranking civil servants, popular newspapers were their primary source of information about developments within their own organization: their perceptions were influenced more by the popular press than by their top management, with whom they were unlikely to have much contact. Journalistic distortion did not help civil servants to understand the approach that Rayner actually brought to the task.

It says something about the lack of public understanding of top management styles in the private sector that the myth took hold. The archetypal figure is the romanticized, individualistic entrepreneur, such as Freddie Laker, pushing his way from rags to riches through a combination of corner-cutting and sheer force of personality. The professional, managerial tradition in which Sir Derek Rayner works is different from this. Successfully guiding large and complex organizations through turbulent times requires sustained effort, a good understanding of people and the systems in which they work, and above all an ability to integrate and produce a coherent and achievable strategy which is then pursued with dedication and commitment. It was the successful exercise of these qualities at Marks and Spencer that provided some of Rayner's credentials for the job he was given. In the minds of many ordinary civil servants and the general public, the Efficiency Strategy is identified with him personally. 'Raynerism' continues to be a term in common use years after his departure and when his successor, Sir Robin Ibbs, is firmly established and injecting his own particular concerns into the Efficiency Strategy.

Rayner had not formed his views in the abstract. He combined management experience at the highest level in the private sector with experience at the same level of the civil service, since he himself had been involved in the Heath reforms. He was one of the businessmen imported into the civil service to apply business management practice in the early 1970s. He was also one of the few successes. He formed and was the first head of the Procurement Executive in the Ministry of Defence, with the rank of Second Permanent Secretary, purchasing being one of the traditional strengths of Marks and Spencer. This experience and appreciation of the reality of Whitehall politics put him in a much better position than past reformers to secure real change. He understood the strength of departmentalism — the relative autonomy of government departments and the weaknesses of interdepartmental coordination. Where better to learn this lesson than in the Ministry of Defence?

The Rayner Programme: Scrutinies and Lasting Reforms

The strategy Rayner proposed avoided what was seen as the major error of previous attempts at reform. Instead of advancing a 'grand scheme', a detailed blueprint for reform, he developed a strategy with two elements. The first was quickly to set in train numerous small-scale initiatives designed to produce discernible benefits in a relatively short time and to demonstrate that there were serious shortcomings in the management of the civil service.

A series of scrutinies was conducted within individual departments aimed at identifying and eliminating areas of waste, inefficiency, duplication and overlap. The scrutiny programme was designed to overcome complacency: it produced evidence of past inefficiency on a wide scale and, by the same token, confirmation of generalized doubts about civil service management. It was also designed to show that something could be done about poor performance and to stimulate the action needed.

The second part of the strategy was designed to consolidate and integrate the evidence from scrutinies and build a case for reform that would be credible within the civil service as well as outside it — lasting reforms that would lead to a better managed, more efficient civil service in the future. Scrutinies might deal with particular examples of inefficiency that had already occurred, but to prevent similar cases occurring in the future a fundamental change in civil service management was required. The long-term goal was lasting reforms of structures, systems, personnel policies and deeply ingrained attitudes and beliefs.

A major assumption in Rayner's strategy was that, to a large extent, reform had to be an internal process. Large-scale change could not be imposed from outside, but required actions to mobilize support for change within the system. The Efficiency Unit he created and the way it set about its task reflected a recognition that commitment to change within departments at both official and ministerial levels was vitally necessary if there was to be a transformation in the whole managerial culture of Whitehall. To generate that commitment, external pressure was required, and the Prime Minister made her backing for her Efficiency Adviser abundantly plain to ministers and senior officials. 'Political clout' was a necessary condition for initiating improvements in public management although not a sufficient one for their success. Only by winning the support of those involved in implementing change would lasting reforms be accomplished (Metcalfe and Richards, 1984b).

The Role of the Efficiency Unit
In order to understand the scrutiny programme and its relationship to lasting reforms of civil service management, it is necessary to look at the Efficiency Unit. The design and functioning of the Efficiency Unit embodies some of the central tenets of Rayner's philosophy. To a substantial degree, they have been retained by Sir Robin Ibbs, although the Efficiency Strategy under his guidance has entered a new phase.

Instead of establishing a large central staff under his own control to go into departments and seek ways of making savings, Rayner set up a small unit within the Prime Minister's office. The role of the Efficiency Unit was to prompt departments into carrying out scrutinies, to ensure that these led to action and to provide a means of learning lessons from individual cases which could be disseminated more widely or used to identify new targets. A determination that the Efficiency Unit should remain small was part of a commitment to the principle of winning support from departments for the idea of improving their own performance. It was evident, both from its small staff and the way it operated that it did not absolve departments from responsibility for improving performance. The Efficiency Unit was the fulcrum of a system for creating task forces within departments rather than a centralized organization geared up to carry out its own independent investigations. In this way, the organization of the

Efficiency Unit and its links with departments sought to combine external pressure and internal commitment to change.

The Efficiency Unit was headed by a chief of staff of under-secretary rank — the first, Clive Priestley, was recruited from the Civil Service Department; the second, Ian Beesley, was promoted from within the Efficiency Unit; and the third, Kate Jenkins, was also promoted from within. The unit has remained small: including personal secretaries and a clerical officer, it does not reach double figures. The staff is a mixture of career civil servants and outside consultants. Selection has favoured individuals with a more specialist knowledge and background in economics, accounting, statistics or computing than would be expected in a typical group of generalist civil servants. Although there was an important strand of continuity in promoting the assistant secretary in the unit, the general civil service practice of moving people on to other jobs after two or three years has been retained.

Originally, the Efficiency Unit was established as part of the Prime Minister's Office and was located physically in the Cabinet Office. It was distanced from the Civil Service Department (CSD), whose future looked in doubt. When the Civil Service Department was abolished in November 1981, its responsibilities were divided between the Treasury and the newly created Management and Personnel Office inherited from the defunct Civil Service Department. The under-secretary heading the Efficiency Unit then took over responsibility for the much larger management and efficiency divisions of the Management and Personnel Office. The Efficiency Unit itself moved across Horseguards' Parade into the Old Admiralty Building where the Management and Personnel Office was housed. When Sir Robin Ibbs took office, the Efficiency Unit moved back into the Cabinet Office. It is the symbolic significance of these moves that matter. Doubts about the standing of the Efficiency Unit, which began to circulate following the relocation and linkage with the newly created Management and Personnel Office, were stilled when it became clear that Sir Robin Ibbs could call on prime ministerial backing if it was needed. Her support ensured that civil servants (and ministers) in departments continued to take the Efficiency Unit's work seriously.

One of the traditionally highly prized skills of senior civil servants has been their ability to read the symbolic significance of apparently mundane events — such as office relocation. An almost intuitive grasp of what does and does not matter, given the prevailing distribution of power, is what distinguishes the generalist who will rise to the top from others who have more demonstrable skills, such as economics or statistics, but who cannot see the political straws in the wind. There are interesting parallels between civil servants, whose lack of formal powers (being the servants of their ministers) leads them to develop skills in interpreting the wishes of their masters, and women, also formally powerless in many societies. In both cases, a subordinate postition encourages the development of intuitive, interpretive skills. Paradoxically, the senior ranks of the civil service remain very much a man's world.

Scrutinies — the Cutting-edge of Raynerism?

The scrutiny programme has received a good deal of attention within government and also in public discussion. It is widely regarded as the cutting-edge of Raynerism, and it is the part of the programme that has had most visible impact in terms of cuts in staff and savings. The scrutiny process itself was designed to ensure that fundamental questions about the costs and results of departmental operations would be asked and recommendations for improvement made to ministers. Ministers and their senior officials in turn are obliged to make decisions on required action within a tight timetable. There are many scrutiny stories to tell, and some form the basis of the later chapters of this book. One of the most graphic illustrations of the need to count costs is the £30 rat. A multi-departmental review of the support services in Research and Development bodies found this creature residing in a Ministry of Agriculture laboratory in Reading. There, rats were being bred in-house for experimental purposes, without any full account of the overhead costs being kept. This figure actually worked out at just under £30 a rat, when a private sector laboratory not far away bred similar rats for only £2 each.

While the savings from scrutinies are not a complete measure of the achievement of Raynerism in that they do not demonstrate anything about the achievement of lasting reforms, none the less the figures are significant in themselves. By the end of 1982, when Sir Derek Rayner relinquished his position, over 133 scrutinies had been conducted. They recommended once-and-for-all savings of £56 million and recurrent savings of £400 million and 21,000 posts per annum. Firm decisions had been reached on £29 million once-and-for-all savings, with annual savings of £180 million and 12,000 posts. The recurrent savings recommended by October 1985 were £600 million, of which £300 million have actually been achieved. A further £145 million have been rejected, and the rest are somewhere in the pipeline (Efficiency Unit, 1985). These figures demonstrate substantial achievements. Even if critics would want to revise them downwards, they are of an order of magnitude that makes them worth realizing.

In creating the scrutiny process, Sir Derek Rayner drew on his previous involvement in government in the early 1970s. He concluded that improved management in government depended substantially on securing the commitment of the civil service to the task. And this meant working with, rather than against, the grain of departmentalism. The modus operandi of the Efficiency Unit was deliberately designed to give departments such as Industry, Environment, Defence and Inland Revenue a considerable role in examining and improving their own performance. The Efficiency Unit provided a framework within which departments would carry out their own investigations and it provided guidelines for individuals to work to. This is illustrated by the opening paragraph of the 'Note of Guidance' which Rayner wrote to explain his philosophy to departments and examining officers responsible for carrying out scrutinies:

> The reasoning behind the scrutiny programme is that Ministers and their officials are better equipped than anyone else to examine the use of the resources for which they are responsible. The scrutineers therefore rely heavily on self-examination; on applying a fresh mind to the policy or activity under scrutiny, unfettered by committees or hierarchy; on learning from those who are expert in it; on supervision by the Minister accountable for it; and on a contribution from my office and me.

Ministerial and departmental commitment is secured through the scrutiny programme in several ways:

1. departmental choice of policies and functions to investigate. Initial choices varied widely. Some departments embraced the scrutiny process as a way of coming to grips with a big problem that had been troubling them for some time. One example would be the Manpower Services Commission's scrutiny of the Skillcentre network. Others hoped at first that it would go away, and chose low-key topics, such as their messenger services, to duck out of the task;
2. departmental selection of scrutineers;
3. ministerial decision on scrutineers' recommendations;
4. departmental action to ensure implementation. Latterly, a named official has been given responsibility for implementation.

Of course, departmental choices and actions are not unfettered. In each respect, there is consultation with the Efficiency Unit. But the onus to do the work rests with departments and especially on the selected scrutineers. The Efficiency Unit role involves agreeing the terms of reference, and intervening to strengthen these where it is considered appropriate. After that, the Unit's staff provide a friendly ear and advice when needed. They also check on progress to ensure the timing is on schedule and comment on draft reports. While the scrutineer reports to the minister responsible in this department, Efficiency Unit agreement is also required. In most cases, that agreement is reached quite easily, but there have been some cases of profound differences between the Unit and the scrutineer and his department. One of the best-known examples of such disagreement was in the case of the Department of Education and Science review of Her Majesty's Inspectorate of Schools. Inspection work, where output is not easily measured or demonstrated largely because it involves preventative or information-gathering work, has been difficult to assess.

Importantly, scrutineers have been chosen not for specific technical competences, but for general ability. The choice of 'bright young principals' has been criticized because there are relevant technical skills, especially in the management services area that could have been called on. In part, choices are a recognition of a need to make political as well as technical assessments of what is acceptable and feasible. But, as the scrutiny programme has evolved, individuals from a wider range of levels and experience have been chosen and increasingly, small teams have been assembled to draw in needed skills. Scrutineers have usually reported that the process of conducting their investigations is quite different from their normal work. Though they are usually 'insiders', the status of scrutineer detaches them not only from normal organizational constraints but also from organizational sources of support. Perhaps because they are so clearly responsible for their diagnosis and the recommendations they make, scrutineers almost invariably feel a sense of isolation and loneliness. The usual civil service practice of clearing proposals within the management hierarchy diffuses and blunts the sense of personal responsibility, rounding off the edges of criticism. The scrutiny process by contrast, with its emphasis on asking basic questions about the need for activities, the costs of activities and the value they add to outputs, is designed to put scrutineers in a strong position to argue their case. Elsewhere we have called the impact of this work on scrutineers the 'Smirnoff Effect': scrutineers are never quite the same afterwards (Metcalfe and Richards, 1984a). They continue to ask the searching questions that the scrutiny process requires. The Smirnoff effect has also influenced at least some departments which have begun to initiate scrutinies of their own.

The impact on scrutineers is strengthened by the insistence on their seeing what is actually done, by talking to the staff involved, and where necessary bringing in outside expertise rather than relying on written reports. There is also a cachet associated with being chosen to conduct a scrutiny. Scrutineers are expected to put forward definite proposals for action and often their reports are published. Civil servants are very conscious of the relative positions of themselves and their peers in the pecking order, especially at a time of organizational contraction when opportunities for promotion are more limited. On the whole, those chosen as scrutineers were the coming men (and occasionally women), thus reinforcing the view that scrutineers' jobs really are high-profile and important. There is little systematic evidence that any of the chosen few have suffered in their promotion prospects and there are many cases of people being promoted immediately on finishing their scrutinies. One individual has described how he was sent on 'gardening leave' following his scrutiny, but in that case Sir Derek Rayner intervened to restore his prospects — with unanticipated political consequences (Ponting, 1985).

Scrutinies are distinguished from the more routine efficiency exercises which were carried out as part of the normal management processes of the civil service, such as Organization and Methods or Staff Inspection. The line of reporting on results is direct to top management, with a named minister (and a permanent secretary) being given actual responsibility. Again, the symbolic significance of this arrangement should not be underestimated. Ministerial and permanent secretary time is a finite commodity and its allocation tells staff what is 'really' important in a way that carries more weight than mere words. This arrangement outflanked those in intervening ranks who had empires to defend. Existing management services had a relatively poor record of achievement, not necessarily because of a lack of technical expertise, but because they did not have the standing to defend their recommendations against the interested parties in the intervening layers of the hierarchy. 'We did it before but without the clout', as one experienced management services official put it. Indeed, they had asked many of the same questions as scrutineers, but had been defeated by departmental inertia.

Development of the Scrutiny Programme: 'Read-Across'
In addition to the political visibility of the scrutiny programme and the publicity that individual scrutinies have attracted, the possibility of making comparisons across departments has put the Efficiency Unit in a position to ensure that departments offer up significant problems. In contrast to the normal dynamics of interdepartmental relations oriented to resource acquisition, the scrutiny programme gives ministerial kudos for making savings rather than increasing expenditure. Furthermore, a department that proposed low-level scrutinies, such as the streamlining of messenger services or the reorganization of registries and filing systems, could be prevailed upon subsequently to tackle more (managerially) substantial areas of activity. The scrutiny programme has retained many of its original features but the concept has broadened. From scrutinies conducted by individuals there has been a move towards small departmental and interdepartmental teams as well as service-wide scrutinies of, for

example, statistics and multi-departmental scrutinies including administrative forms, research and development support services and personnel work.

The scrutiny programme also offers the possibility of more specific comparisons, or 'read-across' where different departments tackle similar problems. Comparisons of performance, whether in the production of outputs or use of inputs, are obviously simpler and more straightforward in a multiple retail store with many similar branches than in government. It is possible to 'read across' the columns on a chart showing the sales performance of all the different stores and the comparisons emerge. There was some hope that the scrutiny programme would identify some common problems which would allow similar interdepartmental comparisons. In the event, read-across did not emerge spontaneously. An appraisal conducted in 1981 by the Civil Service Department to evaluate the extent of read-across and the scope for extrapolation uncovered only limited possibilities.

This in itself indicated the degree of departmental discretion in choosing subjects of scrutiny. Even where cross-departmental exercises such as a scrutiny of departmental running costs were mounted, comparisons did not lead to simple league tables of department profligacy or parsimony. The differences that emerged reflected familiar differences between large and small departments such as Defence and Energy and between primarily executive departments, such as the Department of Health and Social Security, Inland Revenue or Customs and Excise, and non-executive departments, like Environment and the Treasury, which operate mainly through other agencies. The real significance of this exercise was to underscore the need for better and more consistent management accounting, to ensure that costs are known and to provide a base for intra-departmental comparison over time rather than for direct comparisons between departments.

Under Sir Robin Ibbs' guidance the Efficiency Strategy has moved on from relying on the demonstration effect of scrutinies to placing more emphasis on their role as one among several means of upgrading departmental management and performance. As part of the effort that Ibbs has led to inculcate a value for money ethos in government, departments have been encouraged to take a more integrated approach and — an important break with the past — to manage for year-on-year improvements in performance. Instead of performance improvement being the outcome of occasional administrative shake-ups, the objective is to make it a part of the normal responsibility of departmental management to see that there is a continuing search for improvement. In addition, Ibbs brought with him from ICI a clear understanding of the special requirements of managing change in large organizations.

Important though they are, scrutinies are only one part of the broader Efficiency Strategy. Indeed, they acquired much more importance than was originally planned. Scrutinies were intended to be a tool for dealing with the effects of past inefficiency and bad management. Lasting reforms — the other main strand of Raynerism — are concerned with the conditions of effective future management, and in the long term they are the most important part of the strategy.

From Political Clout to Cultural Change
While it is possible to achieve one-off savings through the scrutiny programme by the exercise of political clout with the use of little technical expertise; the more fundamental changes that are necessary to achieve improved management in the longer term can come only from change of a more radical nature. This raises the whole question of the respective roles of political clout and cultural change in instigating lasting reforms. Political clout overrides resistance without necessarily changing established attitudes. Cultural change is concerned with the revision of attitudes and the transformation of practice. Political clout was a necessary condition for initiating an Efficiency Strategy and continues to be indispensable. It ensured that ministers as well as senior civil servants took the Efficiency Strategy seriously from the start. In the eyes of many civil servants and observers it is the main, if not the sole, motivating force behind the drive for greater efficiency. Contrasts are often drawn with the loss of momentum of management reforms during the Heath administration in the early 1970s when prime ministerial interest waned.

But political clout is not enough. Reliance on prime ministerial intervention or support distracts attention from the practical problems of managing change. As the objectives of the Efficiency Strategy become more ambitious and more general the problems of implementation are becoming more complex. Securing support at the top level is only the first stage of implementation. Later stages depend on the capabilities and commitment of civil servants at several levels. For many important problems it is the links between the bridge and the engine room that are inadequate or absent. More sophisticated methods of intervention are needed to ensure that the momentum of change is maintained.

Relying on political clout underestimates the extent to which the obstacles to reform are specifically cultural. The administrative culture is embodied not so much in explicit statements of function as in an almost taken for granted amalgam of beliefs, assumptions and values about the roles and responsibilities of civil servants

(Summerton, 1980). As so often happens, cultural lag means that the ruling ideas appropriate to an earlier age persist and continue to exert an influence on administrative behaviour and organizational structure long after the conditions in which they developed have disappeared. Rayner coined the phrase 'the culture of Whitehall' to draw attention to the inbuilt limitations of civil service thinking about management. His targets were the values and perceptions of the top echelons of the civil service rather than middle levels, where ideas about management are often more sophisticated and informed than those at the higher levels. In the past, the functions of the top levels have been thought of as proffering policy advice to ministers, and not as improving the management of service to publics.

Changing the culture of Whitehall has been a theme of the Efficiency Strategy since the first days of Raynerism. In public and professional discussion of Raynerism, the scrutiny programme has received the lion's share of attention. Nevertheless, in Rayner's view, lasting reforms of civil service management depend on changing the culture of Whitehall to instil a more managerial outlook from the top down.

An Impoverished Concept of Management
One problem in creating a more managerial culture in the civil service has been an inadequate conceptualization of management within the civil service. Although there has been a conscious effort to raise the status of management, this has not been accompanied by a systematic reconsideration of what public management means. Concern about the quality of public management has been expressed in a variety of ways, including the familiar litany of economy, efficiency and effectiveness. Other phrases such as 'a better use of resources' and 'the search for value for money', are now established elements of administrative rhetoric. A definition of management that gives these phrases operational meaning has been assumed rather than stated. Consequently they are interpreted using traditional concepts of management already present in the culture of Whitehall. Instead of drawing on recent thinking about public management, old ideas have been dusted off. Johnson (1983) commenting on recent enthusiasm for management in government noted the continuities between existing prescriptions for better management and much earlier prescriptions for administrative improvement. In addition, he observed how much of the richness and diversity of politics and public administration is excluded from consideration by the perception of management as merely a process of controlling and supervising routine functions. Even without a formal statement of the meaning of management it is possible to infer from published sources and other

material what is generally understood by the term. In summary the main elements are as follows:

— Management is an executive function, i.e. it presupposes the clear definition of objectives, policies and, if possible, corresponding performance measures.
— Management is an intra-organizational process, i.e. it is what goes on within organizations: it is concerned with how work is done within organizations, with internal routines and procedures.
— Managerial control is hierarchical: coordination and control are achieved through well-defined hierarchies of responsibility and authority. Ideally these are structured into distinct cost or responsibility centres.
— There are broad principles of management which apply with only minor adaptation to all organizations. Many of these principles are already known from private business practice.

These elements in combination impose severe restrictions on the scope of management. They limit the role of public managers to programmed implementation of predetermined policies. They disregard the problems of adapting policies and organizations to environmental change. If this is all that management means, giving more weight to it is likely to cause confusion and frustration rather than lead to long-term improvements in performance. In terms of the development of ideas about management, this concept is very dated. It has been superseded by contingency theories and theories of organizational adaptation and learning (Nystrom and Starbuck, 1981). At best, its implementation would drag British government kicking and screaming back into the 1950s.

This is not to say that there is no room for improvement in the economical use of resources by applying readily available techniques which have been developed in business. Government can achieve better resource utilization through improved accounting, cost-consciousness and better information systems. The real question is whether management ends there. It is certainly not the case that such an impoverished concept of management is typical of business. In business, management responsibilities and functions gradually broaden from one level of organization to the next. Top management deals with different problems from middle management, not with the same problems on a larger scale. Top management deals with strategy, with major areas of uncertainty, with the surprise element which can threaten existing operations or open up new opportunities.

Clearly, a broader concept moves public management into some areas that have traditionally been regarded as taboo. It implies that policy and management are intertwined. It is not realistic to suppose that ministers take all policy decisions. There are some that civil servants must deal with and that have a considerable influence on governmental performance. They include objective-setting, which must take account of the political environment as well as available resources. They also include the management of interdepartmental relations and relations with non-departmental bodies. Typically, these inter-organizational networks do not form orderly tidy hierarchical structures. Since the unit of public management is often a network of organizations jointly involved in the delivery of services, competences in designing and negotiating effective working relationships between organizations are vitally important. Skills in 'fighting departmental corners' fall well short of what is needed, though they are what is expected in the culture of Whitehall.

Public management problems at the level of organizational and inter-organizational design have been neglected. Whitehall devotes few resources to machinery of government questions. Even the label 'machinery of government' has a period charm about it. Mechanistic metaphors have been superseded in organizational analysis. The corporatism scare of the mid-1970s and the subsequent Quango hunt did nothing to encourage positive interest. But the population of organizations of which government is composed shows no sign of decreasing in diversity. At this level, policy and management issues concerning the development of objectives and performance standards for multi-organizational units should be handled together (Hanf and Scharpf, 1978, Hall and Quinn, 1983).

The Disbelief System
These are not the only problems. As with any system of beliefs the definition of management built into the culture of Whitehall not only provides a framework for interpreting events but also contains a disbelief system which defines what the holders of a set of beliefs should ignore or reject. In general, a disbelief system acts as a psychological defence against proposals or events that threaten the stability of the belief system (Rokeach, 1960).

The disbelief system, which buttresses the impoverished concept of management in the culture of Whitehall, contains at least three elements which many civil servants would regard as almost self-evidently true. One has to do with proposals for alternative forms of organization. There is extreme scepticism about such proposals for restructuring government, commonly expressed in phrases which referred to the futility of 'tinkering with institutions'. There can be no doubt that in the past organizational changes have been made for reasons that have little to do with administrative efficiency or good management. Frequently changes have been made for cosmetic political reasons or to provide a job for an influential politician. But this does not mean that a great deal of work on the design of organizational structures, the development of new forms of organization and the emergence of contingency (as distinct from universalistic) approaches to organization can simply be dismissed out of hand. At present there are few indications that they are being used systematically.

A second associated strand of scepticism is the belief that reforms fail. It assumes that whatever may be the intentions of politicians or administrators, reform efforts are essentially short-lived. Their value is not that they produce significant lasting changes, but that they provide an occasional jolt that keeps people up to the mark. There is a good deal of historical evidence that supports such beliefs. Even so, a record of failure does not mean that failure is inevitable. An alternative interpretation is that it demonstrates an inability to learn from experience and a strictly limited competence in managing change.

The third element in the disbelief system is the refusal to take seriously management concepts and ideas that address broader or longer-term issues. Characteristically, ideas such as strategic management or organizational design are regarded as so much meaningless jargon. Again, experience lends credibility to these beliefs. The experience of most civil servants is of pressure to deal with short-term problems and resolve immediate crises rather than address long-term issues. But this is a self-fulfilling prophecy. If management is inadequate there will always be crises to maintain the vicious circle of ineffectiveness.

Lasting Reforms and the Culture of Whitehall
Rayner believed that, in order to make the civil service more efficient, it was important to concentrate on solving particular problems in particular cases. However, having demonstrated the need for improved efficiency through the scrutiny programme, he believed that there were larger issues to be addressed. He took the opportunity of giving evidence to the House of Commons Treasury and Civil Service Sub-committee, in July 1981, to make a public statement on what those underlying issues were. He called for a number of 'lasting reforms' which would 'produce desirable changes and developments in the managerial culture of the civil service' (House of Commons, 1982a).

He divided his recommendations into the changes needed in relation to people and those relating to institutions. While responsibility for some of these reforms rested with other parts of the centre of government — the Treasury or the then Civil Service Department — he saw them all as contributing to a change of management climate in the civil service. The Marks and Spencer emphasis on personnel factors was very

evident in his remarks on 'people'. The main points related to the
need to plan careers so that those occupying senior posts, particularly
the principal finance officer and the principal establishment officer,
and of course the permanent secretary, should have acquired
appropriate managerial skills and experience during their previous
careers. Such people were responsible for the system of management in
departments: if they were not expert themselves, how could they be
managerial leaders? More generally, there should be recognition for
achievement in the managerial field, with 'accelerated advancement'
for those who make a success of it. Changes in structures, systems and
techniques provided the main thrust of the lasting reform proposals.
One of the themes to emerge from scrutinies was decentralization —
that responsibility must be pushed down the line to where the costs are
incurred, thereby avoiding overlap and duplication, excessive checking
and unnecessary paperwork, all of which contribute to slowness and
inefficiency.

This process of decentralization had to be underpinned by new
management accounting developments. The story of the £30 rat has
been mentioned already in this chapter. Those expending resources
needed information about costs that would allow them to be cost-
conscious, and therefore to make the best use of the resources under
their control. They also needed training to equip them to use new
costing information. A decentralized system calls for clearer definitions
of responsibility and accountability at all levels including clarification
of the respective roles of minister and permanent secretary in the
management process. Permanent secretaries had interpreted their roles
in various ways, and Rayner was concerned to increase the proportion
of their attention they gave to managing their departments, 'close to the
customer' rather than 'close to the minister'. Permanent secretaries
form a collegiate leadership for the civil service, although one of their
number has the formal title of Head of the Home Civil Service. They
are not used to being evaluated. One permanent secretary nicely
encapsulated the traditional culture of Whitehall in his reply to an
Efficiency Unit request for a job description — defining the duties of
permanent secretaries and spelling out what they must do: 'Must! Is
must a word to be addressed to Princes?' (Elizabeth I to Robert Cecil).

Rayner also talked about 'closing the loop' on ministerial and civil
service responsibility. In effect, since ministers have many concerns
other than management, the civil service should accept 'a heavy
professional and moral responsibility for good management' (House of
Commons, 1982a). There is more than a hint here that there is a need
not only for a clarification of the roles of ministers and civil servants,
but also for a change in that relationship. Permanent secretaries, in
their role as accounting officers, are already directly responsible

themselves, rather than through ministers, to Parliament. Do the requirements of good management require an extension of direct accountability? Rayner put this issue on the agenda. It is politically difficult to take it further because, in spite of the inadequacies of the doctrine of ministerial responsibility, members of Parliament regard it as their way of holding the executive to account.

This book examines the way the Efficiency Strategy has evolved and considers the issues and problems emerging from it. Individual chapters discuss particular cases which illustrate general themes and go on to explore the implications of recent developments in public management for the traditional concerns of public administration. Chapter 2 provides a basis for subsequent analysis by discussing key concepts employed in the quest for better management in government. Chapter 3 discusses one of the best known of the innovations to emerge from the Rayner programme, the MINIS system, which has led to the development of top management information systems in government departments. Chapter 4 concentrates on one of the classic issues of public administration, decentralization. It examines the conditions of successful reorganization to achieve greater decentralization with improved central control.

Substantial improvements in efficiency may require investments of resources in reorganization. Chapter 5 examines one such case, the scrutiny of the system for paying benefit to the unemployed, and the obstacles to implementation at the inter-departmental level. Chapter 6 explores a pioneering effort to implement a multi-departmental review. The review of statistical services was a departure from the individual scrutiny and established a precedent which was followed in a series of other multi-departmental reviews. It also deals with the management of professionals, a major issue in government. Chapter 7 outlines the evolution of multi-departmental reviews, and considers their advantages and the special problems associated with carrying them out effectively. Chapter 8 focuses on issues associated with privatization and the application of a more commercial approach to management within government.

Chapter 9 gives an account of the origins and development of the Financial Management Initiative, evaluates its impact, and assesses its future prospects as the major embodiment of lasting reforms. Chapter 10 offers an overall assessment and draws out some of the major questions and challenges that will have to be faced in the future to enrich the concept and improve the practice of public management.

2
Management and Efficiency in Government

Scrutinies enabled the Efficiency Strategy to make rapid and newsworthy initial progress. Results were reported in a matter of months. As we observed in Chapter 1, scrutinies had a swift impact because they were mostly going with the grain of departmentalism. The scrutiny programme was shrewdly designed to take advantage of the existing institutional framework rather than provoke resistance from it. Departments identified areas of administrative work where gains in efficiency could be made quickly and cheaply. Few civil servants would dispute that there were some embarrassingly easy pickings. Nevertheless, scrutinies are likely to yield diminishing returns as successive rounds mop up pockets of inefficiency. And in any case, compared with the whole problem of improving public management, the scrutiny programme can only scratch the surface.

Lasting reforms, the other strand of Raynerism, depend upon developing a more broadly based strategy for modernization and the skills to implement it. Whereas scrutinies can be mounted using existing skills and competences, lasting reforms demand a more sophisticated approach and the application of management concepts and tools which senior civil servants in particular have not felt the need to acquire in the past. Progressive improvements require a capacity to manage structural change and carry through major reorganizations. Apart from anything else, this means that a realistic time scale for lasting reforms is measured in years and not, as with the scrutiny programme, in months.

New management competences cannot be acquired overnight. In large part, their development depends on facing up to the complexities of public management problems and revising established beliefs about management and efficiency in the process. Civil servants need a richer and more precise language for diagnosing complex management problems and developing workable solutions to them. The impoverished concept of management and the various elements of the disbelief system that buttresses the orthodox culture of Whitehall should be superseded by more refined and flexible concepts. Otherwise, management development atrophies in slogans and parrot-cries.

If you want to know whether a particular policy is really important to your superiors, examine the vocabulary that surrounds it; if it is rich, full of synonyms and active verbs and new phases, the policy is alive — it will float. If the policy is conveyed only by set phrases, with no distinctive context of supporting words — let it sink; it is not an active premise for decision. Where snow is only an occasional inconvenience, as it is for Londoners, there is only one word for it; by contrast when people's lives or recreation depend on it, as with Eskimos and skiers, there are many words for snow. (Perrow, 1977: 12)

The task of this chapter is to further the process of developing new tools for thought about public management. Some of the material is already available but it needs to be brought together in an accessible way. There is a great deal of leeway to make up. One reason for this is that there is something of a bias in the academic world against what is often called 'managerialism'; a concept not far removed from the impoverished concept of management discussed in Chapter 1. There are also influential critics of the civil service who will regard elaborating concepts of public management as a digression from the real task of cutting government down to size. Critics often appear to espouse a 'health farm' concept of reform. The aim of a leaner and fitter civil service, this implies, can be accomplished by a combination of crash diet and harder work. What government needs to trim the fat from bloated bureaucracies and slim down administrative overheads is reduced inputs and a strict regime. Leaner means fitter. Savings are a good proxy for improved efficiency and effectiveness. In this best of all possible worlds, reducing inputs of money and manpower reduces costs directly and also stimulates productivity by forcing officials to cut out waste and irrelevance.

There is enough truth in the health farm concept to lend it a degree of plausibility. Governments have certainly needed to do some belt-tightening. But this virtuous circle of increasing efficiency by reducing bureaucracy is an incomplete and misleading diagnosis. Paradoxically, adherence to it would bureaucratize the Efficiency Strategy by giving too much weight to the scrutiny programme as an established routine and too little weight to more difficult problems where real innovation in public management methods is needed. The long-term development of the Efficiency Strategy would be compromised if the health farm concept became accepted dogma. By concentrating heavily on reducing inputs, it largely disregards the urgent need to build flexibility to manage change. Just as businesses in the 1970s found that they had to define new strategies rather than just scale down output, employment and costs, government is now finding that cut-back management is only part of a larger and more complex adjustment process.

Equating management reform with tightening up the operation of existing systems would mean that the Efficiency Strategy would fall short of what is needed. To be sure, reducing costs is vital. The decline of North Sea oil revenues in the late 1980s and 1990s will ensure that cost constraints will, if anything, increase. But there is a concurrent need to create capacities for responding quickly and efficiently to change. New public management competences are needed to keep policies attuned to emerging problems. Sometimes this means managing major discontinuity, rather than tightening up the existing system. 'Especially when conditions change by jumps and trend-turns occur — it is necessary to move to new policy curves, rather than try to optimize on old and perhaps sinking curves' (Dror, 1985: 11).

Being efficiently prepared to fight the last war is as wasteful in its way as not being well prepared for anything. There is a need to consider how the Efficiency Strategy should develop to serve the objectives of lasting reforms. In the long run, efficiency gains depend on improving the quality of public management. This is a challenge that calls not only for greater persistence in seeking solutions in familiar areas but also for the willingness to question preconceptions and extend the scope of attention to a wider range of issues.

Cost-consciousness versus Flexibility

The basic dilemma of public management reform is coping with rapidly changing problems while living within tight resource constraints. This dilemma is all the more acute because their previous experience has not prepared public managers for it. A decade and more ago, governments perceived their main problem as planning the growth of basically stable programmes. Cuts were perceived as temporary setbacks, not precursors of fundamental change. After an extended period of austerity and turbulence, the prospect is one of continuing hard times. There is no easy way out of the dilemma created by the need to curb expenditure while simultaneously responding to new problems. If resources were more abundant it would be easier to deal with unanticipated problems. However, throwing resources at problems is no longer economically or politically feasible. If problems were more amenable it would be easier to adjust to resource constraints; but arbitrarily cutting back across-the-board is not a long-term solution when problems and priorities are undergoing sudden shifts.

Public management reform has come into vogue because it promises to alleviate the economic pressure on resources and the political pressure for tough and unpopular policy decisions. Even so, improving management and raising efficiency do not provide a magic formula for producing quarts from pint pots. An effective response will be one that takes account of the qualitative as well as the quantitative facets of governmental overload. Cuts and more cuts will not provide a long-term solution to what Deutsch (1981) described as the crisis of the state.

Deutsch advanced the thesis that we are witnessing a transition from the welfare state of the second half of the twentieth century to a new pattern of governmental organization appropriate to handling a sustained rapid rate of social change. 'What of the state of the near future, say about 2000 AD? In today's highly developed countries, it may have to put heavy stress on adaptive social learning, together with the power to implement its results, followed by a heightened concern for integration and coordination' (Deutsch, 1981: 338). Enhanced public management capabilities are essential to ensure flexibility and adaptability in a rapidly changing and increasingly interdependent world.

Even without projecting ourselves forward this modest distance into the future, it is apparent that giving operational meaning to better management in government raises a host of conceptual and practical problems. Some of the problems are familiar. They are frequently and inconclusively discussed. Others are de-emphasized or assiduously ignored. The development of performance measures and the design of incentive systems fall into the former category. The lack of a bottom-line, the absence of quantitative measures of performance and the inappropriateness or unfeasibility of linking financial rewards to results are old chestnuts. Whatever the position in business — and private sector practice is frequently described in oversimplified terms — developing adequate yardsticks of efficiency and establishing positive motivation to improve performance are very difficult in government. Other problems of public management, including organizational design, strategic management and management of change, have never received the attention they deserve. The difficulties they present have not been properly assessed. Nor is their role in facilitating structural, as distinct from incremental, change well understood. The familiar problems are in the area of cost-consciousness. The unfamiliar ones are in the area of flexibility.

This maldistribution of attention reflects assumptions and beliefs about the role of management in government that are explicable historically but likely to be less and less appropriate to future tasks. As the Efficiency Strategy moves into uncharted territory, managing for flexibility will make new demands on civil servants and success will depend increasingly on their active and informed commitment. There is uncertainty about whether civil servants can and will offer the positive cooperation that fundamental reform requires. After an extended period of staff cuts and low pay settlements during which the civil service has been a political whipping boy, morale is very low. Good people have been leaving at an excessive rate, and high-fliers have been increasingly difficult to recruit. Sporadic industrial action in hard-pressed areas like social security, the prison service, customs and excise and revenue collection have become commonplace. Senior civil servants have had to recognize that their self-image as hard-working, loyal, dedicated and competent public servants is not widely shared by the public at large, let alone by those sectors of the public influential with the government. Civil servants have also been forced to realize that their constitutional position is ill defined, anomalous and vulnerable. The administrative reality of responsibility for large organizations delivering services in important fields such as health, welfare, education, defence, industry, trade, foreign affairs, environment, agriculture and law and order contrasts with the constitutional fiction of an anonymous, politically neutral service, totally subordinate to the political will of ministers. The gap between constitutional convention and governmental practice has widened visibly since 1975, when Wright observed:

> it has become increasingly difficult to conceal that the constitutional position of the civil servant vis-à-vis the Minister, and through him Parliament and the public, has given rise to some anxiety in recent years; particularly, the difficulty of attaching personal blame for policy failure or administrative mismanagement. (Wright 1975: 363; see also Fry, 1981)

Recent debate about the politicization of the higher reaches of the civil service has muddied the waters still further. But there is little recognition that these increasingly incompatible expectations are symptoms of general problems.

Public Management and Conviction Politics

Public awareness of the discrepancies between civil servants' formal status and what they are expected to do in practice has been heightened by some recent *causes célèbres*, such as the break-out from the Maze prison in 1983, the Clive Ponting trial and the Westland saga. In the sound and fury of party political points-scoring, little real attention has been paid to the structural origins of the role conflicts to which civil servants are exposed. Instead, established constitutional conventions have been reaffirmed in a way that avoided addressing the underlying problems of managerial competences and managerial authority. Civil service acquiescence in inconsistencies of practice that serve the short-term interests of politicians pays little regard to the consequences for management or for their own credibility. In responding to public criticism civil servants face a double jeopardy: they are accused of being too powerful and also of being too weak. Criticisms of excessive power stem from traditional assumptions about total ministerial responsibility. Ministers are answerable to Parliament for what their departments do. Criticisms of weakness stem from new expectations of managerial competence. Civil servants should exercise power as accountable managers. Redefining the roles of administrators and politicians is difficult because principles of accountable management sit uneasily with doctrines of ministerial responsibility. This conflict is more a product of culture-bound assumptions about management and accountability than a product of inherent conceptual restrictions. Time after time, the unfamiliar or untried is equated with the impossible.

At present, the attempts to reconcile these conflicting principles without structural reform presume that the difficulties can be circumvented by shifting the focus of top civil servants' attention from policy advice to the management tasks of achieving results. Conviction politics supposedly reduces the need for civil servants to debate what goods to deliver and concentrates their energies on actually delivering the goods. This confines public management to implementation. Far from being a new departure, it reasserts the familiar, but obsolete, distinction between policy and administration, restating orthodox assumptions in a different language. However appealing the idea that the world can be divided on some Cartesian principle into thinkers and doers, policy-makers and managers, this supposed separation of functions is liable to have an increasingly adverse effect on performance. In a changing environment there are great dangers in structuring government departments into separate policy divisions and executive divisions, staffed by officials with different orientations, outlooks and career aspirations. It is the interdependence of policy and execution that sets the main coordinating tasks of management. The role of management is to maintain interaction between them rather than keep them apart. A serious reform strategy will have to break out of old and outmoded categories and propose new concepts of public management.

We do not suggest that Whitehall is an intellectual desert so far as sophisticated thinking about management is concerned. There is an increasing range of ideas under examination. The main problem is that new ideas do not get a ready hearing. Within the Whitehall culture, narrow preconceptions about management impose excessive limits on what people believe their colleagues believe. This is particularly dangerous when the management problems confronting government are becoming more complex because it slows the pace of management innovation.

To escape these constraints, this chapter examines key ideas that recur in discussion of public management. It seeks to clear away some of the conceptual confusion that surrounds the use of terms such as efficiency, effectiveness, management, control, accountability and organizational culture. No-one could expect to achieve complete agreement on terminology but, at the very least, it should be possible to differentiate mere variations in vocabulary from significant conceptual distinctions, and to develop a language in which the full range of public management concerns can be discussed.

Four Key Ideas: Efficiency, Management, Accountability, Culture

Four key ideas — efficiency, management, accountability and organizational culture — recur in the discussion of public management. Each of these ideas may be interpreted in different ways, and each requires closer analysis. Management and efficiency are ideas so vital to the development of the Efficiency Strategy that it is essential to be clear about what they mean; otherwise, political rhetoric which allows everyone to make their own interpretations will diverge ever more widely from administrative reality. There are particular dangers that both efficiency and management are defined too narrowly and even incorrectly. If this happens reform efforts lose credibility and opportunities to make significant improvements will be overlooked or mishandled.

As we have already indicated, diagnoses cannot stop short of questioning institutional and cultural assumptions. Introducing broader concepts of management and efficiency exposes the limitations of conventional concepts and established procedures of accountability. Yet there is almost a taboo on pursuing the implications of new concepts of public management into areas that transgress established assumptions about public accountability. This is most obviously the case in those instances where a basic constitutional convention such as ministerial responsibility comes into question. Frequent discrepancies between practice and precept only serve to prompt ritual and hypocritical reaffirmation. More seriously, there are wide areas where the mismatch between organizational function and forms of accountability is great enough to arouse concern about its effects on the integrity of management and the implications for performance.

Organizational cultures bind together particular ideas about efficiency management and accountability. As we pointed out in Chapter 1, the established beliefs of the senior civil service form a coherent system of belief and disbelief with its own particular strengths and weaknesses, its virtues and its blindspots. The myth and ritual of the administrative culture institutionalize distributions of authority and responsibility that are exceedingly difficult to change.

Before considering efficiency, management, accountability and culture more fully, it is worth noting that we are not intent on establishing authoritative definitions of what each term really means. The four key ideas are convenient labels for clusters of concepts which need elaboration in order to deepen understanding of each and of the relationships among them.

Efficiency
Of the four key concepts, efficiency is the appropriate one to start with because of the prominence it has received in political debate. The term 'Efficiency Strategy' symbolizes the enhanced importance Mrs Thatcher's government attached to improving administrative performance. It denotes a continuing effort to see that public resources are used to good effect rather than signifying a one-off cost-cutting campaign. The connotation of efficiency as a politically neutral, no-nonsense way of improving performance is a useful weapon in political debate. Efficiency, portrayed as a purely technical, instrumental means to politically approved ends is often presented as an unqualified good like apple pie or motherhood. Political opponents are easily wrong-footed and put on the defensive when efficiency is portrayed as a neutral concept. Their criticisms appear merely carping, or leave them vulnerable to the counter-accusation that they are prepared to defend waste and inefficiency.

Efficiency and the associated cluster of concepts — economy, effectiveness and value for money — with their emphasis on cost-consciousness are on their way to achieving an established place in administrative practice as well as in political rhetoric. Administrators are having to learn a litany of resources–results ratios which define economy, efficiency and effectiveness and the relations among them. Figure 1 illustrates the ways in which these terms are being used to provide a technical framework for rational choice.

FIGURE 1: *Distinctions Between Economy, Efficiency and Effectiveness*

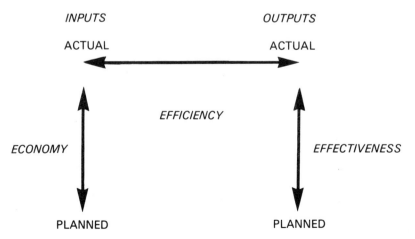

Taking efficiency first, the generic definition — the ratio between outputs and inputs — establishes a technical point of departure. Improvements in efficiency may be achieved by increasing outputs relative to inputs, reducing inputs relative to outputs or, ideally, doing both at the same time. Within this framework greater economy is achieved by making savings in actual resource inputs relative to planned resource inputs. Effectiveness is increased by achieving a better ratio between desired objectives and actual outputs. A similar framework was set out in the Third Report of the House of Commons Select Committee on the Treasury and Civil Service (1981-2), which interpreted effectiveness as 'the definition of objectives, the measurement of progress towards achieving those objectives and the consideration of alternative means of achieving objectives', and efficiency as, 'given the objectives and the means chosen to pursue the objectives the minimizing of inputs to the programme in relation to the outputs from it' (House of Commons, 1982a).

Rational Choice and Political Judgement
These various ways of achieving better results presume the existence of a firm framework of politically defined objectives. Even if we disregard, for the moment, the difficulties of actually establishing a policy framework that eliminates ambiguity about objectives, efficiency is a less straightforward concept than it at first appears. Political and technical considerations are always interwoven in the search for greater efficiency. Political judgements are involved in deciding whether to seek improvements in efficiency ratios by increasing outputs, reducing inputs or pursuing excellence by doing both at the same time. Political judgements are also involved in setting the time scales for producing results. Investments in human capital through reorganization and training or in information-processing hardware may produce large long-term benefits. These spend-to-save results are attainable only at the price of increased short-term costs which conflict with attempts to reduce current public spending. Politics, in short, sets constraints as well as indicating what to optimize.

Because technical and political considerations are always interrelated, the main focus of interest shifts from efficiency in general to what is actually done. The positive political connotations of improving efficiency lose their force if there is evidence that practice fails to follow precept. Efficiency becomes a dirty word if outcomes are in some significant sense inefficient. As Mintzberg (1982) noted, efficiency gets a bad name if in practice it is equated with measurable efficiency. Concentrating exclusively on measurable efficiency has three undesirable consequences. First, because costs are more easily measured than benefits, efficiency often reduces to economy. Savings in money and manpower become the sole measure of improvement; the quest for efficiency becomes a search for cuts. Second, because social costs are more difficult to measure than economic costs, externalities are often ignored. Individual units concentrate on improving their own efficiency even though the overall effect is suboptimal. Third, economic benefits are more easily identified than social benefits and efforts to increase efficiency lead to a redefinition of performance criteria in ways that lend themselves to easier measurement. The pursuit of efficiency degenerates into a numbers game. As Gray and Jenkins (1985) put it, 'Today we suspect it means minimizing inputs almost regardless of outputs. We doubt this is efficiency at all, as the essential input–output relationship is now of less significance than the reduction of inputs as such.'

These dangers are not specific to government. But the diversity of governmental functions, the problems of formulating objectives and the difficulties of setting and maintaining priorities present major challenges to improving efficiency in government that cannot be wished away. In order to disentangle the real issues that governments must grapple with in improving performance, several efficiency concepts need to be borne in mind: technical and economic efficiency, allocative and productive efficiency, and static and dynamic efficiency.

Technical and Economic Efficiency
The distinction between technical and economic efficiency is of fundamental importance. Technical efficiency measures the physical use of resource inputs in relation to physical outputs, while economic efficiency measures the cost of using inputs in relation to the value of outputs. Disparities can arise between the dictates of technical and economic efficiency. The most technologically advanced equipment may be very costly. In the present climate of governmental austerity it is clear that economic efficiency is the central concern. The shift from technical to economic efficiency is evidenced by the negative connotations civil servants now attach to 'Rolls-Royce' standards of service and 'gold-plated proposals'. Excellence is no longer sought in standards of service that are set independent of costs. Cost-consciousness and value for money are the watchwords in the quest for least-cost solutions. The greater prominence of professional accountants in government in recent years, the introduction of management accounting tools and the use of management consultants with an accounting orientation are also symptomatic of this cultural change.

Within the sphere of economic efficiency there is another important distinction between allocative and X-efficiency. Allocative efficiency is the optimal distribution of resources, guided by prices where possible, to ensure that resources are distributed among producing units to serve consumer wants in ways that reflect costs of provision. X-efficiency is about productivity in the utilization of resources — producing at minimum cost. X-efficiency — or, strictly, X-inefficiency — is economists' jargon for poor management. Traditionally, economic theory focused on allocative efficiency assuming effective organizational incentives to minimize costs. Hence it avoided addressing institutional and managerial problems. X-inefficiency occurs when organizations fail to minimize costs because of managerial inadequacies and it is clear that it is very relevant to public management concerns. Notwithstanding current policy changes towards privatization and contracting-out designed to increase allocative efficiency and reduce X-inefficiency, the efficiency of government depends more on the performance of organizations than on that of markets. Organizational and managerial factors are major determinants of the efficiency with which public policies are implemented. Whatever the allocative efficiency of budgetary processes in distributing resources in line with political priorities, major problems remain in ensuring that resources are well used.

Peacock (1983) pointed to several familiar difficulties in eradicating X-inefficiency in government. He suggested four reasons: outputs are difficult to define let alone measure; the output indicators available are flawed by their inability to pick up qualitative differences in performance; the incentives and opportunities for managers to seek ways of minimizing costs are limited by agreements and regulations that restrict managerial discretion; and finally, administrators cope with these uncertainties by withdrawing from the task of evaluation. They make little use of empirical evidence about performance. Rather than basing judgements on measures of performance they base them on the style and elegance of argument. 'Bureaucratic politics becomes frequently "the art of the plausible"' (Peacock, 1983: 133). Like much of the contribution of economists to organizational analysis, this is a clear statement of familiar management problems rather than a striking new insight into ways of solving them.

Operational and Adaptive Efficiency
Extending this hierarchy of efficiency concepts leads to a further distinction between operational and adaptive efficiency which ties efficiency even more closely to improvements in management. Efficiency has different organizational and managerial implications in a stable environment from those in a dynamic, rapidly changing environment. In the former case, operational efficiency stresses cost-consciousness in performing existing functions. Measures include a tight specification of objectives and performance standards, increased task specialization and standardization of procedures.

Stability justifies the elaboration of long-term plans and detailed programmes of activity. Conversely, adaptive efficiency involves increasing flexibility. This depends on the reformulation of objectives and a speedy adjustment to environmental change. Adaptive efficiency is aided by creating temporary structures and promoting information flows that give early signals of the need for change. The organizational imperatives of operational and adaptive efficiency are, at least partially, at odds with one another. In stable environments organizations can be solidly designed with long-term investments in specialized structures. In changing environments, temporary structures that are easy to change are more appropriate (Hedberg, Nystrom and Starbuck, 1976). It is a matter of judgement where the balance should be in particular circumstances. The answer may be different at different times and in different spheres of governmental activity. But the traditions of government and the Efficiency Strategy give too much emphasis to operational efficiency. There is now an increasing need to equip public organizations to adapt to rapid and unpredictable environmental shifts.

Efficiency and Effectiveness
Emphasizing resilience and flexibility draws attention to the limitations of the model of rational choice based on given objectives. Adaptive efficiency embraces the revision and redefinition of objectives. This opens the door to a consideration of effectiveness in setting objectives as well as in achieving objectives. Conventionally, effectiveness has to do with the extent to which desired goals are achieved. Recent surveys of the theory and practice of organizational effectiveness have been stronger in rejecting the rational model than in reaching agreement on a new one (Goodman and Pennings, 1977; Cameron and Whetten, 1983). Yet this is a critical area for public management. In government, objectives are notoriously difficult to define, are frequently in conflict and are often subject to change. Coping effectively with ambiguity, conflict and instability are strategic tasks of public management that cannot be assumed away. To anticipate the discussion of management, goalsetting is a particular problem of public management because it is an inter-organizational process and not just an intra-organizational process.

The rational model echoes the conventional but obsolete distinction between policy and administration. It makes effectiveness logically prior to efficiency, but by the same token it makes the assessment of effectiveness dependent on a prior definition of policy objectives. In practice, the situation is far less clear-cut. The boundary between efficiency and effectiveness is a permeable one. Attempts to improve efficiency may lead to a clarification or redefinition of objectives, and it has certainly not been the case that the Efficiency Strategy has eschewed consideration of policy issues. The orthodox view is that, despite the difficulties, every effort should be made to tighten up and clarify objectives to provide a basis for assessing effectiveness and improving efficiency. The Management by Objectives movement assumed that progress in this direction was both a feasible and a desirable condition of improving public management. As with many other tools and techniques intended to increase the rationality of governmental action, it assumed that the most appropriate place to break into the public management cycle was at the stage when objectives were defined. This view was buttressed by the widespread belief that good business practice results from sharpening up and clarifying objectives. But, as business was forced to adapt rapidly to adverse economic circumstances in the 1970s, the limitations of the orthodox rational model became apparent. Business was forced to reformulate the concept of organizational effectiveness because environmental change frequently rendered objectives obsolete.

As these changes in organizational environments have taken place, research and theorizing have moved to ask different questions and reformulate the problem of organizational effectiveness. Instead of assuming given objectives and conceptualizing organizations as goal-seeking systems, effectiveness is increasingly defined in terms of innovativeness, adaptability, organizational learning and the capacity to manage change. There is a strong emphasis on flexibility. This has given rise to a number of variations on the theme of organizational adaptability — the self-designing organization (Hedberg, Nystrom, Starbuck, 1976; Weick, 1977), the self-evaluating organization (Wildavsky, 1976), the self-correcting organization (Landau, 1973) and the experimenting organization (Staw, 1977) — or emphasis on the central importance of organizational learning (Argyris and Schon, 1974; Hedberg, 1981) and, within that perspective, to the critical role that strategic management of the relations between organizations and their environments plays in facilitating learning (Metcalfe, 1981).

This is not just a restatement of the rational model, at a higher level of abstraction, with adaptability inserted as a higher level goal. Goal-seeking is a partial model which is applicable only within an evolving framework of policy norms and values (Vickers, 1970). Furthermore, the focus on adaptability is leading to constructive thought about how to achieve effective performance in organizations with ill-defined performance criteria (Nystrom and Starbuck, 1983). Since one of the commonest observations about public organizations is that their objectives are ill defined, it is an interesting development for public management.

Civil servants may find this both comforting and disquieting. Comforting, because there is an element of 'we told you so' in acknowledging the difficulties, in a political environment, of presetting objectives and ensuring the stability needed to achieve optimum efficiency and effectiveness in pursuing them. Disquieting, because acknowledging these difficulties is not a counsel of despair but a challenge. It does not dispose of the tasks of devising criteria of effectiveness or organizing action to improve efficiency. Instead, it transforms the problems in ways that will tax the intellectual and social skills of public managers. What is very clear is that the route to greater efficiency and effectiveness is through better management.

Management

Lasting improvements in efficiency and effectiveness are inextricably bound up with better management. However, shifting the conceptual focus from efficiency to management is like jumping out of the frying pan into the fire. For an idea that connotes a no-nonsense, matter-of-fact, down-to-earth, action-oriented approach, management is surprisingly elusive. The widespread belief that better management holds the key to improved governmental performance owes more to a low estimation of what governments currently achieve, and to an equally low opinion of the management competence of civil servants, than to an agreed concept of management. As a slogan for reform, management promises positive action and better results. In practice there are divergent views and some clear misconceptions about management in general and public management in particular.

Debate about public management runs along contradictory lines. The similarities and differences between public and private management are a constant source of controversy and confusion. For some, public management is just public administration carried on under another name. For others public management can be subsumed under a generic concept of management governed by universally applicable principles. Another view is that private business practice offers a set of ready-made solutions to public management problems. Yet others see sharp contrasts in context and process between public and private which largely preclude the adoption of private sector practice. Whatever position is taken, the explicit or implicit assumption of most management reformers is that management offers a more logical, rational and orderly approach to improving performance in government than existing administrative practice. The superiority of a management approach is supposed to reside in applying proven principles to create neatly structured organizational hierarchies with well-defined tasks and clearly allocated responsibilities. Orderly management is superior to muddling through because it establishes firm control, streamlines processes and defines purposes.

Tidy-minded prescriptions such as those just mentioned have little empirical support in government and are at odds with the findings of recent investigations of business management. The rhetorical appeal of slogans like 'back to basics' is the presumption that principles of good management have been lost sight of, but can be revived. This has little justification. The contemporary situation of public management is not one in which old truths can be reasserted. It is one in which new principles have to be developed. Government must face the challenge of innovation rather than rely on imitation. Improving public management is not just a matter of catching up with what is already being done in business: it also involves breaking new ground.

Taking Responsibility for the Performance of a System
Because of persistent confusion over the meaning of management, there is a temptation to duck the question of definition altogether or to settle for a conventional definition such as 'getting things done through others'. Greater clarity is possible. Simon (1961) defined management as decision-making by extending the concept of decision-making from the final moment of choice to 'the whole lengthy complex process of alerting, exploring and analyzing what precedes that final moment'. Simon analyzed decision-making into three principal phases: an intelligence phase, concerned with searching the environment for conditions calling for decision; a design phase, concerned with devising alternative policy responses; and a choice phase, concerned with selecting a preferred course of action. For good measure Simon threw in implementation, since a broader policy decision creates a new condition which calls for more decision-making activity. 'Executing policy, then, is indistinguishable from making more detailed policy' (Simon, 1961: 4). Aside from anything else, this neatly converts the dichotomy of policy and management into a continuum of responses to problems of different degrees of importance and specificity.

More recently, Leavitt, emphasizing skills, competences and perceptions as well as decision-making, proposed a threefold division of the managerial process into pathfinding, problem-solving and implementing. Pathfinding is about asking the right questions, selecting problems rather than solving them; problem-solving entails reducing complex problems to simpler forms and setting up choices; implementation concerns the delivery of services. 'Pathfinding then, is about mission, innovation, vision; problem-solving is about analysis, thought, reason; Implementing is about acting, changing, doing. Good management not only requires competences in each of these areas but also skills in managing the relationships among them' (Leavitt, 1983: 4). Both Leavitt and Simon define management broadly enough to include all phases of the policy process and their coordination to achieve overall purposes.

With these concepts in mind, we propose a general definition of management as taking responsibility for the performance of a system. Like any general definition, it poses a series of questions — in this case, about responsibility, performance and the unit of management. First, management in a normative sense is 'where the buck stops' and managers individually and collectively are those who accept responsibility for the performance of a system. Managers may delegate implementation responsibilities but they cannot legitimately abdicate responsibility. This is reflected in the way that recent discussion about management in government has been framed in terms of accountable management, a concept clearly related to the allocation of responsibility. The second question concerns performance criteria and the role of management in setting and achieving goals. Managers do not just operate within a framework of objectives. As pathfinders and problems-solvers, they participate in defining what is attainable and accept responsibility for achieving results. The third question, about the unit of management, deliberately places the emphasis on the system managed rather than on the manager as an individual. At some levels, the unit of management may make it appropriate to fix on the responsibilities of individual managers; but often, in a public management context, systems are much larger and the appropriate unit of management is not just a single department but a network comprising several different organizations. If management in general entails getting things done through others, public management entails getting things done through other organizations. Steering the activities of systems composed of several interdependent organizations is one of the distinctive challenges of public management.

This definition has more practical implications than might at first appear. On the one side, it distinguishes management as a purposeful process from the mutual adjustment characteristic of 'muddling through', where the overall performance of a system is the unintended consequence of interaction among component subsystems; whether or not it embodies the intelligence of democracy (Lindblom and Braybrooke, 1973), disjointed incrementalism is not management because there is no locus of responsibility for system performance. On the other side, much discussion of management confuses it with control. Control itself is an extremely slippery term, sometimes equated with accountability (as in parliamentary control), sometimes with financial management (as in Treasury control), sometimes meaning acceptance of ministerial direction (as in political control) and sometimes economy (as in budgetary control). Confusion between management and control is particularly common. This error is evident in many prescriptions for the use, or perhaps one should say the misuse, of a variety of familiar techniques, such as PPBS, PERT, MBO and variations on the theme of management information systems.

Landau and Stout (1979) argued that far from being synonymous and interchangeable terms, there is a fundamental distinction between management and control: to manage is not to control. Control techniques are valuable in situations where actions can determine outcomes; where routines can be confidently established and programmes elaborated to deal with foreseeable problems. Predictability is the condition of control. Management comes into play where non-routine responses are needed. Actions are adjusted and responses improvised to take account of changing circumstances and feedback about earlier performance. 'There is an inverse relationship between the ability to control and the necessity to manage. A controlled situation is one in which there exists both well-defined objectives and a technology capable of achieving them' (Landau and Stout, 1979: 149).

Control links with efficiency and cost-consciousness rather than flexibility. Control is improved by tighter specification, clearer definition and greater standardization:

> The *raison d'être* of control systems is to increase the likelihood that people will internalize organizational goals and thus behave in ways that lead to the achievement of these goals. Supervision, standard operating procedures, position descriptions, performance measurement and performance-related reward systems are all useful means to predefined ends. (Flamholtz, Das and Tsui 1985: 36)

Too much of current discussion of public management wrongly identifies management with control. Where conditions for control do not obtain these 'means to predefined ends' are apt to be counterproductive, increasing rigidity in situations where flexibility is needed. Management is an adaptive process. It requires discretion to respond to change and stimulate innovation, whereas control procedures quite deliberately programme behaviours and predefine responses. Control techniques presume a greater degree of stability than is frequently found in the politically charged atmosphere of public management. In themselves, they offer too narrow a base for making improvements in the performance of public organizations.

Nevertheless it is wrong to over-react and throw the baby out with the bath water. Not using control techniques where they can work is as counterproductive as using them where they cannot. One task of public management proper is to establish conditions in which control techniques and methods can work.

Actual managerial behaviour does not correspond with the clean-cut image of control so frequently presented. The concept of management as a less tidy adaptive process in which experimentation, search and trial, error and error correction play important roles is in keeping with the findings of empirical studies of managerial behaviour. These portray management as a fragmented, episodic but purposeful process, frequently involving the laborious tying up of many loose ends, rather than as a unified and tidy process of planned and programmed action. The picture that emerges is

> not of a manager who sits quietly controlling but [who] is dependent upon many people, other than subordinates, with whom reciprocal relationships should be created; who need to learn how to trade, bargain and compromise; and a picture of managers who, increasingly as they ascend the managerial ladder live in a political world where they must learn how to influence people other than subordinates, how to manoeuvre and how to enlist support for what they want to do. (Stewart, 1983: 96-97)

This resembles an account that traditional senior civil servants might give of their work in the upper reaches of administration. It is hardly surprising that the model of control, masquerading as management, which they feel is being foisted on them seems quite inadequate. However, it would be wrong to infer that senior civil servants have been managers all along without realizing it. As Strand (1984) showed, public administration practice tends to confine the legitimate role of officials too narrowly to meet the challenges of the world in which they now work. Strand's analysis, summarized in Table 1, distinguishes four public management roles appropriate to different tasks and contexts. He characterized the four roles as administrator, producer, integrator and innovator.

TABLE 1: *Public Managers' Role*

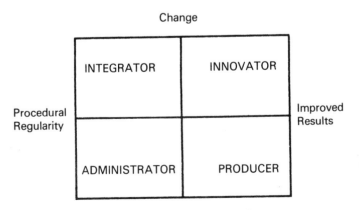

(Based on Strand, 1984)

Traditionally, expectations and assumptions have focused on the administrator role, emphasizing procedural regularity and ensuring stability. The administrator performs what is largely a system maintenance function, interpreting and applying general principles to particular cases and working within given policy parameters. The public manager as producer displays more concern with results than the administrator but still works within established policy constraints. The producer role is the most widely articulated view at present of the meaning of public management. It fits most closely with Simon's post-decision phase of management and Leavitt's implementer role, and is also consonant with the resolute approach of conviction politics — the belief that the problem is getting things done rather than continually debating what to do.

Committed producers are indispensable to sustained improvements in performance, especially if year-on-year gains in productivity are being sought. They give priority to ensuring operational efficiency and seeking ways of reducing costs. However, it is not their responsibility to advise on new policies or initiate responses to change; those are the tasks of the innovator and integrator. Public managers with competences in these roles are needed to create flexibility by designing new systems and managing change. The emphasis is on Simon's pre-decision phases of information-gathering, problem formulation and generation of new solutions, and on Leavitt's pathfinder and problem-solver roles. The innovator, being results-oriented, places the emphasis on developing new policies to achieve existing objectives better or to prompt strategic changes of direction. This goes well beyond proffering policy advice to ministers. Innovators seek to stimulate action, alert decision-makers to the need for change and advocate new responses.

Real flexibility in public management also requires integrators, to complement the assertive activities of innovators. Sometimes changes can be imposed from above, but often their success depends on mobilizing widespread support and building a base of lasting cooperation. Since public management entails getting things done through other organizations, coordination is achieved through non-hierarchical means. Integrators exercise networking skills to negotiate the terms on which different organizations participate, to clarify organizational roles and to ensure that the vision of the innovators is translated and communicated in terms that are meaningful in a variety of organizational contexts. Integrators are the people with skills in managing the transition from old to new systems. If innovators produce and develop the new policy proposals, it is integrators who make them work. Flexibility requires both.

Definitions of public managers' roles are rarely as clear-cut in practice as this categorization might suggest. However, it is not intended to force individuals into this or that box: its main value is in pointing to the range of options and posing the question of whether the existing balance is right and whether today's civil servants are acquiring the skills and the legitimacy to meet the challenges of tomorrow's problems. Leavitt argued that businesses and business schools had given too high a priority to analytical problem-solving skills to the detriment of implementation skills and the substantial neglect of pathfinder skills. Overemphasis on the producer role in an era of major change may leave public management short of the innovators and integrators required to build much needed flexibility. This is an issue the Efficiency Strategy must face.

Before leaving the theme of management, a comment on a question that has attracted a good deal of attention is in order — that of the minister as manager. Few ministers have embraced the idea of being a manager with great enthusiasm; Michael Heseltine was exceptional. Perhaps this is because the culture of Westminster shares many of the restrictive assumptions about management enshrined in the culture of Whitehall. These negative attitudes are based on serious misconceptions. As the foregoing analysis sought to show, management is a broad concept including all phases of decision-making, extending to the higher reaches of political leadership and including policy innovation and development across as well as within organizational boundaries. Ministers already play management roles, whether they are aware of it or not. For obvious reasons, they prefer the more publicly visible aspects of management where their presumed political skills in presentation, communication and debate show to best advantage.

In place of the either/or questions like, 'Should ministers be managers?', it makes more sense to ask, 'Which management roles should ministers play and which roles should be played by others to ensure that departments perform well?' Pitching the question at the level of roles allows for differences in personal preferences and competences while avoiding the wooden and restrictive detail of formal job descriptions. It also allows for a more objective and systematic analysis of problems of overload and role conflict which are currently veiled by constitutional conventions of anonymity, secrecy and ministerial responsibility.

Mintzberg's fine-grained analysis of management roles provides a useful language for clarifying who is doing what and where organizational structures and political conventions leave gaps and create role conflicts, role ambiguity, role strain and role overload. Mintzberg distinguished nine management roles clustered into three subsets: interpersonal, informational and decisional. The interpersonal roles, which in public management are often played in an inter-organizational context, include the symbolic and ceremonial functions of figurehead, leader and liaison. Their principal locus is the minster and his private office in close conjunction with the permanent secretary. The informational roles of monitor, disseminator and spokesman set the pattern of communication networks and information systems that govern internal flows of information as well as flows of information to and from the environment. The decisional roles are: entrepreneur, developing new policies; disturbance-handler, resolving disputes and conflicts and alleviating tension, allocating resources and setting priorities; and negotiator, advancing departmental interests and setting the terms of interdepartmental cooperation.

It would be interesting to see a thorough role analysis comparing ministers, private offices, permanent secretaries and other senior officials in different departments. This would highlight real managerial differences between departments and provide a basis for evaluating reform proposals such as those advanced by the Institute of Directors' group led by Sir John Hoskyns for expanded private offices along the lines of ministerial *cabinets* in other European countries. If ministerial overload is the problem, is it because ministers have to play too many roles or because they do not or cannot delegate some of the detail? Is overload the basic problem or is it symptomatic of other, more deep-seated, problems within departmental management structures? Or to anticipate the next key idea, is it traceable to obsolete patterns of accountability?

Accountability

Accountability is the other side of the coin of managerial responsibility. Public managers, who are entrusted with the resources allocated to policies and programmes, are necessarily involved in the exercise of public authority. But they do not have unfettered discretion in exercising the authority delegated to them. They operate within a framework of accountability which is intended to ensure that authority and resources are properly used. Proper use of power and resources cannot be left to the good intentions and public spiritedness of politicians and officials. In broad terms, the function of accountability is to keep organizational performance up to standard. To insure against an abuse of organizational power and yet promote its effective use is one of the classic problems of modern government. To many, it poses an irresolvable dilemma.

> Democracy generates a dilemma of bureaucracy and the bureaucrats who run it, because democratic rules are self-contradictory and put bureaucracy in a double bind. By such rules, bureaucracy is expected to be both independent and subservient, both responsible for its own actions and subject to ministerial responsibility, both politicized and non-politicized at the same time. (Etzioni-Halevy, 1985: 87)

A large part of recent public discussion about the role of the civil service and civil service ethics centres on this dilemma. The issues are real, but the dilemma poses a false choice between accountability and effectiveness. It is cast too much in either–or terms, leading to the belief that public management and public accountability are inherently in conflict. We do not deny the difficulties of designing appropriate frameworks of accountability, but we do reject the pessimistic assumption that this invariably means attempting to reconcile the irreconcilable. The source of error is a failure to recognize two aspects of accountability; a negative, preventive aspect and a positive motivating aspect (Metcalfe, 1981). Well-designed accountability arrangements can have a constructive influence in ensuring effectiveness and responsiveness to external reference groups if they pay as much attention to the latter as to the former.

Good design is lacking at present. The framework of constitutional myth and ritual in which accountability processes are embedded and from which they derive their legitimacy is now an object of scepticism and cynicism. Current disenchantment with the practice of public accountability and confusion about theory have deep roots. Much of the institutional framework of accountability predates the growth of big government. It fails to come to terms with the organizational facts of governmental life. Accountability processes are concerned mostly with guaranteeing legality and financial regularity in a formal sense. Questions of efficiency, effectiveness and value for money have been on the periphery for some time, but the basic structure of the system gives them low priority. Even then, the system is not good at doing its traditional job. Despite the weight of accountability procedures, it is weak, often inappropriate, and sometimes capricious in its operation.

In some cases the accountability system has proved so inadequate that those in positions of power have been able to hijack it and use it to mask their abuse of power. One of the most notorious British examples is the Crown Agents' case (Hood, 1978). Behind the facade of complete respectability symbolized by the name, it proved possible for those in charge to operate in financial markets in a way that was quite at variance with expected standards of corporate conduct, public or private. Cases like this call forth political demands for more draconian measures to prevent future abuse. They concentrate on closing the stable door after the horse has gone rather than on providing the stimulus for more positive consideration and constructive development of new forms of accountability.

Advocates of public management have not displayed much positive interest in accountability. Public management reforms have often been discussed as if they had no relevance to the broader constitutional framework. The authors of the Fulton report were precluded from considering any changes that overstepped established constitutional conventions. Fry (1981), in his apt comments on the conservatism of the Fulton report, quoted the insistence of the then Prime Minister, Harold Wilson, that

> the Government's willingness to consider changes in the Civil Service does not imply any intention on its part to alter the basic relationship between Ministers and Civil Servants. Civil Servants, however eminent, remain the confidential advisers of Ministers, who alone are answerable to Parliament for policy; and we do not envisage any change in this fundamental feature of our parliamentary system of democracy. (Fry, 1981: 142)

This ruled out any real consideration of the impact on public management of ministerial responsibility.

By and large these inhibitions persist. Civil servants habitually preface consideration of management or organizational issues by dismissing any options that question the institutional framework within which they work. The habit is reinforced by the disbelief system of the Whitehall culture. 'Tinkering with institutions' is portrayed as mere political cosmetics and not as a serious contribution to improving public management. The existing system of public accountability is perceived as a cross that civil servants have to bear. From a public management point of view, this is a dangerous limitation because it removes an important potentiality for coping with change. The long-term progress of lasting reforms depends on using accountability frameworks actively as manageable variables to open up new strategic options rather than regarding them passively as straitjackets that impose conformity. Stability and continuity are desirable properties of institutions of accountability, but this is no reason to make a fetish of them. Unqualified loyalty to the established order can easily convert stability into rigidity.

The capacity to adapt patterns of accountability has a particular importance in creating flexibility to deal with structural, as distinct from incremental, change. So long as incremental change can be absorbed gradually and slowly, there may be no need for the accountability framework to change. It is when rapid structural changes occur that a flexible redirection of policy and reorganization of powers and responsibilities are needed. These transformations will not succeed unless they are underpinned by changes in the accountability framework. The grain of truth in 'tinkering with institutions' is that technical changes in structures and functions on their own have little impact on behaviour.

Accountability and the Right to Manage

Coping with structural change is an exercise in what Gowler and Legge (1983) termed the 'management of meaning': not in the superficial sense of public relations and political window-dressing, but in a deeper sense of generating new commitments to wider social values and public purposes. The pragmatic language of management incorporates a rhetoric that 'constructs and legitimizes managerial prerogatives'. The management of meaning 'contributes to management as a political activity concerned with the creation, maintenance and manipulation of power and exchange relations' (Gowler and Legge, 1983: 198). In short, it provides a justification for the right to manage.

The management of meaning by tying the right to manage to accountability symbolizes the interpenetration of politics and management. Doctrines and the process of accountability link the dignified and the efficient sides of the constitution. But at critical junctures old formulations no longer work: the rules of the game come into question; competing interpretations of organizational purpose and alternative rationales for the right to manage emerge. Negotiating these periods of turbulence is a major task of public management. It is no accident that structural problems are provoking precisely these kinds of questions now. Civil servants are publicly claiming the right to manage without fully explaining the doctrine of legitimacy on which their claims rest. Nor is it clear whether they square with broader constitutional doctrines.

The starting point for remedying this is to recognize fully the organizational scale, diversity and complexity of modern government. Individual government departments can be large and they share the managerial problems of all large-scale organizations. There is probably more diversity among public organizations than among private ones. The heterogeneity of public organizations is under-recognized, so far as accountability is concerned. They are complex structures, and there is often substantial interdependence among organizations operating within the same policy field or even in different policy fields. Patterns of interdependence are not confined to the Whitehall village community of government departments; they ramify through the public sector and beyond, domestically and internationally.

Scale, diversity and complexity set difficult accountability problems. Even if some public organizations can be scaled down or dispensed with by discarding functions, privatizing or contracting-out, large-scale organization remains a technical necessity for conducting the business of government. Nor are organizational diversity and interdependence likely to decline. Consequently the old formulas of accountability will prove less and less appropriate. Simply trying to reassert them will be of no avail. In a way, the 'quango hunt' of the late 1970s and early 1980s was a forlorn attempt to impose standard solutions on non-standard organizations. At one level it was a generalized attack on proliferating bureaucracy; at another level it was an expression of frustration with the organizational diversity and interdependence of modern government. It sought, unsuccessfully, to impose a Procrustean strategy on government, forcing organizations into traditional institutional moulds and stigmatizing misfits and deviants; maintaining doctrinal simplicity in the face of administrative complexity (Johnson, 1982).

There is little sign that these attitudes are changing. Mrs Thatcher, unlike some of her predecessors, has shown little interest in machinery-of-government questions. Within the Efficiency Strategy, efforts to improve accountability have concentrated on accountability within departments. Moreover, internal accountability has been given a very specific meaning, centring on the appropriate delegation of authority within departments, a prominent feature of the Financial Management Initiative (discussed in Chapter 9). The idea itself is not new. Accountable management has been an integral part of civil service thinking about management reform at least since Fulton. Its intellectual pedigree as a management concept goes back much further, into US business history in the 1920s (Chandler, 1962). Garrett (1981), who was closely associated with the production of the Fulton report, has supplied a concise statement of this concept of internally accountable management:

> An accountable manager is one to whom specific authority over part of an organization's resources has been delegated and who is required to answer for the results he has obtained from the deployment of those resources. Accountability implies the delegation to managers of authority over money and manpower; a form of organization in which managers can be made responsible for the activities of sub-units; a strategic planning framework in which the objectives of those managers can be related to corporate objectives; an arrangement of control information so that progress towards the attainment of those objectives can be monitored; and a procedural system for securing managerial commitment to unit objectives and for reviewing results. (Garrett, 1981)

Although these prescriptions could improve performance in many specific instances, they have significant limitations as a general philosophy of public management. They address problems of operational efficiency. They focus on the individual manager and presuppose a low degree of interdependence between managerial units. Hence they assume a very limited need for coordination. Accountable management in this sense is a recipe for the management of independence rather than the management of interdependence. Even ignoring these limitations, there is the more general problem that systems of internal accountability are not freestanding: they rest on the foundations provided by the system of external accountability. Internal accountability — and, indeed organizational performance — can be no better than the institutions of public accountability allow.

This is not an encouraging prospect. Institutions of accountability should be major variables in defining constructive relationships between public organizations and their political environments. Their actual role is limited because they are taken as givers rather than strategically important sources of flexibility. The system of accountability is discredited. The dead hand of ministerial responsibility is the most important instance of deterioration and obsolescence.

The notion that civil servants are politically neutral, anonymous and powerless agents of ministerial will is far removed from the facts of contemporary administrative life. However appropriate this doctrine might have been when public organizations were tiny and officials nothing more than personal servants of the minister, it falls well short of what is needed now to ensure the responsible and effective exercise of public authority. The deficiencies of ministerial responsibility are apparent when serious mistakes are made. When a number of prisoners escaped from a high-security wing of the Maze prison, the then Northern Ireland secretary, James Prior, was not compelled to resign, nor did he accept responsibility for allowing the break-out to occur. The gloss given to the doctrine of ministerial responsibility was that ministers are responsible for policy and resources but not for mistakes made by officials in using the latter to implement the former. Protests from prison officers that policy issues were involved, because ministers had insisted that some Republican prisoners were made orderlies and issued with keys that eased the escape, were quickly silenced. Whether prison officers' complaints were justified or not is beside the point. This interpretation of ministerial responsibility drove a coach and horses through traditional concepts of accountability. It is seriously inconsistent in limiting the scope of ministerial culpability, laying the blame on officials and then denying them the right to defend themselves.

Ministerial responsibility, in some form, remains essential, but it is inadequate on its own to meet the needs of accountability in a positive and constructive way. It is too simple and limited a doctrine to comprehend the diversity of public organizations and it does nothing to instil a sense of commitment and purpose in officials who often feel that they have nothing to gain and much to lose from its operation. Despite widely acknowledged deficiencies, reform is exceedingly difficult. Britain's long history of political and administrative continuity which maintains old institutions has 'contributed to the atrophy of any language in which we can talk about constitutional issues, of rules or the principles of public law' (Johnson, 1977). The waning of constitutional understanding is, one hopes, close to its nadir.

Doctrines of accountability have been so watered down to accord with political and administrative practice that they no longer provide standards to work to. Despite the weight of accountability procedures, their real impact at the political level is often reduced to mere answerability and their impact on management is rarely thought through. Accountability as answerability means no more than having to justify and explain what has been done — taking the political flak and fielding parliamentary questions — but without serious fear of longer-term consequences. For our purposes a stronger meaning of public accountability is needed which includes answerability but carries

> an additional implication: the answer when given, or the account, when rendered, is to be evaluated by the superior or the superior body, measured against some standard or some expectation and the difference noted; and then praise or blame are to be meted out or sanctions applied. It is the coupling with information with its evaluations and the application of sanctions that gives "accountability" or "answerability" or "responsibility" their full sense in ordinary organizational usage. (Dunsire, 1978)

This stronger sense of accountability goes some way towards what is needed, but it still places the emphasis on the negative function of accountability. As a contribution to lasting reforms, new institutions of accountability must respond to two challenges: the challenge of matching forms of accountability to diverse kinds of organization and the challenge of balancing the positive and negative components of accountability.

Matching and Balancing

Public accountability should mirror the diversity of public organizations. Instead of standard forms, there should be networks of accountability that correspond with the variety of public organizations (Barker, 1982). If diversity is important in serving different needs accountability arrangements should reflect this. They should not whittle away the power or compromise the legitimacy of management. All too often this is what has happened in the past — most damagingly with nationalized industries, but also in many other cases. As Richard Wilding remarked,

> The central dilemma of the accountability of fringe bodies is therefore this. The more we increase their accountability, the larger the number of things we make them account for to the Minister, since this is the only way our arrangements for accountability are channelled to flow. (Wilding, 1982: 42)

If 'arrangements for accountability' were to flow in other directions than up the administrative hierarchy, the progressive loss of managerial autonomy would not need to occur. A first step in this direction is an analysis of the characteristics and functions of each organization, and especially the relations between it and its various publics (Metcalfe, 1981). The characteristics of these relationships, whether superior–subordinate, professional–client, customer–supplier or constituent–representative require matching types of accountability, as Table 2 shows. This typology does not describe types of organizations: it defines types of relationships which may be combined in different ways. Its applications to particular cases involves careful consideration in order to decide on the relative priority of external hierarchical accountability, peer group evaluation, internal membership control and competition. These strategic organizational design issues are of more far-reaching importance than would appear from the cursory treatment they have received in the past. Preconceptions and homespun theories have played a larger role than organizational analysis in manipulating the government machine (Pollitt, 1983). Some of the heat of the ideological debate about privatization is due to the fact that the protagonists place unqualified faith in markets or hierarchies as modes of accountability. By oversimplifying and stereotyping, they avoid the complex task of matching modes of accountability to organizations which rarely, if ever, fall into neat categories.

TABLE 2: *Power and Accountability*

	Type of Power			
	Hierarchical Authority	*Expert Authority*	*Influence*	*Exchange*
Form of Accountability				
Structural Constraints	Upward account-ability for delegated authority	Peer-group evaluation of performance	Internal, membership control of representatives	Competition among customers and suppliers
Doctrine of Legitimacy	Authoriz-ation by higher authority	Professional commitment to client welfare	Consensual agreement on policies	Mutual gains from self-interested trading

The challenge of balance arises because each of the four modes of accountability works through two countervailing processes: structural constraints, which act as checks on poor performance and the misuse of power, and cultural doctrines of legitimacy or codes of conduct, which motivate and guide the exercise of management responsibilities. The former operate reactively and intermittently as negative feedback processes, correcting unacceptable departures from policy and performance norms. The latter operate continuously and pro-actively as positive feedback processes which set the values and norms from which policies and standards derive. Structural constraints are more obvious and intrusive, and there is over-reliance on them in government. But just tightening constraints does not assure progressive improvements in performance. After a point they have the opposite effect, because they emasculate and impede managerial action. Reinforcing commitment through an internalization of legitimate values and codes of conduct is much more important in inculcating positive motivation. Shifting the balance from negative to positive avoids the conventional dilemma of accountability. Excessive reliance on structural accountability constraints leads to poorer performance.

Emphasis on legitimacy, values and culture leads naturally to our fourth key idea.

Organizational Culture
Organizational culture is the last of the four key ideas in the current debate about public management which warrants closer analysis and elaboration. It is appropriate to leave it to last because it is a latecomer to the management scene. Although there is a history of research into organizational culture, organizational climate, ideologies, belief systems and related topics, it has been peripheral to the mainstream of management thinking until recently. In the hard-nosed quantitative scientific management tradition, harking back to the work of F.W. Taylor, culture and related concepts such as myth, symbol and ritual seem suspiciously soft, if not actually wet. Perhaps we have not yet reached the stage at which managing directors feel they should have an anthropologist rather than an accountant at their elbow, but there has been some movement in that direction.

Organizational culture has not been regarded as an issue or problem within the civil service. The hubris of the high civil service has meant that, apart from a few despairing acknowledgements of the difficulties of changing attitudes, it has been treated as an object of pride rather than concern. Now, the situation has changed. As Rayner recognized, in coining the phrase 'the culture of Whitehall', this matrix of assumptions and practices exerts a considerable and by no means wholly positive influence on the way the business of government is conducted. The *Yes, Minister* television series brilliantly satirized the higher reaches of government as a context in which appearances and presentations are crucial and reality breaks through only by accident. Humour catalyzed and legitimized a wider public interest and prompted debate about civil service reform along the lines of Rayner's criticisms of the lack of cost-consciousness, lack of reliable information about responsibilities and a tendency to view management as a second-rate function separate from and subordinate to policy-making.

The culture of Whitehall is not synonymous with the civil service culture; it refers to the values and beliefs that shape the behaviour of the higher civil service who work in and around Whitehall. Nevertheless, it exerts a strong influence on the functioning of the whole system. As Wiener, in his perceptive exploration of a familiar theme, English culture and the decline of the industrial spirit, observed:

> Elites have disproportionate influence upon both the effective climate of opinion and the conduct of affairs. The values of the directing strata, particularly in a stable, cohesive society like modern Britain, tend to permeate society as a whole and to take on the colour of national values, and a general mentalité. (Wiener, 1981: 5)

While questioning whether Britain is now either a stable or a cohesive society, we agree with the emphasis on the pervasiveness of elite values. The strategic position of the higher civil service means that any limitations or blind spots in its ways of thinking and acting are amplified in their effects. There is a great deal of uncertainty and disorientation, accompanied by heart-searching, about civil service ethics, about roles and responsibilities and about accountability. There is a strong sense that the traditional assumptions about what it means to be a civil servant are crumbling rapidly, despite some rear-guard efforts to reinforce them. In this crisis of confidence and legitimacy there are no leaders willing or able to guide the management of meaning to articulate a new image which fits the circumstances and has external as well as internal credibility. The profession of government, at a critical juncture, lacks pathfinders with the vision to set the direction of change.

Significantly in this situation, management reformers are inclined to brush the problem aside; to rely on political clout to overcome resistance to change. This underestimates the extent to which improved organizational performance, and particularly managerial performance, depends on firm belief and active commitment rather than grudging acquiescence. As we noted in Chapter 1, political clout is a necessary but not sufficient condition for improving public management. Many of the obstacles to change are specifically cultural. The implicit and taken-for-granted assumptions about what is and what is not done impose hidden constraints on performance. Political clout may temporarily override some of these, but other, more considered, interventions, designed to reduce resistance to change and mobilize support, are needed in the long term (Argyris, 1971).

Culture is not an easy or readily accessible concept to use. It is defined in a number of ways, from the banal and uninformative 'the way we do things round here' to highly generalized and esoteric concepts from which it is difficult to draw specific implications. Fortunately, it is not culture in general that we are concerned with, nor even all aspects of the civil service culture. Our focus is on the organizational culture and especially its implications for the definition of managerial tasks and responsibilities. Harrison (1971) emphasized that cultural values and norms do more than provide prescriptions and prohibitions. They provide a rationale for organizational members' conduct towards one another and a *raison d'être* for the organization as a whole in relation to the environment. The unifying and guiding power of organizational cultures arises because they enshrine the theories of organization and management that people in organizations use to interpret events, frame problems and coordinate action. Effective or strong cultures provide shared frames of reference and firm mutual expectations, which simplify problems of communication and decision-making as well as channelling energies into implementation. Because cultural assumptions are acquired by learning from everyday experience what is approved and disapproved, what is valued and rewarded and what is disapproved and punished, they are difficult to evaluate dispassionately. Indeed, in the context of bureaucratic politics, it is unwise from a tactical point of view to challenge them or even entertain the idea that things could be different.

Culture-bound organizations are overcommitted to their current theories of practice. They are especially prone to find adjustment to structural change difficult. Many businesses experienced the painful consequences of a failure to recognize the need for substantial and rapid adaptation to cope with the adverse and turbulent conditions of the 1970s. Studies of businesses in crisis indicate the stranglehold that managerial beliefs exert on efforts to promote organizational adaptation. Trying harder in familiar ways is psychologically and politically easier than venturing into new and unexplored territory.

The need, in business, not just to have a corporate strategy but to have a capacity for changing corporate strategies has been increasingly recognized. As a result consultants and 'strategy boutiques' have moved strongly into the organizational culture field (Perry and Lorenz, 1983). Growth of interest in organizational culture was prompted by

Peters' and Waterman's book *In Search of Excellence*. They examined the attributes of US corporations whose cultures enabled them to cope effectively with rapid change without a loss of organizational identity and cohesion when rivals were falling apart at the seams. Drawing as much, if not more, on recent organizational research as on evidence from excellent companies, and blending the ingredients (somewhat inconsistently) with a fashionable back-to-basics philosophy, they distilled eight distinctive features of the culture of corporate excellence:

1. managing ambiguity and paradox;
2. a bias for action;
3. closeness to the customer;
4. encouraging autonomy and entrepreneurship;
5. productivity through people;
6. hands-on commitment to product or service;
7. simple form, lean staff;
8. know your business.

There are many questions that might be raised about the meaning and significance of these criteria as guides to organizational action or the corporate equivalent of 'How to Win Friends and Influence People'. It is not altogether clear whether cultural change in these directions is a means of improving performance, a concomitant of improving performance or a means of maintaining high performance levels once achieved. As careful surveys show, drawing prescriptive conclusions from descriptive studies is a hazardous business (Beyer, 1981; Sproull, 1981). However, it is rather clear that the values underlying the eight criteria are not much in evidence in the traditional civil service culture. In several cases, the traditions of the civil service run counter to concepts such as encouraging autonomy, knowing your business and displaying a bias for action. It is not even clear that the Efficiency Strategy and the Financial Management Initiative always take them into account. They give more emphasis to the clarification and specification of responsibilities than to the management of ambiguity and paradox. Yet, the latter is highly pertinent in government where objectives are multiple, conflicting, unstable and often ill-defined.

To take another example, government pays very little attention to human resources management. Even though public service delivery depends critically on productivity through people, the civil service now displays many of the symptoms of a demoralized and demotivated workforce. At a time when businesses are moving to the view that their staffs are much more product-motivated than profit-motivated, government is toying with performance-related financial reward systems. Furthermore, there are some clear public–private differences. The relationship of government organizations to their publics is often not that of a supplier to a customer. Evolving public management cultures of excellence will have to embrace relationships with clients, subjects, citizens, suppliers, inmates, taxpayers, recipients of benefits and grants as well as customers. Closeness is not invariably a desirable characteristic of these relationships. The important issue for public management is to design appropriate relationships between organizations and their publics.

Bearing in mind these qualifications, the current discussion of organizational cultures draws attention to three general points of importance to public management. First, it highlights the role of values and norms in guiding, motivating and legitimizing managerial behaviour, especially, in situations where operational objectives are conflicting and changing. Without these higher level reference points, changes in objectives are apt to create serious and costly disorientation. A strong culture creates organizational flexibility by providing symbols of continuity in the midst of change (Pondy, 1982). Second, introducing the idea of excellence has provided a long-overdue corrective to the model of administrative man as satisficer. Satisficing is widely regarded as implying that levels of aspiration are both low and immutable. Excellence opens up the question of how aspiration levels are set and how they relate to more general performance criteria which differentiate public management from business management (Metcalfe and Richards, 1985). Coupled with concepts of organizational experimentation and learning, excellence leads to a culturally defined orientation towards seeking year-on-year improvements in performance. Third, a well-developed public management culture should help to widen the options and increase the prospects for success in managing change. Efforts at planned change always rely to some extent on external pressure — force of circumstances or political clout — to overcome resistance. However, it is often more efficient managerially and less costly in terms of political reputations to unfreeze old attitudes, unlearn obsolete habits of mind and create expectations that changes will present opportunities and can be successfully managed. Internal commitment to shared cultural values reduces the felt need to resist change and the positive motivation to implement change.

Having said this, cultural change is no easy matter. Established cultural values are deeply entrenched in beliefs and institutions. They are regularly reasserted and enforced by constitutional procedures within which officials work. Administrative action is habitually embedded in 'things more general than words which can be used to speak powerfully at higher levels than those of social chat and instrumental cooperation. I summarize these as myth, symbol, ritual and ideology' (Mackenzie, 1978: 151). In government, the actions that speak louder than words are embodied in the myths and rituals of parliamentary control and accountability, ministerial and collective cabinet responsibility and the administrative assumptions and practices stemming from them. Although the disparities between myth and reality are often commented on and it is common to speak of 'empty ritual', their importance should not be underestimated.

New Directions
There is a chicken-and-egg problem. Moving in new directions requires changes in the culture of Whitehall, and changes in the culture of Whitehall are needed to permit and facilitate movements in new directions. Progress is an evolutionary process in which new competences are gradually developed in the process tackling new problems. Reform is not an all-or-nothing choice. Viewing organizational culture as the theory of management that practitioners work by, one of the ways of gauging progress is to look for greater sophistication in the way public management issues are formulated and tackled. The traditional culture of Whitehall selects too narrowly from the clusters of concepts discussed under the headings of efficiency, management and accountability. Received ideas and the institutions and practices that embody them display a bias towards limited concepts of operating efficiency; they tend to avoid the difficult effectiveness issues, misdefine management as routine control, and confine the search for improvements within established patterns of accountability.

The order in which the four key concepts have been considered in this chapter suggests a progression in complexity and generality which should be taken into account in the development of the Efficiency Strategy. Efficiency is simpler than management. Culture is more general than accountability. At the efficiency end of the scale, changes are guided principally by consideration of cost-consciousness. At the culture end of the scale, flexibility is the prime consideration. The former is oriented more to tightening up operational systems in the short term; the latter, to long-term adaptation to environmental change. The Efficiency Strategy should take account of this by gradually developing managerial capabilities that enable more basic and long-term changes to be made. The following chapters consider how far it has been possible to move in this direction.

3
MINIS:
Management Information and the Minister as Manager

Encouraging departments to create or improve management information systems is one of the most prominent features of the Efficiency Strategy. From the beginning, the Rayner programme pinpointed inadequate information about results and costs as an important constraint on the bid to improve governmental performance. Within the Financial Management Initiative there is an across-the-board move to create top management information systems to serve the needs of ministers as well as senior officials. All government departments are now under an obligation to improve the provision of information to management. Early in 1985, the Financial Management Unit issued a report documenting the progress that central departments had made in developing top management information systems. Based on work with 16 major departments during 1984, this report surveyed the advances made in refining the systems for planning improvements in value for money, resource allocation and monitoring performance. Top management systems serve the needs of senior officials and ministers in assessing and reviewing policies and programmes, preparing for the annual Public Expenditure Survey, approving operating plans and budgets down the management line, and monitoring performance against plans and budgets within years. A top management system is, or ought to be, the buckle that joins operational management within departments to more long-term strategic consideration of future developments. In order to perform this function effectively, it must synthesize information about current performance and plans, prospective environmental changes and available resources needed by top management to form judgements about the feasibility and desirability of alternative courses of action.

The initial impulse for the development of information systems came from the creation of 'MINIS', the 'Management Information System for Ministers' in the Department of the Environment. In retrospect, it seems a natural evolution, yet in some ways it is surprising that top management information systems are becoming part of the Whitehall landscape. Even after the initial publicity surrounding MINIS, few practitioners or observers forecast any significant follow-up. Management information systems were not given the consideration they warrant in traditional Whitehall thinking. Their vigorous development owes a good deal to the pioneering efforts of Michael Heseltine; when he was Secretary of State at the Department of the Environment he provided the impetus for the creation of MINIS. However, the story of MINIS is not just a record of personal achievement; it is, as this chapter seeks to show, a case study of the politics of innovation in public management.

MINIS came into being because Michael Heseltine found no adequate system in the Department of the Environment for giving ministers a clear picture of what was going on in the department. Lines of responsibility were confused, and there were inadequate data for making decisions and assessing costs. MINIS was intended to remedy this by clarifying who was responsible for what, why activities were undertaken, and what the costs associated with them were. Although some commentators have presented MINIS as a parallel development to the Rayner programme and as more or less a personal Heseltine initiative, it emerged from a Rayner scrutiny on 'The Provision of Management Information to Ministers'. The scrutiny proposed procedures for assembling detailed basic information about existing departmental activities, objectives and patterns of responsibility. These procedures were swiftly put into operation. At ministerial insistence, and to the consternation of officials, the documentation produced by directorates for the first MINIS round was published. Its publication was used as an occasion to propagate Mr Heseltine's view of the minister as manager, assembling the information base to ensure that he was fully in charge of what his department was doing.

The broad pattern laid down at the beginning — preparation of statements for each directorate within the department by the responsible under-secretaries, review meetings to consider the statements, with ministers and top officials participating, and action flowing from the review meetings — has settled down into an annual cycle, with a number of modifications and refinements. The further evolution of MINIS is discussed later.

MINIS symbolized Mr Heseltine's personal commitment to the idea of the minister as manager. It subsequently became a public symbol of the government's commitment to management reform. The purpose of this chapter is to trace the development of MINIS and explore some of the issues it raises about the role of information systems in public management.

Information, Interpretation and Attention Management

For anyone familiar with recent thinking about management, the prominence given to management information systems in the development of the Efficiency Strategy is not at all unexpected. Information and communication are subjects that permeate contemporary discussion of management theory and practice. Managers at all levels need information to keep track of day-to-day operations, evaluate performance, assure control, adjust to change and plan for the future. These various needs are not automatically met satisfactorily by spontaneous information flows; nor is it possible for managers to have first-hand knowledge of what is happening. Deliberate arrangements to provide requisite information have to be designed. Several common features of large-scale organization increase the need for planned provision of information to management: managers are remote from the direct delivery of services, and intervening levels of organization may distort and delay reports of what is really happening; the scale of operations means that large quantities of data have to be collected, classified and presented compactly, otherwise top management is unable to see the wood for the trees; the complexity of decisions, and the multiplicity of values and interests involved, call for correspondingly diverse sets of data. Added to remoteness, scale and complexity, rapid rates of change make information obsolete more quickly. In a changing environment, managers have an increasingly difficult task in keeping abreast of developments, and management information systems are tools to assist them in doing so (Tricker, 1982).

The development of new information technologies has given most attention to the creation of data bases, storage and retrieval. But it is the use to which information is put that ultimately determines the contribution information systems make to organizational effectiveness. Weick and Daft (1983) placed the emphasis not so much on the data as on its interpretation. In all organizations there are culturally patterned interpretation systems which give meaning and significance to information about what is happening within the organization and in its environment. Events are categorized as relevant or not; patterns are recognized or misinterpreted.

> Organizations are much more than input—output, resource-consuming, goal-seeking systems. Organizations also have mechanisms to interpret ambiguous events and providing meaning for participants. Organizations are as much meaning systems as they are input—output systems. They transform the equivocality and randomness outside the organization into specificity and direction within the organization. (Weick and Daft, 1983)

From a theoretical standpoint, organizations are increasingly conceptualized as information-processing systems. Management can almost be defined in terms of information-processing, punctuated into data collection, transmission, analysis, storage, retrieval and use in decision-making, monitoring and evaluation. One indicator of the advance of this information-processing concept is that the emphasis of organizational design has shifted from the problem of allocating responsibilities and determining the organizational division of labour to the problem of attention management, ensuring that limited management information-processing capacities are intelligently used and not flooded with indigestible data or starved of crucial evidence (Simon, 1973). The division of worrying is displacing the division of work as the central problem of organizational design.

Within this perspective, new information technologies and computer-based decision support systems are widely advertised as the key to enhanced effectiveness. We are accustomed to hearing about the information revolution and the information society in which effective organizations base their success on employing the latest developments in computer technology to aid management functions. However, there is a real danger that information technologies become a panacea, a technological fix, which supposedly provides a short-cut to improved performance without the trials and tribulations of managing changes in attitudes, roles, structures and methods. In reality, the productive use of computer hardware depends on supporting organizational and managerial changes in the way information is used.

Information and Power
The direction of organizational change needed to take advantage of new information technology is becoming increasingly clear. It involves a shift in organizational culture from static operation to evolutionary operation (Box and Draper, 1969). Static operation is a control process aimed at maintaining given levels of performance, whereas evolutionary operation is a process of managing change and searching for ways of improving performance. In a stable environment static operation is adequate: organizations can be designed to perform a specific task; information systems monitor and report on the performance of that task. In a changing environment, organizations require systems to generate information about how to adapt activities and improve performance when performance criteria themselves may be changing. Evolutionary operation is partly a response to environmental changes which exert an influence on what organizations should do as well as how effectively they do it. It requires a fundamental change of attitude, to act on the assumption that there are always ways of improving performance. This contrasts with the long-held civil service assumption that acknowledging room for improvement implies criticism of past performance. Evolutionary operation is linked to thinking and theorizing about self-correcting organizations, adaptation and organizational learning (Landau, 1973; Argyris and Schon, 1974; Hedberg et al., 1976; Metcalfe, 1981).

Recognizing the central role of information in the management process points up a recurrent dilemma of reconciling conflicting principles of access and security, freedom of information and confidentiality, which are matters of great public interest. This dilemma certainly did not arrive with the advent of the computer; computerization has, however, redefined and sharpened the issues which, in the British context have traditionally been resolved in favour of secrecy rather than openness.

The dilemma can be formulated in terms of two diametrically opposed sets of beliefs and assumptions about the relationship between information and organization. First, there is a belief that all organizational problems are reducible to failures of communication. If conflicts of interest and divergent policy positions derive from misunderstanding, the recipe for improvement is better information and greater openness leading to joint problem-solving and ultimately to consensus on what action to take. If implementation fails because political intentions were not communicated, the recipe for improvement is greater clarity, precision and fidelity in transmission. Second, there is a contrasting belief that knowledge is power. Control of information and secrecy are strategic weapons in the political battles over policy and resources. This more Machiavellian assumption prescribes a guarded attitude towards the disclosure of information and the maintenance of information disparities that serve to enhance the bargaining position of one group vis-à-vis another.

The rationale of MINIS sought to resolve this dilemma by combining elements of each set of assumptions. It drew on the belief that, on purely technical grounds, existing information flows in the Department of the Environment were inadequate and insufficiently coordinated to give ministers and senior officials a comprehensive picture of the department's activities. As Heseltine stressed, without some additional source of information he did not really know what was going on in his department. But the motivation for MINIS was not purely technical. In addition to remedying weaknesses in existing systems, it also sprang from a political concern that established departmental practices, by accident or design, were obstructing ministerial access to important information. De facto, this maldistribution of information placed power in the hands of permanent officials in a way that is inconsistent with the doctrine of ministerial responsibility. Creating an information system for ministers provided a way of correcting this imbalance. Asserting the role of minister as manager was a means of restoring substance to the constitutional forms of ministerial responsibility and public accountability.

Innovation, Information, Accountability

MINIS is one of only two exceptions to the general rule in this book of avoiding initials or acronyms. The other is the FMI, the Financial Management Initiative, which is discussed in Chapter 9. The reason for making an exception in the case of MINIS is clearly not the aptness of the acronym, but the symbolic significance it acquired in the process of public management innovation. MINIS might have become a shorthand term used to refer to the subset of information systems designed specifically for ministers. But it has not become standard terminology. Departments have asserted their independence by producing many and diverse acronyms for their information systems. It is a moot point whether this diversity reflects significant differences in technique and concept or merely obscures underlying similarities.

Particularly in a system so notoriously secretive and closed as British government, MINIS put management information on the political agenda. It provided a rallying cry for the proponents of management innovation in government, and found allies in the advocates of open government. It provided a point of reference and an initial agenda for debate about the role of information systems in government. It forced other departments to review the appropriateness and adequacy of their own information systems. The evolution of MINIS is, therefore, of general interest for public management from three distinct points of view, summarized under the headings of innovation, information and accountability.

1. *Innovation*: MINIS illustrates some of the general requirements and difficulties of innovation in government. The politics of management reform in government are more complex than they are in business because worthwhile progress often requires parallel changes across several or all departments. Innovation goes against the grain of departmentalism.

2. *Information*: much of the discussion about MINIS presumed a concept of management information systems and a view of the role of information in organization that are too restrictive to do justice to the needs of public management. Some broader questions about the link between management information and policy analysis need examination because it is artificial to try to separate the two.

3. *Accountability*: changes in information systems are not neutral in the sense that they leave organizational structures and the distribution of organizational power as it was. The impact of new information systems is not limited to their manifest functions of improving the quality, reliability and timeliness of information available to decision-makers. In addition, information systems have significant implications for accountable management and public accountability which call into question established constitutional conventions.

The Background of MINIS

MINIS was launched early in 1980 following the lines of recommendations made in a Department of the Environment Rayner scrutiny of 'The Provision of Management Information to Ministers'. Its purpose was to provide the Secretary of State and his ministerial colleagues with detailed information to review the work of the department. Mr Heseltine saw it as the third element of an approach to managing, broader than 'day-to-day administration', and comprising:

— setting clear objectives;
— a strategy to reach those objectives;
— a method of monitoring progress to ensure one is not losing momentum or, if one is, that one can adjust to new circumstances deliberately and quickly. (Heseltine, 1980: 62)

It is worth noting at this point that the Department of the Environment consists of two rather different components. In the traditional Whitehall terminology it is partly a policy department and partly an executive department. The Department of the Environment (Central) is concerned mainly with formulating policy on a wide range of environmentally related matters, including the construction industry, the water industry, housing, physical planning, local government finance and the care of historic buildings. The other part of the department is the Property Services Agency which has executive responsibility for the management of the government estate — offices, courts, prisons and defence establishments at home and abroad — and encompassing responsibility for design, construction and maintenance as well as the supply of office furnishings for these establishments. MINIS was originally developed for the Department of the Environment (Central) and not for the Property Services Agency. The latter does take part in the MINIS process, but the information on which its participation is based is drawn from the Agency's existing computerized management information system and differs in some details from the MINIS system.

MINIS required that the directorates that form the main sub-units of the department each provided information on:

— their activities and objectives;
— the priorities attached to these activities;
— the cost associated with them;
— an assessment of the directorates' performance on each activity;
— a forward look to set standards for future performance.

In the first MINIS round in 1980, directorates were also required to provide an organization chart and describe any important links with other directorates. This information gave a comprehensive overview of the structure and functions of the department as a basis for assessment against ministerial priorities. The second MINIS round, which followed soon after in the autumn of 1980, also included manpower budgeting and was used as a vehicle for deciding where manpower cuts could be made to meet government targets for manpower reductions by 1984. Subsequent MINIS rounds have taken place on an annual basis.

There is a familiar cycle of events coordinated by the 'MINIS Unit'. Information is prepared and submitted by each directorate in a standard form. A series of meetings then takes place between senior officials and ministers and the heads of each directorate to discuss the reports and make decisions. The third phase of the process is implementation. Subsequently, performance is reviewed at the beginning of the next MINIS round. There is nothing strikingly new about this account of a familiar feedback/control loop. Indeed, it is a description of an elementary form of control loop sometimes referred to as 'thermostat control' (Lawler, 1975). What was different, so far as British government is concerned, was, first, the involvement of ministers in the process and, second, the publication of the reports. The process of monitoring and reviewing performance was much more public and visible than had previously been the case. There were other, less obvious and unintended, consequences of the MINIS process which modified the roles and relationship of officials and ministers. These are considered later.

The process has been elaborated since the first MINIS round, and now, instead of a single meeting, there is a preliminary meeting between directors and the permanent secretary prior to the meeting with the secretary of state and other ministers. Briefings for these meetings are provided by the MINIS Unit drawing on the data generated by the system and other relevant information from, for example, staff inspections and Rayner scrutinies. Over time, the coverage of MINIS has broadened, but the process has remained basically the same.

Civil Service Responses to MINIS
MINIS was specifically addressed to the needs of the Department of the Environment, but it soon began to attract wider attention — positive from outside government and sceptical from other departments. There was a variety of defensive responses to MINIS from within the civil service. Taken together, they illustrate rather well some of the features of the disbelief system of the culture of Whitehall which come into play when reforms are proposed. As described in detail by Likierman (1982), they were a mixture of the ad

hoc and the ad hominem. The ad hoc included the argument that MINIS was over-elaborate, that it was too costly, that the system was specific to the Department of the Environment and was not transferable — or, alternatively, that it embodied general principles which might be transferable but did not give specific prescriptions for other departments. Finally, there was always the argument that MINIS was nothing new. Other departments already had adequate information systems — 'we are doing it anyway' — and the Department of the Environment was a laggard rather than a leader. The ad hominem criticism was that the whole MINIS system depended too much on the personal style and commitment of a particular minister and was therefore unlikely to survive Heseltine's term of office in his department, let alone transfer readily to other departments.

That these sources of resistance did not bring progress to a standstill was due to the way in which the politics of management reform developed. Possibly the most important factor was that the issue of management information systems did not remain within the closed politics of the civil service. Because of Heseltine's association with it, MINIS broke out of the confines of the culture of Whitehall and gathered external support which outflanked internal resistance.

Ideas in Good Currency
Because most interest has been on the mechanics of the MINIS process, the way in which management information systems became a significant issue has received rather little attention. As Schon (1971) pointed out, for an idea to come into good currency it must overcome the dynamic conservatism of institutions. Organizations do not merely display inertia; that is, they do not just tend to maintain momentum in a given direction: they fight to remain the same by neutralizing new ideas which threaten their integrity. Embryonic proposals have a high mortality rate. There is a major threshold to surmount in moving from invention — the formulation of a new idea — to innovation — its embodiment in practice. Ideas in good currency have to survive this obstacle course.

> Underlying every public debate and every formal conflict over policy there is a barely visible process through which issues come to awareness and ideas about them become powerful. The hidden process by which ideas come into good currency gives us the illusory sense of knowing what we must worry about and do. (Schon, 1971: 123)

Improving public management depends upon a more systematic understanding of the process of innovation. Rogers and Kim (1985) summarized the findings of recent research on innovation in organizations. They identified five sub-processes through which new ideas gain acceptance, two concerned with initiation and three with implementation:

I. *Initiation*
1. *Agenda-setting*: formulating and recognizing a need for innovation.
2. *Matching*: the fit between a specific problem on the organization's agenda and an innovative solution is evaluated.
II. *Implementation*
3. *Redefining*: the innovation is 'translated' into a more appropriate form to fit organizational needs (Lewis, 1984). This may not be just routine specification: it may require reinvention also.
4. *Structurizing*: adapting organizational structures directly involved to accommodate and use the innovation. This may involve creating a new unit to manage the innovation.
5. *Interconnecting*: integrating the innovation into the total functioning of the organization so that it becomes part of regular operation and ceases to have a distinct and separate identity.

This framework provides useful guidelines for monitoring and evaluating the progress of any organizational innovation. At the very least, it provides practitioners with a basic check list of the problems they have to solve in managing innovation. The history of MINIS shows how this was done, but with a more political emphasis to take account of the fact that, in public management, innovation is the adoption of new methods by a set of organizations rather than just a single organization.

MINIS, as an example of public management innovation, is examined below by distinguishing three overlapping phases: initiating, stabilizing and diffusing. The first of these centres on bringing a new concept to public attention, the second on establishing the legitimacy of the proposed innovation, and the third on moving from prototype or pilot project to general application. Innovation requires more than invention: it requires skills in mobilizing support for ideas and securing their adoption and implementation. It is a long-standing criticism of British culture that it is more fruitful in the sphere of invention than it is productive in the sphere of innovation. For a variety of reasons, that criticism is particularly applicable to the civil service. Hence, the fact that MINIS moved beyond the initial phase is especially instructive.

Initiating
The most important factor in bringing MINIS on to the political agenda was that it was not just an idea: it was an idea with a powerful

champion, a minister who was a political heavyweight heading a major department. There is an analogy with the notion of a product champion in business. The product champion is committed to bringing new ideas to fruition. Typically, the product champion is personally committed to the successful implementation of an idea and is willing to weather failures that would deter others from proceeding further (Schon, 1963). Because of the need to persist in the face of disappointments and to counter informal resistance to change, product champions must have a strong personal belief in the value of a new idea. They may not have originated the idea themselves but they must be convinced and convincing advocates. They must volunteer for the role rather than be press-ganged into it. Such qualities are rare and not altogether approved of in Whitehall; though some civil servants have been known for their entrepreneurial qualities, the norm is a wait-and-see attitude. Persistent enthusiasm in the absence of consensus is apt to be regarded as evidence of lack of balance and objectivity and a sign that the judgement of the individual concerned is not entirely sound. In Whitehall parlance, 'thinking aloud' is one thing, but having 'a bee in one's bonnet' — that is, being identified with pet projects — is quite another. Since mistakes are punished and successes are not rewarded, risk avoidance is prevalent.

Politicians are in a different position. Championing new policies is a role that ministers like to be seen to play. Ministers, ambitious to further their political careers, like to be identified with new policy initiatives. However, it is very unusual to find a minister who acts as a champion for an innovation in management. In the past, the rewards for this kind of innovation have been as meagre in the culture of Westminster as they are in the culture of Whitehall. Because this kind of entrepreneurial behaviour is rather rare and undervalued, there is a tendency to dismiss it as a temporary enthusiasm that will soon pass. But this proved not to be the case, partly because of Heseltine's own approach and partly because of the response of other political actors.

If displaying enthusiasm deviated from the norms of the Whitehall culture, Heseltine compensated for it by presenting his proposals within a framework of impeccable constitutional orthodoxy. He did so by combining two rhetorics of administrative reform: a management rhetoric which emphasizes orderly structures, the elimination of overlap, duplication and the design of clearly articulated systems to serve predefined objectives; and a political rhetoric, which emphasizes the need to change the balance of power between contending interests and to establish a different pattern of control. The details of the MINIS proposals described earlier fall into the former category. In the simplest terms, they involved clarification of responsibilities, definition of objectives and regular flows of information to monitor and review results — hardly the stuff to capture the public imagination. The concept of the minister as manager falls into the latter category. This rhetoric conforms closely with the conventional view of ministerial responsibility and provided a means of presenting a new management technique as restoring power relationships to what they should be. The political rhetoric also helped to stimulate public interest and give the whole venture visibility. MINIS was to make clear to the civil service who was running the show.

Stabilizing

Having a minister as a champion ensured that MINIS would, at least for the duration, have a localized success in the Department of the Environment. However, the process of innovation in public management is even more complex and untidy than it is in business. In business, a product champion with the right patrons and sponsors may be able to push through all the way from advocating an idea to securing its implementation. In government, the entrepreneurial process is less individualistic and depends to a large extent on mobilizing support in the right places. Giving a lead is one thing; acquiring a following is another. Some stabilizing and consolidating processes are needed to ensure that innovations survive. A number of sources of support combined to create a niche for MINIS and to consolidate the idea of management information systems as a change worth making. One source of support, somewhat surprisingly, was parliamentary interest. In its Third Report on Efficiency and Effectiveness in the Civil Service, the House of Commons Select Committee on the Treasury and Civil Service recommended that all departments should adopt MINIS or a clearly equivalent management information system. A second factor, interacting with parliamentary interest, was media interest. Journalists were quick to seize on the fact that MINIS brought a great deal of information into the public arena. Given the general orientation towards secrecy rather than disclosure of information in British government, the ready availability of detailed information — especially in the early MINIS rounds — came as a surprise. Journalists were less quick to make use of the information made available than to comment on its availability.

Even if efforts to bring an idea into good currency overcome initial sources of resistance, its survival is not assured. Ideas in good currency may disappear as quickly as they arrive. The British political culture epitomized in Harold Wilson's remark that 'a week is a long time in politics' is notoriously limited in its horizons. As Dahrendorf (1982), with the benefit of a comparative perspective, remarked:

short-term thinking is a popular British pastime. It may or may not have its origin in Parliament; but Parliament certainly demonstrates it to the full. The rim of the saucer beyond which the House of Commons [never (authors' addition)] looks, is rarely even the next election, rather the next budget. Once, a group of parliamentary lobby correspondents asked me whether I could help them find out about experiences with federalism. When I recommended a seminar in a few months' time, they were rather taken aback. Oh no! they needed to know by Monday week. They did not say so, but they might have added that after Monday week they would no longer be interested. (Dahrendorf, 1982: 93)

Surprisingly, in the case of MINIS, parliamentary interest was not evanescent. On the contrary, through the medium of a select committee it helped to consolidate the idea of management information systems as a worthwhile development. Newspaper coverage by specialist journalists helped to keep MINIS in the forefront of public attention and provided them with a peg on which to hang other stories.

Diffusing
The third phase in the process of innovation is diffusion from the original source to other departments. If this had depended on voluntary departmental decisions, it is extremely unlikely that many, far less all, departments would have chosen to embark on introducing management information systems. However, the launching of the Financial Management Initiative in 1982 established a secure niche for MINIS. At the insistence of the Prime Minister, all departments were required to bring forward plans for instituting top management information systems broadly along the lines of MINIS. Some of the results of the ensuing work in this field are reviewed in the Financial Management Unit report referred to at the beginning of this chapter. It was made clear that this did not mean a slavish imitation of the Department of the Environment system. The functions and circumstances of government departments vary widely, and so, therefore, do their information requirements. Some departments had already given a good deal of attention to developing management information systems while others had ground to make up.

However, there was no explicit comparative framework available to departments for evaluating existing information systems or prescribing appropriate ones for the future. The process of innovation, as described above, left unanswered many questions about the forms of management information systems needed in different contexts. Moreover, implicitly rather than explicitly, it confined the role of information systems too narrowly. There are several questions about what information systems in government should do and how they should be designed to do it which warrant closer analysis. The following section considers some of them.

Information Systems for Public Management

One of the paradoxes of innovation is that conditions that favour progress at an early stage may subsequently become an obstacle to development. Realizing some opportunities may inadvertently foreclose a wider range of options. Promising developments lead into blind alleys. Overcoming resistance to change partly depends on operationalizing a new concept and showing that it can work. In doing so, the general idea is given a specific form, and it may be difficult to disentangle those features that are generic from those that happen to be appropriate to the case in point. This creates a danger that no basis for systematic comparison between different needs and circumstances is ever established. The original model is oversold and imitated more widely than it warrants, or else ad hoc variations are introduced from case to case without the benefit of any intervening theory to discriminate between appropriate and inappropriate diversity.

The debate about management information systems in government, prompted by MINIS, exemplifies this. A good deal of internal civil service debate and related public discussion revolved around a lowest common denominator concept of a management information system. Discussion was confined to information systems for performance review, principally, if not exclusively, intended to serve predefined objectives and taking policies as given. The role of information under this concept is largely confined to reporting actual performance in relation to plans and targets. Without wishing to deny the need for such systems, they provide only for a portion of the needs of public managers. Indeed, bearing in mind the analysis of key concepts in Chapter 2, it can be argued that this concept applies to control information in the context of routine operations rather than management information. Because of this initial emphasis, there has been only limited progress in considering the kinds of information systems needed for strategic management purposes. In fairness, a wider perspective could have developed than that which has become common currency. The accounts of MINIS by Bradley (1983), who conducted the original Rayner scrutiny that paved the way for MINIS, and Likierman (1982) show that there was no intention to foreclose options. The consolidating and diffusing phases narrowed the concept and gave an incomplete picture of the actual operation of MINIS as it evolved in the Department of the Environment.

To consider the potential of information systems in public management, a perspective is required that takes full account of the need to review objectives, strategies and policies in the light of environmental change and emerging problems. But conceptualizing information systems as an aid to strategic management as well as operational management encounters some influential criticism. Wildavsky (1979), for example, incorporated a sharp distinction between policy and management in his well-known aphorism 'policy analysis is what information systems are not'. However apt this may be as a comment on the specific systems he had in mind, which we would classify as control systems, it is misleading as a general statement. A more useful and relevant distinction is between information systems designed to improve the operational efficiency and effectiveness of existing organizations — by monitoring inputs and outputs, by uncovering ways of adapting to environmental fluctuations and by promoting more effective internal coordination — and information systems designed to improve adaptive efficiency and effectiveness, in recognizing the need for more fundamental strategic adjustment, and aiding processes of organizational learning that facilitate a reformulation of problems, a redefinition of objectives and the evolution of new policies. Broadly speaking, in the former case the role of information systems is to provide negative feedback — correcting departures from desired objectives. In the latter case the role of information systems is to provide positive feedback — prompting change, reinforcing movements away from previous policies, and searching out new objectives.

Much of the work on management information systems has, quite legitimately, focused on systems designed on negative feedback principles rather than on positive feedback principles. In so far as governmental organizations seek to maintain existing policies, this is appropriate. Improvements in operating efficiency are an important concern, but they are not all-important. A balance always has to be struck between improving efficiency in operational management and improving adaptive efficiency in the strategic management sense of recognizing early warnings of the need to change and adapt. Judging where the balance should be is one of the decisions to be made in assessing the relative importance of flexibility and cost-consciousness to organizational effectiveness.

Hedberg and Jönnson (1978) observed that most management information systems in business are strongly biased towards stabilizing current activities. Conventional systems tend to confirm the validity of what is being done and to seek improvements in pre-established directions. 'They filter away conflicts, ambiguities, overlaps, uncertainty, etc. and they suppress many relevant change signals and kill initiative to act on early warnings' (Hedberg and Jönnson, 1978:

47). These authors suggest several ways in which the design of information systems could counteract excessive stabilizing tendencies by incorporating deliberately destabilizing features into their information systems such as encouraging experimentation, promoting variety in communication and evaluation criteria, and implanting review processes to promote change. Especially in times of apparent stability, information systems should trigger investigation and act as sources of criticism of established policies rather than simply assuming their indefinite continuance.

Anti-hubris devices are especially important when political and organizational processes show tendencies towards groupthink. As Janis (1972, 1985) observed, potentially serious and costly errors arise when political leaders or managers form a tightly knit group which seeks internal concurrence on strategies, rejects evidence or ideas that do not fit the group perspective and protects preconceptions from external challenge. Even if signals for change are strengthened, they may be disregarded because the frames of reference that people bring to interpreting events embody strong preconceptions and fixed expectations. McCann (1977) identified a number of ways in which belief systems are protected from information and events that threaten them. When events depart significantly from expectations disparities are treated as temporary aberrations. Exceptions prove the rule. Management by exception allows departures from the norm to be treated as random errors of no policy significance. When incongruities are acknowledged to be real rather than aberrant they may still not prompt any revision of ideas that makes them comprehensible and may just be treated as oddities that must be tolerated. Another reason for discounting changes is, paradoxically, repeatedly erroneous claims that catastrophic events or crises are about to occur. Crying wolf dulls responsiveness to real crises. But political opponents are not always wrong. Most insidious of all is the persistence of obsolete frames of reference which maintain a myth. Information that challenges the myth is treated as inadmissible evidence, often with damaging consequences. The myth of self-regulation, which justified a minimal supervisory role for the Bank of England, was a contributory factor in the 1973-4 secondary banking crisis (Metcalfe, 1981). Strong faith in self-regulation is still a feature of the City of London financial community.

Once one considers the role of information systems as an aid to strategic management in prompting policy changes, the whole orientation becomes more active. Instead of being just reporting systems, they become enquiring systems, defining what information to seek and how to conduct the search as well as guiding interpretation. Mitroff and Pondy (1974) argued that, in public management especially, a single approach to information systems is inappropriate.

As with forms of organization, there is not 'one best way'. Radically different approaches to gathering and using information may be needed in different situations, and the management of enquiry involves the selection of appropriate forms of organizing information and a combination of these forms to meet different needs. Choice of information systems is closely related to methods of policy analysis rather than being sharply separated.

The management of information systems raises the further question of the replacement of obsolete systems. At a time when the main concern is with establishing information systems, talk of obsolescence may seem premature. But no information system lasts for ever, and sometimes the process of development is so slow relative to the rate of change of the problems that the system is obsolete by the time it is operational. Identifying obsolescence and initiating the task of renewal are significant concerns (Starbuck, 1973). No information system operates at peak efficiency from the start, and none retains peak efficiency for ever. It may be useful to think of the half-life of a system as the period during which it is 50 per cent efficient. The half-life or a higher standard might be a criterion for deciding when action should be taken to prepare a successor system. A key question in a rapidly changing environment is how to smooth the process of developing new systems and phasing out old ones. Creating a series of discrete and separate information systems, one after another, results in discontinuity and in distinct periods of poor performance. A more attractive, but managerially more difficult, approach is to move towards self-designing systems which monitor their own effectiveness and have a built-in learning capacity which enables new systems to evolve as existing systems become obsolete. Developing such systems, which are in the spirit of evolutionary operation, has far-reaching implications not only for the design of information systems themselves, but also for the organizational frameworks in which they function. The impact of changes in information systems on organization is discussed in the following section.

Information and Accountability
The development of management information systems is a direct response to the problems of large-scale organization. As we argued above, their design should allow for the familiar distortions that information flows through organizations are subject to. In addition, it should be borne in mind that the relationship between information and organization is a reciprocal one. The impact of information systems on the organizational framework should be considered as well as the impact of organization on information. As we indicated at the beginning of this chapter, one of the motivations behind MINIS was to

enable the minister to live up to the expectations embodied in the doctrine of ministerial responsibility. In launching MINIS, Heseltine shrewdly cloaked organizational innovation in traditional constitutional garb. The underlying thesis was a simple and direct one: the doctrine of ministerial responsibility needed to be reasserted. To bring reality into line with doctrine, the balance of power had to shift back to ministers and away from officials. Ministers needed regular detailed information about the whole range of departmental work, not just data about policy areas in which they had decided to take an interest. In short, information restored power to its rightful place. Admittedly, this required the minister to extend his managerial role, but in contemporary conditions this additional load was a burden that ambitious and effective politicians should be prepared to shoulder.

Given the premise, the argument works. As an element of rhetoric in the initiation phase, it provided a politically impeccable foundation for introducing change. In practice, the association of managerial innovation and constitutional orthodoxy is much less strong and clear-cut. Indeed, it is very likely that MINIS and other top management information systems will create pressures for change not only in patterns of departmental management but also in the constitutional framework of public management. Bearing in mind the wide disparities between the myth of ministerial responsibility and the realities of public management, pouring new managerial wine into old — and flawed — constitutional bottles is unlikely to extend their life: on the contrary, it is likely to accentuate the need for constitutional renewal.

MINIS is not just a tactical ploy in a zero-sum power game between politicians and officials within a given structure. Its main significance for public management lies in a more extensive redefinition of roles and relationships which has the potential for increasing organizational effectiveness by clarifying mutual expectations, stabilizing responsibilities, and linking resource allocation and performance assessment. Bradley (1983) perceptively explained the way in which the new departmental procedures for discussion and evaluation of performance and decision-making coordinated by the MINIS unit introduced 'due process' into departmental management.

Due process is an important and apt concept for public management, given its associations with US constitutional theory and the functions it can perform in organizational governance (Scott, Mitchell and Peery, 1981). Formally, due process defines a set of procedures through which management responsibilities, resource allocations and performance standards are set and changed. In other words, it is an integral element of the process of accountable management.

Substantive due process within an organization helps generate consensus about values. This consensus is necessary for legitimizing organizational

values, allocative decisions, rules and regulations... Procedural due process
provides a judicial function and includes review and appeal process which
protect lower-level organizational members from the arbitrary use of power
by superiors. (Scott, Mitchell and Peery, 1981: 147)

These two aspects of due process correspond with the distinction
drawn earlier between the positive, motivating, legitimizing role of
accountability processes and their restraining role. Due process
establishes constraints upon managerial discretion at the same time as it
accords legitimacy to it. Importantly, this applies equally to ministers
and civil servants. While on the one hand the procedures enhance
ministerial power in precisely the way Heseltine intended, by
establishing definite intervals at which explicit decisions have to be
made, on the other hand they set limits to ad hoc ministerial
intervention. Due process establishes in specific circumstances the right
of officials to manage. For the departmental management system to
retain credibility as a framework for action and assure the integrity of
the accountable management structure, ministers as well as civil
servants have to abide by the rules of the game.

Thus, MINIS and systems like it are not just introducing better
information into the processes of decision-making: they are also
leading to changes in the way government departments are managed.
These changes, in turn, will call into question established constitutional
doctrines. To the extent that MINIS procedures succeed in instituting
due process in departmental decision-making, they represent a significant move towards establishing accountable management. They pave
the way for clear delegation of authority and responsibility and provide
a mechanism for differentiating systematically between levels of policy
decision within departments. If practice conformed with this concept, it
would instigate a significant cultural shift away from the particularistic
'treat every case on its merits' attitudes which frequently create
ambiguity and lead to overcentralization. It would be wrong to
overdramatize the effects of occasional and unavoidable ad hoc
political interventions; but when exceptions become the rule, the
unintended result is excessive centralization, a collapse of managerial
accountability and a reversion to seat-of-the-pants management — in
other words, to the problems that reform was supposed to remedy.

Another unintended organizational consequence of MINIS is to
reinforce tendencies towards greater openness in government. To the
extent that government departments assemble information on a
systematic basis for their own purposes, the argument that open
government is too costly loses a lot of force. The initial acceptance of
MINIS was due partly to the fact that the returns disclosed information
not previously available to the public. If the flow of published
information dries up, public support for improving public management

will turn to criticism. The adverse reactions to the non-disclosure of cost information about proposed changes in welfare benefits by the government in 1985 exemplifies the kind of pressure for greater openness that the development of information systems will bring.

Finally, openness and accountability are linked. The more civil servants are held accountable internally for what they do as a result of MINIS-type processes, and the more the information base on which decisions are made is generally available, the less tenable will be the doctrine of ministerial responsibility as a sufficient channel for public accountability. Attempts to hold the line on conventional concepts of external accountability while introducing changes in internal accountability will set up increasing strains and tensions. This is not to argue for throwing out ministerial accountability: it is an argument for reconstructing the doctrine and practice of public accountability along lines that correspond with the actual exercise of public authority and that support efforts to improve performance.

Conclusions

The development of MINIS has played an important role in lodging the idea of management information systems in the culture of Whitehall. Nevertheless, the use of information systems in government will overcome the substantial scepticism that remains only if they demonstrate the ability to satisfy the real information needs of managers at all levels. Top management systems are only one element, though a crucial one, for the following reasons. Future development should take account of the political environment of public management. If information systems fail to reflect the political dimension and do not link with policy analysis they will lose credibility and fall into disuse. Public interest and support have played an important role in the development of information systems. This should be reflected in public accountability processes that strengthen accountable management within departments. The sheer complexity of the problems that government faces presents a real challenge to the development of new types of information system. If necessity is the mother of invention, there is little doubt that public management will be a forcing house for new ideas about the form and function of management information systems.

The process through which MINIS evolved indicates some of the alternative pathways that future reforms of public management may follow and which have different implications for the management of change. Innovation follows different courses, depending on whether innovation decisions by the organizations involved are optional, collective or authoritative (Rogers and Kim, 1985). Optional decisions rely on individual organizations to form judgements and make commitments to action. Collective decisions are choices made by consensus. Authoritative decisions are made on a higher level, and compliance is required. MINIS moved from optional to authoritative decision when it was incorporated in the Financial Management Initiative. At the time MINIS was conceived, consensus decision-making, the preferred Whitehall style, would have rejected it. It will be interesting to see whether in the future the culture will be more supportive of innovation.

4
Centralize in order to Decentralize

Decentralization of authority and responsibility is one of the most common prescriptions for improving efficiency and effectiveness in large organizations, public or private. In the private sector, decentralization is often advocated as a means of setting managers free from excessive controls and enabling them to use their initiative. The thesis is that decentralized structures can recreate the conditions in which innovative and entrepreneurial talents can flourish. From Schumacher onwards, 'Small is Beautiful' has supplanted glorification of big business and led many large companies to seek ways of simulating conditions associated with small business. In the public sector, decentralization is generally prescribed as a means of liberating managerial potential shackled by bureaucratic restrictions. Public organizations are regularly taken to task for having too many hierarchical levels and displaying a reluctance to delegate decision-making down the line. Bureaucratic rigidity and inefficiency are often attributed to excessive centralization. Not surprisingly increased delegation was one of the clear messages propagated in the Rayner programme. It was a message that many, inside and outside government, welcomed and it is a prominent theme of the Financial Management Initiative.

Never the less decentralization in government is problematic: it prompts anxieties and scepticism when attention shifts from general principle to specific cases. Administrators at top levels fear a loss of control. They perceive conflicts between the implications of increased delegation of authority and the requirements of public accountability; the inefficiencies resulting from excessive centralization are often seen as the unavoidable price of public accountability. In British government, the personal responsibility of ministers to Parliament for everything that happens in their departments sharpens their concern with accountability and accentuates the difficulties of achieving decentralization. Elaborate processes of internal and external accountability can stultify the exercise of administrative discretion. Concern with satisfying accountability requirements can lead people to a preoccupation with avoiding errors. More accurately, perhaps, passing the buck — avoiding responsibility for errors — rather than improving performance is the main preoccupation.

A justifiable concern with public accountability should not be allowed to obscure the significant failure to attain the degree of decentralization that is achievable. Many of the criticisms of overcautious and defensive management in government have a substantial degree of validity. Poorly designed procedures and management systems produce duplication, overlap and a confusion of responsibilities, or leave unrecognized loopholes. Staff are faced with too many unanswered questions, or given too little clear guidance to deal promptly and efficiently with the flow of work. Instead of a clear delegation of responsibilities, answers frequently have to be sought by referring up the hierarchy. Real authority to make decisions may be reserved at levels well above the point where facts are assembled and assimilated. Perversely, the congestion and overload caused by centralization are often given as reasons for adding more support staff and extra supervisory levels to the hierarchy — a duplication of functions which increases delay and inefficiency. Everyone is too absorbed in coping with day-to-day problems to consider how to improve the situation.

In view of this, there seems to be a clear-cut case for identifying and overcoming the obstacles to greater decentralization. It would be reassuring if organizational research on centralization and decentralization confirmed conventional wisdom and offered prescriptions; yet a major survey of organizational research on decentralization showed that firm conclusions are unwarranted. While, at a general level, large organizations decentralize more than small organizations, and unimportant decisions are more readily delegated than important ones, the evidence assembled by Jennergren (1981) poses as many questions as it answers. The meaning of decentralization is not self-evident: different definitions are used in different contexts. The measurement of decentralization presents problems even when one is clear about what is being measured. The form of decentralization is not preordained. In stable environments functional decentralization appears more appropriate, while the evidence shows that divisional decentralization is more appropriate in changing environments. Employing the term 'appropriate' suggests a link with performance, yet Jennergren concluded that the evidence of a positive relationship between performance and decentralization is unclear and difficult to disentangle from the effects of other structural variables. Indeed, he questioned whether prescriptions for decentralization could be implemented without, at the same time, transforming many other aspects of organizational functioning.

Bearing this in mind, and also keeping in mind the forces working to maintain excessive centralization in government, it is clear that there is a need to tread carefully and not simply regard decentralization as an easy and self-evidently beneficial prescription for improving public management. Before going further, some basic points are worth restating lest they cause confusion. After this it will be useful to consider a particular case of successful decentralization conducted within the framework of the Rayner programme. The case in question is the scrutiny of the Department of Industry's Regional Development Grants Administration. The outcomes of this scrutiny give some useful guidance about the possibilities and problems of decentralization.

Either-or, or a Question of Degree?

Because the bias of discussion is so often towards the assumption that decentralization is good and centralization is bad, it sometimes seems that two quite different models of organization are being counterposed; one characterized by tight unified control at the top and the other by great autonomy and initiative at the bottom. In reality, we are never talking about polar opposites presenting such a clear choice. Some central direction and control is always present, otherwise organizations simply fragment and disintegrate. Some local discretion is always present, otherwise nothing gets done. The problem is how to combine them in a way that contributes to greater efficiency and effectiveness.

Seeking a combination of decentralizing and centralizing tendencies frequently leads to the view that the problem is one of degree — a balance between opposites. The question is how much delegation of authority is possible without threatening overall managerial control. At what point does delegation become abdication? Politically and managerially there is an awkward problem of reconciling the irreconcilable. The trade-off or conflict between maintaining control and improving performance recalls the earlier discussion of dilemmas of accountability. Greater efficiency and effectiveness can only be bought at the price of reduced control.

A Difference of Kind?

Fortunately, it is not necessary to remain locked within the conflicts created by this formulation of the problem. There is a more fruitful and constructive way out of the centralization/decentralization dilemma. Differences of kind as well as of degree are involved. The question is not simply, 'How much decentralization?' It is what kinds of controls and management processes should be instituted to assure overall direction at the same time as effective delegation? Instead of sacrificing one aim to achieve another, the manager as integrator seeks solutions which serve both. Perhaps the clearest analysis of how to deal with the problem was proposed by Perrow (1977). He argued that the dilemma is largely a product of outmoded ways of thinking about organization. The bureaucratic paradox is that efficient organizations centralize in order to decentralize:

We are in a bind that insists that the idea of a centralized-decentralized bureaucracy is a contradiction in terms. Yet the fact is that our terms are about a half-century out of date. Organizations have changed, but changes in terminology to reflect those changes in organizations have not been forthcoming and are long overdue. (Perrow, 1977: 5)

In order to make centralization and decentralization complementary components of an efficient organization, three types of controls, serving different purposes, have to be combined. Perrow termed them first-order, second-order and third-order controls. First-order controls are direct, detailed face-to-face requests and orders from superiors to subordinates. They are essential features of direct supervision and are applied on a case-by-case basis. From a managerial standpoint they are both expensive, because superiors are constantly involved in making or reviewing subordinates' decisions, and they are obtrusive, because subordinates have to seek approval time after time or have their boss looking over their shoulder. A great deal of managerial time is absorbed in operational decision-making.

Rules and regulations, another form of first-order control, can reduce the burden because they give general directions. But rules and regulations enshrined in forms, standard operating procedures and working instructions easily proliferate to the point where they may themselves become a source of error and confusion. Red tape is just as frustrating for insiders as it is for outsiders, possibly even more so. It is also a potent source of overcentralization since it leaves many lower level staff unsure what they should be doing and unwilling to make decisions.

Second-order controls are needed when direct supervision and general rules are not up to the job, either because the scale of operations or the complexity of the task is too great. Standardization and specialization are two major forms of second-order controls. Standardization involves classifying the types of problems that organizations deal with and establishing specific criteria for dealing with subsets of cases. Standardization focuses attention, prepares responses and thereby paves the way for specialization. Once it is clear what problems people have to deal with it is worth investing in training and selection to improve performance over a specified range of case-work.

Specialization also has a hierarchical dimension. It is worthwhile designing structures which differentiate simpler and less important problems from complex and more important problems. Instead of treating all cases in the same way, which may mean some of them are tackled several times before someone has the expertise or authority to handle them effectively, clear demarcations among levels can indicate where incoming problems should be routed.

These second-order controls embody some of the most frequently reiterated Rayner principles of specification of objectives: the clarification of responsibilities and the definition of line management structures. In one sense, they may be seen as creating more bureaucracy. They do. In another sense, they are a means of providing a clearer framework within which people know what is expected of them and know what to expect of others. Standardization, specialization and hierarchy, by reducing ambiguity, increase subordinates' sense of autonomy within their zone of discretion and at the same time increase superiors' sense of control.

First- and second-order controls do not install, maintain or change themselves. Third-order controls are needed to design, sustain and modify their operation. The application of third-order controls is especially important as a function of top management — though it is not their exclusive preserve. Communication channels, corporate values and cultural norms about coordination, rewards and reinforcements, and feedback about performance are powerful, though often unobtrusive, variables which influence behaviour by changing the working assumptions underlying decisions and actions. In contrast with first-order controls they work indirectly by changing the premises on which people make judgements and by re-framing their perceptions and attention. Instead of requiring constant management by direction, they provide management by design. Unless top management pays attention to the impact of these contextual variables — which can only be modified at the organizational level — they will fail to create the conditions for either decentralization of authority or central control.

With these distinctions in mind, we proceed to consider the scrutiny of the Regional Development Grants Administration. The following pages give a short account of the scheme: the way the system was administered before the scrutiny, and the scrutineers' diagnosis and recommendations. This is followed by an assessment of its wider relevance and applicability to other areas of public management.

Empirical Focus
The empirical focus is the 1980 Department of Industry scrutiny of the Administration of Regional Development Grants. This scrutiny is of general interest for a variety of reasons. It revealed scope for simplification of procedures and information needs in dealing with applicants and recipients of grants. It led to a reduction of duplication among administrative units. It showed that there were opportunities for decentralizing the administration of grants. Furthermore, the scrutiny provided insights into how to achieve decentralization, and to create the scope for improving both service and efficiency. It is as interesting as a study in the management of change as for the decentralization it achieved.

The choice of the Regional Development Grants Administration for scrutiny did not mean that it was an area of gross inefficiency. On the contrary, the scrutineers were at pains to state that the system was not expensive in relation to the amount of grant paid or by comparison with other similar administrative systems. But it was large, costly and, because of its size and substandard performance, criticized by industry. It administered about one-third of the Department of Industry's budget and employed a substantial proportion of its staff. Because the system was highly visible it had encountered criticisms from the Public Accounts Committee, Parliament's main 'watchdog' body.

Although things changed later, at the time of the scrutiny the problem facing the scrutineers was not whether to scrap the whole system or initiate root and branch reorganization. A change of emphasis was needed to promote greater efficiency and remove the self-protective procedures which had crept into the operation of the system. Sensitivity to external criticism and concern with avoiding mistakes had created a climate in which people were reluctant to accept responsibility. The process of dealing with applications for grants had become clogged and overloaded. There were no significant incentives to improve operational efficiency. If, as we suggested earlier, management means taking responsibility for the performance of a system, and one major element of management is ensuring that first-, second- and third-order controls are appropriate to the task, management responsibility had not been effectively discharged.

The Regional Development Grants Scheme

The Regional Development Grants Scheme came into existence as the main instrument of regional industrial policy under Part I of the Industry Act 1972. The 1972 Act made grants available for capital expenditure by businesses on new plant and buildings in special development areas and development areas. Eligibility for grants under the Scheme was deliberately defined in broad terms. The scheme was designed to provide a source of capital finance that could be built into investment planning and which businesses could be sure that they would receive and receive promptly. The operation of the scheme was intended to be automatic so that applicants would be assured that, if they met the criteria, they would be certain of obtaining grants. From the applicants' point of view it was supposed to be intelligible, predictable and quick.

In 1979/80, the year before the scrutiny took place there were almost 40,000 applications for grants. The grant payments approved in the same period totalled approximately £440 million. This was a substantial part of the total Department of Industry budget. Further details of the scheme will be explained later after the apparatus created to administer the scheme has been described. This description is based on the scrutineers' account and subsequent interviews with staff.

The Regional Development Grants Administration
The Regional Development Grants scheme was administered by an organization consisting of a headquarters unit and four regional units, covering Scotland and Wales as well as England. The four Regional Development Grant Offices were at Billingham, Bootle, Cardiff and Glasgow. The small headquarters unit formed part of the Regional Policy and Development Grants Division of the Department of Industry and was located in London. The London-based headquarters was responsible for policy matters, forecasting, and advice to the Regional Development Grant Offices. It was also responsible for the pursuit of cases where grant was recoverable and legal proceedings or write-off action had to be considered.

The Regional Development Grant Offices were responsible for receiving applications and examining them, giving approval where appropriate, paying grants and monitoring compliance with the conditions on which the grants were given. Management responsibility in each Regional Development Grant Office was focused on a director at senior principal level who normally had two assistant directors. The internal structure of each office consisted of an Examination Unit which processed grant applications and approved payment of grants on eligible applications as well as checking whether industrial premises qualified for grants. About three-quarters of all Regional Development Grant Offices' staff worked in the Examination Units. The rest of the staff of the four Regional Development Grant Offices was divided among a number of small ancillary units. An Audit Unit checked a sample of approved applications, before payment was made, to guard against fraud by applicants and to check on inconsistencies in decision-making. A Payments Unit had formal responsibility for issuing grant payments, seeking recovery of grants where necessary and performing accounting functions within the Regional Development Grant Offices. The staff of an Inspection Unit visited premises on which grant had been paid to ensure that the conditions about the use of assets were complied with. In addition, there was a Common Services Unit responsible for office accommodation, typing and offices services, and for collating data on work flow to report to the Regional Development Grants Administration headquarter's office. Above these units was a policy unit to advise the Examination Unit. Figure 1 shows this arrangement in chart form.

FIGURE 1: *Regional Development Grant Administration*

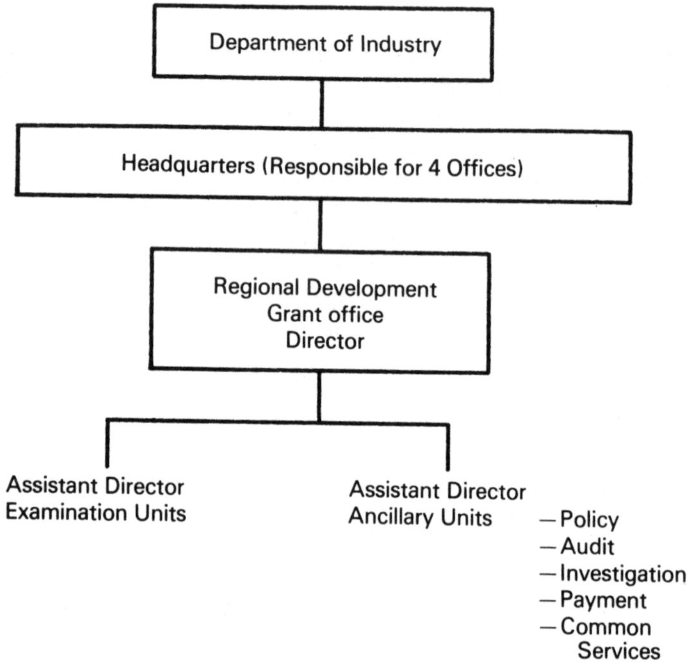

```
        ┌─────────────────────────────────────┐
        │       Department of Industry        │
        └─────────────────────────────────────┘
                          │
   ┌──────────────────────────────────────────────┐
   │   Headquarters (Responsible for 4 Offices)   │
   └──────────────────────────────────────────────┘
                          │
            ┌───────────────────────────┐
            │   Regional Development     │
            │      Grant office          │
            │       Director             │
            └───────────────────────────┘
                          │
      ┌───────────────────┴───────────────────┐
Assistant Director                    Assistant Director
Examination Units                     Ancillary Units      — Policy
                                                           — Audit
                                                           — Investigation
                                                           — Payment
                                                           — Common
                                                             Services
```

The Process of Administration

The process of administration can almost be inferred from the foregoing description of the organization and its task. It is worth providing a short statement of this, because this will help to identify the areas where the scrutineers discovered weaknesses and opportunities for improvement. The description outlines the flow of work as it was before the scrutiny took place.

The process began with applicants completing a form and submitting it to the Regional Development Grant Office to be checked by the Examination Unit for errors and omissions prior to considering eligibility for grant. Any errors in filling in the forms had to be corrected by communication with the applicant. No matter how large or small the amount of money the applicant requested, the same procedure for assessing applications was followed, on grounds of equity and accountability. Although the scheme was intended to provide grant on a quick, predictable and almost automatic basis, the process could take a long time because of the accretion of practices that had grown up for handling particular cases: examination of eligibility was conducted in the light of a considerable 'case-law' built up over a period of years.

After consideration by the Examination Unit, applications were either rejected or approved for payment. If approved, some would be checked by the Audit Unit then passed on to the Payment Unit if audit criteria were met. Grant was then paid to eligible applicants who, as recipients of grants, were liable to have their premises inspected by the staff of the Inspection Unit in order to ensure that the conditions of grant were met and that no conditions of default arose which might lead Regional Policy and Development Grants to seek a refund in part or in whole. Inspections were made at intervals during the period of the grant, which was four years. This was the system whose working the scrutineers set out to examine.

Terms of Reference and Diagnosis
The scrutiny began in February 1980 as a standard 90-day departmental scrutiny with the following terms of reference: 'to examine the administration of regional development grant work at the Department's four Regional Development Grant Offices and at headquarters; to consider how far changes in or greater standardiz-ation of procedures in Regional Development Grant Offices could lead to greater efficiency; to have full regard to the outcome of recent reviews of this area of work by Organisation and Methods, Staff Inspection and Internal Audit teams; and to make recommendations.' The importance of the reference to standardization for the process of decentralization will emerge as the discussion proceeds.

In accordance with the general scrutiny guidelines, the scrutineers spent some time familiarizing themselves with the scheme and discussing its operation with the staff involved and with others in the department. Deliberate efforts were made to obtain the views of the staff involved about how to improve efficiency. As the terms of reference indicate, it was also possible to take advantage of recent work done by management service groups within the Department of Industry. If a general point may be interjected here, this is an example of the way the Rayner programme has built on existing efficiency work in departments, and given impetus to making changes that might otherwise have had low priority.

The departmental and local trade union side in each of the four Regional Development Grant Offices were informed of the terms of reference of the scrutiny and given the opportunity to submit their views. Their input to the formulation of scrutiny recommendations was small in comparison with that of staff members. Indeed, to begin with, doubts about the intentions of these scrutineers in particular, and Raynerism in general, provoked hostility. Union representatives had no intention of associating themselves with a cut-back exercise, and in the civil service as a whole, union policy was to remain suspicious of the 'job-enriching' claims which accompanied many scrutinies. They displayed more positive interest in the implementation phase.

As a result of their inquiries, the scrutineers identified a number of problems which, in combination, constituted significant obstacles to efficiency. They started from the design and content of application forms and included the working practices of Examination Units, the relations of Ancillary Units to Examination Units, the duplication of work in the management hierarchy and the lack of coordination and consistency of practice among the four regional offices. There was scope for improvement in each of these areas. More important, from a management point of view, there was the possibility of achieving greater improvements by integrating solutions into a new pattern of organization.

The first problem area was the design and content of the application form itself. Experience showed that applicants found the forms difficult to complete satisfactorily, and therefore unnecessary delays and errors occurred in processing them. Apart from unclear instructions and inadequate layout, the completed forms did not provide all the relevant information. Additional information had to be sought through correspondence or telephone communications with applicants. This gave rise to delay and possibly also to errors. Furthermore, separate forms had to be completed for grant applications for plant and machinery, as distinct from grant applications for building and works. The distinction sounds obvious. But, in fact, the administration of the scheme revealed grey areas where classification of capital investment projects was difficult and where disputes arose about the appropriate categorization of particular assets. These disputes had policy and resource repercussions: different conditions and rates of grant applied to the two categories. Any changes in the specification of information requirements raised further problems in clarifying the conditions for the eligibility for grant. If these problems were not resolved the work of Inspection Units at a later stage became unnecessarily complicated.

The next problem area the scrutineers identified was the modus operandi of Examination Units. In part, the procedures employed followed from guidelines laid down when the policy was introduced. But practices had also developed in response to the particular problems and pressures encountered in running the scheme, and it was these adjustments which gave rise to inefficiency. Although, in principle, the scheme was intended to be predictable and simple to administer, an elaborate system of case-law gradually developed and was embodied in a three-volume, 600-page instruction manual. Formally, the status of the instruction manual was advisory, but a tendency developed within the Regional Development Grants Administration for staff to regard it as authoritative and binding. Going by the book gave a sense of security and a feeling that errors were being avoided, even if the process was slower, more cumbersome and less efficient than it might otherwise have been. Staff could go against precedent if they were prepared to accept responsibility. Going by the book seems to have been both a cause and a consequence of excessive centralization. Problems were passed up the hierarchy for solution because it was unclear who had authority to resolve them. The solutions arrived at in different cases did not effectively establish general principles that could guide subsequent decisions at lower levels.

The discretion of Examination Units was further restricted by the encroachment of ancillary units, such as the Audit and Payments Units, on their work. Insofar as Audit and Payment Units followed up the work of Examination Units, they were an immediate source of face-to-face criticism for errors made. Examination Unit staff had to justify their decisions to the Audit and Payment Units and behind these lay the more remote threats of (at the time) the Exchequer and Audit Department and the Public Accounts Committee. Thus, while there were no obvious direct rewards for improved efficiency, there was a possibility of rapid identification of particular errors which might prove embarrassing if pursued by departmental auditors, or by the Exchequer and Audit and the Public Accounts Committee. The accountability system was biased towards negative evaluation.

Defensiveness and overcentralization were reinforced by unsystematic and excessively-detailed management supervision. Although all applications, large and small, simple and complex, were supposed to receive the same treatment, claims for large amounts of grant naturally attracted more senior management attention. Their handling involved a duplication of effort up the management hierarchy. Instead of being identified immediately, they were sifted through the management hierarchy and inevitably this caused delays in the treatment of large applications, without necessarily resulting in better or different decisions. Ad hoc centralization increased the likelihood that the system would develop a substantial backlog of unprocessed applications, which it did. At the time of the scrutiny, there was a backlog of several months applications.

Finally, to complicate the situation still further, the relative autonomy of the four Regional Development Grant Offices meant that each developed somewhat different procedures and practices for dealing with similar cases. This was confusing and frustrating to applicant companies who might make similar applications to more than one office. These divergences also made it difficult to introduce changes across the system as a whole because there was a lack of firm management from headquarters about how to secure a uniform approach.

Scrutiny Recommendations

Having identified these various impediments to efficiency, the scrutineers made an integrated set of recommendations for removing them. They recommended that the application form should be redesigned in order to make it easier for applicants to understand; they also recommended an improvement in the comprehensiveness and appropriateness of the information obtained so as to minimize the need to go back to companies for further information at a later stage. Another recommendation was to combine the separate applications for plant and machinery grants, and for building and works grants. A common set of conditions applying to both these categories was designed to achieve greater clarity and simplicity.

From the standpoint of achieving more decentralization, the recommendation that Examination Unit staff exercise greater judgement was of particular importance. At the time of the scrutiny, applications for grants of £5000 or less accounted for a large proportion of the work-load and a small proportion of the budget: 40 per cent of the applications but only 1.5 per cent of the grant actually paid. Pursuing detailed enquiries in all these cases with the same intensity as in cases where applications were for hundreds of thousands or millions of pounds was not cost effective. The scrutineers recommended a more selective approach to applications so that smaller and relatively straightforward applications could be dealt with more quickly. They proposed that Examination Unit staff should exercise discretion in deciding whether or not to allow applications. In line with the terms of reference of the scrutiny, this entailed establishing clearly defined categories and setting levels at which to make decisions.

The major implication of exercising greater judgement in the Examination Units was the need to rewrite the instruction manual so as to provide more systematic general guidance and indicate more clearly the areas in which discretion could be exercised. Work on this had begun even before the scrutiny took place. It became clear during the scrutiny that much of the input to this process could come from within the Regional Development Grant Offices. Even so, the task of separating general principles from responses to particular, and not necessarily representative cases, would have to be undertaken by management in order to ensure consistent standards across the whole system. Once again, decentralizing individual decisions without loss of consistency called for management to establish a clear framework.

Changes in the scope and discretion of the Examination Units had consequences for the relations between them and other units in the Regional Development Grant Offices, and between staff at different levels. Allowing Examination Units to exercise greater judgement meant redefining the role of the local Audit Unit: the recommendation was that they should act as a systems audit rather than as an extra supervisory group picking up individual errors and mistakes. The intervention of the Audit Unit in the past had weakened the responsibility of line management for ensuring that staff did their jobs correctly. The scrutineers sought to strengthen line management responsibility. The scrutineers' observation of the overlap between the work of local Audit and Payments Units led to the recommendation that the units should be merged so as to improve the efficiency of the control process. Further duplication of functions could be eradicated by giving responsibility to the Inspection Unit for following up cases where the possibility of recovering grant arose, and by excluding Payment Units from this area.

In order to ensure that large and important applications received prompt treatment, the scrutineers also proposed standards to indicate the levels in the hierarchy at which applications for particular amounts could be approved. Routing applications to the appropriate levels avoided the situation in which the same applications were subject to review at each level of the hierarchy.

This account makes no attempt to list the numerous detailed recommendations that emerged from the scrutiny — a full listing is available in the scrutineers' report. What it has sought to do is to highlight those factors of general relevance in promoting efficiency in government, especially those that provide ways of achieving greater administrative decentralization. The general thrust is quite clear: there should be a deliberate shift from reliance on first-order controls, such as direct supervision and case-by-case decision-making, to second-order controls, such as clarification of decision-making criteria, definition of responsibilities and demarcation of roles.

Conduct and Implementation of the Scrutiny
The guidelines issued by Sir Derek Rayner to staff conducting scrutinies stressed, in general terms, the importance of 'going and seeing' what was actually happening. Scrutineers were instructed not to rely on second-hand information from reports and written sources. They were instructed to go and see for themselves, and to draw their

own conclusions based on first hand knowledge acquired by talking to those involved at ground level. Beyond these general prescriptions, they were not given specific guidance on how to proceed. Scrutineers were left to make up their own minds about how to go about their task. This approach is open to criticism on the grounds of being unnecessarily hit-or-miss, depending on the imagination, aptitudes and skills of individual scrutineers. The line of least resistance is the arms-length external consultant approach, strong on prescriptions but weak on implementation. In the present case, the scrutineers adopted a different approach which led to a highly successful scrutiny from the point of view of process as well as substance.

The scrutineers approach to their task drew heavily on the knowledge and insights of the people working in the system. Their investigations went well beyond consultation to acquire basic information. Indeed, many of the recommendations incorporated in the final report originated with staff working in the Regional Development Grants Administration rather than being dreamed up by the scrutineers. As a result the report, when it was submitted, did not contain recommendations that surprised officials working in the system. To a substantial degree, it reflected views about problems and solutions that were widely shared within the system though not on the top management agenda for action.

This does not mean that the scrutiny itself was unnecessary or added nothing to what was known already. First of all, merely cataloguing the views of different people rarely, if ever, provides a basis for organizational action. The scrutineers played an important integrative function: they synthesized and organized the ideas presented to them in a set of mutually consistent proposals for improving performance; they identified orderly ways of achieving decentralization at the same time as they proposed systems to enable top management to see the wood rather than just the trees.

Besides putting together a coherent package of proposals that could be applied in practice, the scrutiny helped to pave the way for implementation. How it was conducted, rather than what it proposed, did much to engender a positive reception. Involving staff in the processes of diagnosis and proposing solutions had a catalytic effect in mobilizing support for implementation. Not only did staff know what to expect of the report, but, at least in some degree, they had played a role in producing it. This is not to suggest that the whole process was sweetness and light. There were disagreements, divergent views and hostility to being singled out as a target for scrutiny. Nevertheless the scrutiny was conducted well enough to avoid a sharp polarization or to leave a residue of bitterness that would have obstructed implementation. Over a number of years, this scrutiny has been used as a case study in teaching at the Civil Service College. During that time, several middle-managers from the Regional Development Grants Administration participated in the courses, and their comments on the scrutiny process have been universally favourable — a good indication that this was a job well done.

Combining, in this chapter, a discussion of the conduct of the scrutiny with a description of its implementation reflects what actually happened. The senior scrutineer was promoted and made responsible for the implementation of the scrutiny's recommendations. Without his initially constructive and positive approach it is possible that this appointment could have backfired. In the event, it greatly assisted the process of implementation. There was no delay while someone new become familiar with the recommendations and the reasons for them — a process which middle managers in the civil service who have suffered under transient senior management refer to as 'learning to answer the examination questions'. Nor was there the associated problem of building up relationships almost from scratch.

Finally, because of the confidence he acquired in understanding the problems and his commitment to producing viable solutions, the senior scrutineer chose, in some instances, not to implement his own recommendation. In the light of subsequent evidence some of the conclusions on which recommendations were based turned out to be faulty. Investigations in the course of introducing changes showed that, for example, the distribution of applications of different sizes was not what had been thought and compensating organizational changes had to be made. Even so, implementation took longer and presented more difficulties than was originally expected. But that, paradoxically, is only to be expected.

Conclusions

Three kinds of conclusions flow from the analysis of this scrutiny. The first, central, conclusions have to do with the centralization–decentralization issue. Second, the conduct and implementation of the scrutiny throws light on the strategies that can be employed in managing change in government. Third, the scrutiny shows how the larger governmental context impinges on the management process and how successful internal change involves supporting changes in external expectations and constraints.

First, these three kinds of conclusions are important in their own right and also because of the way they interact in a particular case. The scrutiny recommendations and their implementation fit the framework Perrow proposed; they show the complementarity of centralization and decentralization. The overall impact of the recommendations was to shift away from reliance on first-order controls, such as direct instructions, detailed supervision and checking and the ad hoc solution of individual problems, towards greater reliance on second-order controls. Standardization is, of course, one of the strategies of second-order control together with a formalization and specialization of functions and personnel. These measures permitted an orderly process of decentralization without loss of central control. In order to implement them key decisions had to be made centrally. Centralize in order to decentralize. As the foregoing discussion has shown, this scrutiny gives a very clear picture of how delegating authority can strengthen top management control. The changes required include: clarifying responsibilities, simplifying procedures, sharpening up objectives, eliminating duplication and overlap. Standardization and other second-order controls create a framework which gives positive guidance to decision-makers at lower levels, and reduces the need for negative error correcting first-order controls.

Putting these precepts into practice required new third-order controls. The scrutiny itself was the instrument for creating a new definition of the situation to which staff in the Regional Development Grants Administration had to respond. It is important to appreciate that it did so not simply because it was a report with recommendations that had the backing of top management and therefore was assured of prompt implementation. The manner in which the scrutiny was conducted and the seriousness with which its implementation was treated were very important factors in changing the premises of decision of people actually working in the system. The point bears repeating that, although it is top management that is strategically placed to create and modify premises of decision, their efforts produce results only if they pervade the whole organization. It is not just top management's premises of decision that must change.

Second, this scrutiny did not conform to the conventional image of a consultant's report — conducted by outsiders, based on little familiarity with the organization, presented to top management and unconcerned with implementation. There was already a background of management consideration of how to deal with problems. The scrutineers put in enough work to gain the confidence of staff and to engender a readiness to change. The scrutiny process was catalytic rather than purely prescriptive: it prepared the way for changes which, to some degree, people were ready to make but which lacked a mechanism for facilitating change. The catalytic style of the initial intervention did not make subsequent management of change easy, but it did make it easier than it would have been if the scrutineers had not troubled to mobilize support and build commitment within the organization. The general point is that there are a number of possible methods or styles of intervention which are appropriate for different problems and circumstances. A catalytic or facilitative intervention was right in this case. In other circumstances, a more prescriptive, or a confronting style, might be appropriate. Within the development of the Efficiency Strategy, this is an important area of choice in which more explicit guidance could be given to scrutineers than at present. The continuity of responsibility for the scrutiny and its implementation was another important factor in ensuring positive staff responses in the face of the difficulties of organizational change. On the one hand, there was someone in charge who knew the background and had a commitment to seeing through the task. On the other hand, a clear grasp of what the scrutiny was intended to do allowed him to adopt a flexible attitude when new evidence showed that the problems were different from what had at first been thought, and that the proposed solutions seemed less appropriate. Ticking off the numbers of recommendations implemented, as if they were items on a checklist, was not used as a proxy measure of success in this case. Implementation was treated as an adaptive process and not as a programmed process.

The third set of conclusions concern the management of relations between the Regional Development Grants Administration and its environment. This has been covered, at least by implication, in the discussion of decentralization, because the motivation for change was to provide a better service to the businesses applying for grants. However, the public served is only one element of the environment: there are other important elements within government whose actions and expectations affect the quality of service provided. Most obviously, they include internal and external audit and accountability agencies. To ensure that planned internal changes really took effect they had to be underpinned and reinforced by changes in the basis of evaluation. At the implementation stage the proposed changes in internal organization were discussed fully with auditors, and new procedures and criteria for evaluation agreed. As we pointed out in Chapter 2, just because the existing system of accountability inhibits good management, it does not follow that all systems of accountability necessarily do so. Changes in internal organization and management should be accompanied by appropriate changes in accountability processes.

Taken on is own terms, this scrutiny should be counted a success. It achieved savings and improved the service. It offers some clear and important lessons which have general applicability throughout government. At the same time it is appropriate to add a postscript in 1987. The legislative basis of the grant scheme was the 1972 Industry Act. This put great emphasis on the provision of investment incentives as the main route to improved industrial productivity. Now, unemployment is the main problem, and employment creation is the top priority. Following a major review of the effectiveness of government support to industry there was a policy change. Grants were linked to job creation rather than capital investment. The new scheme was selective rather than automatic. The Regional Development Grants Administration was abolished and the new selective scheme was transferred to the (now) Department of Trade and Industry's main regional office. The specific benefits of the effort put into reforming this part of government were short-lived. The operation was a success, but the patient died.

This may seem a disappointing note on which to end. In a way it is. It would have been nice to report that the reorganization was an unqualified success producing all the long-term benefits that were foreseen. Sceptics may feel that events confirm their doubts about the worthwhileness of efforts to improve public management. If gains can be wiped out so quickly, all the hard work seems wasted. Such a conclusion is not justified. In the first place, the conduct of the scrutiny and its implementation showed a real concern for the quality of service provided to the public and the quality of the working environment of the staff providing the service. Both are important values of a public management culture even if they have not featured strongly in the culture of Whitehall. Second, the general lessons retain their validity whatever the outcome in the particular scrutiny. In designing new organizations and planning changes, top management would do well to consider what kinds of controls they should institute to achieve an effective combination of decentralization and control. The distinctions between first-, second- and third-order controls do not give detailed blueprints, but they do provide a common language for diagnosis and prescription which enable managers working in different organizational contexts to communicate effectively and learn from each other's experiences. Finally, it is appropriate to enter a reminder of one of the main points made in Chapter 2. Improving public management always involves taking a stand in relation to the cost-consciousness versus flexibility dilemma. In this case, the emphasis was on cost-consciousness. The scrutineers were not asked to consider the implications of major policy change or fundamental reorganization. Perhaps, in future, flexibility considerations should receive more attention even if they offer less immediate savings.

5
Spend to Save

In May 1985, the Comptroller and Auditor General reported to Parliament on the means by which the government pays benefits to unemployed people. He concluded that:

> ...many claimants have to deal with two or more offices to get all the benefits to which they are entitled, and for a number of claimants, no one office is aware of their full benefit entitlement. The arrangements are cumbersome and involve some duplication of effort and overlap. (National Audit Office, 1985)

These criticisms are couched in language that reflects a typically British preference for understatement. Four years earlier, in March 1981, a joint scrutiny team from the Departments of Employment and Health and Social Security had recommended sweeping changes to the benefit system, propounding a 'one-office concept' and proposing to do away with much of the duplication of effort (Department of Employment, Department of Health and Social Security, 1981). The scrutineers were invited to 10 Downing Street by the Prime Minister to give a presentation of their findings and recommendations to members of the Cabinet. Positive political support for their proposals seemed assured, particularly because in the long term they would produce substantial administrative savings and reduce the number of civil servants.

The scrutineers had found a system under severe strain, buckling under the weight of 1.3 million unemployed people. Yet four years later, with the numbers of unemployed people claiming benefit at 3.24 million, the central recommendation of the scrutiny had been abandoned. What went wrong? Why was the 'one-office concept' not put into effect? This chapter presents the story of ambitious proposals for managerial change which failed to be implemented despite having initial political approval. While the Efficiency Strategy has its successes, which we report in other chapters, there is also much to be learned about the complexity of public management from its failures. Many of the detailed recommendations of the scrutiny of the system for 'payment of benefits to unemployed people' were implemented, but the main one was not, and it is with that fact and the reasons behind it that we are mainly concerned.

Two of the principles of organizational excellence discussed in Chapter 2 are 'closeness to the customer' and 'lean staff, simple structure' (Peters and Waterman, 1982). Scrutineers would have had a hard job to find a part of government that violated these principles more than the system for paying benefits to the unemployed. Few claimants felt that the system worked in a way that made any concessions to their convenience or their interests. Few staff felt that their working environment enabled them to give the service of which they were capable or to have the job satisfaction that is supposedly one of the intrinsic rewards of a civil service career. Staff at least have the dubious advantage of understanding some of the labyrinthine complexity of the organization on their side of the counter. Improvement, therefore, involved change of a fundamental nature. It raised issues of wider importance for public management, particularly the politically sensitive issue of investment in organizational change and the administratively sensitive issue of interdepartmental relations.

Cost-cutting is the predominant public image of Raynerism. But improvements in the performance of complex administrative systems and long-term reductions in costs can often be achieved only by the investment of substantial resources in reorganization. The slogan that forms the title of this chapter, 'spend to save', sums up the idea that in order to reap longer-term benefits, spending in the short term may need to be higher. Not to spend in certain instances is false economy. In fighting for the 'spend to save' principle in this particular scrutiny, Rayner came up against the shorter time perspective which he castigated as part of the culture of Whitehall. Another aspect of this culture, 'fighting your corner' or 'departmentalism', was implicated in the ultimate demise of the scrutiny's main proposals, and raised questions about how interdepartmental conflicts should be handled as far as the Efficiency Strategy was concerned.

The first sections of this chapter will cover the context, remit and methodology of the scrutiny, a description of the system and a diagnosis of its faults, and an outline of the main recommendations for change made by the scrutineers. We will then go on to the progress made in implementation and the general issues raised.

Context: Three Offices, Two Benefits

To understand the origins of present problems we must go back forty years. Paying benefit to the unemployed had involved more than one department since 1945, when one predecessor of the Department of Health and Social Security, the Ministry of National Insurance, was made responsible for benefit policy but had negotiated an agency agreement with the then Ministry of Labour and National Service to continue paying out unemployment benefit through its local office network, which also served as local employment exchanges. This made good administrative sense, since registration at the employment exchange, to demonstrate availability for work, was a condition of the receipt of benefit. Unemployment benefit was insurance-based. It was not expected at the time that many unemployment benefit claimants would need means-tested benefits to supplement their insured benefits.

The logic of this arrangement disappeared, however, in 1974, when the Employment Service was separated off from the delivery of benefits. A network of bright, 'High Street' Jobcentres, run by the newly created Manpower Services Commission, was established in order to facilitate labour market efficiency by encouraging people to move jobs. Getting away from the stigma of the Employment Exchange was an essential part of this plan. However, it remained part of the unemployment benefit system that claimants had to register for work at the Jobcentre. This involved claimants in going to two offices, now located separately, and a resulting flow of communications between those two offices about the claimant. The respective secretaries of state agreed in principle that the time had arrived for the end of the agency agreement, and for the payment of benefit to the unemployed to be done through the Department of Health and Social Security local office network. However, since the Department of Health and Social Security was already undergoing major organizational change and the Department of Employment was splitting off its Employment Service work, it was decided to defer the change. As time passed, so did this example of interdepartmental accord. When the issue was reconsidered in 1978, the Department of Employment had developed alternative plans.

Large numbers of claimants were having to add a third office to their list of visits on making a claim for unemployment benefit. The insured benefit did not cover their basic needs, and they required in addition the Department of Health and Social Security-administered supplementary allowance, part of the system of means-tested benefits. The Department of Employment proposed improving the level of unemployment benefit and taking over full policy responsibility for the scheme (National Audit Office, 1985). While this idea might have appealed to the outgoing Labour government, it was no part of the programme of the new Conservative government to raise the level of unemployment benefit. Indeed, one of its early actions was to abolish earnings-related unemployment benefit, which had kept sizeable numbers of people out of means-tested benefits in their early months of unemployment.

Terms of Reference and Methodology
Thus, the scrutiny team took on a big problem with a long history. The team consisted of three officials, two from the Department of

Employment and one from the Department of Health and Social Security. Previous scrutinies had fallen mostly within the spheres of particular departments, and had usually been 'one-man' operations. The team approach was in recognition that this was a problem of a different order of magnitude. The timetable was still extremely tight for the task in hand, although it did allow for more than the ninety working days of popular legend. The terms of reference were broad: 'to report on whether the organization and methods by which unemployment benefit and supplementary benefit for unemployed people are delivered can be made more effective'. The team identified five criteria against which to evaluate the operation of the existing system. It should be able to:

1. provide a network of offices giving reasonable access to the great majority of unemployed people;
2. establish quickly and reliably the claimant's entitlement to benefit;
3. pay benefit regularly and promptly to those continuing to be unemployed;
4. ensure that people who are not entitled to receive benefit do not receive it;
5. ensure that those receiving benefit do not neglect opportunities of jobs.

The methodology involved the Rayner principles of engaging high-level support and interest, and then going out to talk to people in the field about the operation of their systems. The initial study plan was cleared with responsible ministers in the two departments and Sir Derek Rayner, and the team then embarked on a series of visits to forty local offices, fifteen area regional offices and two computer centres. They also broadcast a more general plea for staff suggestions, consulted departmental trade union bodies, claimants and their representatives, academics and those involved in policy formulation. They commissioned a survey of 1000 claimants in order to uncover attitudes to claiming benefits, claimants' understanding of the nature of benefits and the conditions of their receipt, and attitudes towards looking for work (Department of Employment, Department of Health and Social Security, 1981).

A major difficulty arose in the field work through the actions of department trade union bodies. They were consulted at the initial stage of drawing up a study plan, but objected strongly to the scrutiny when ministers decided that they would not necessarily see the full report. This policy of non-cooperation by the unions was particularly strong in the Department of Health and Social Security. The Department of Employment section of the Society of Civil and Public

Servants submitted comments on the scrutiny which are appended to the published report. A further difficulty arose because the remit included a clause insisting on no net increase in public expenditure, a factor that caused some outside bodies, notably the Child Poverty Action Group, to have nothing to do with the scrutiny.

Payment of Benefits to Unemployed People — the System in 1980

The scale of the unemployment benefits system was startling. In 1979/80, the year before this scrutiny was undertaken, the amount of grant paid to unemployed people was £1400 million. The administrative costs of making these payments were estimated at £135 million per annum, being the direct and indirect costs of employing 35,000 people full-time in the Department of Employment and Department of Health and Social Security, along with the partial involvement of 10,000 people in Jobcentres. The sheer complexity of this operation is equally startling. Even experienced civil servants find it daunting. The background material on this system has been used as part of a teaching exercise on the Efficiency Strategy at the Civil Service College. Experienced middle managers from other parts of the civil service have difficulty coming to grips with the complexity of the system. 'A governmental spaghetti junction' was the term coined by one official to describe the flowchart he had drawn up to represent the elements in the system and the interconnections among them. A simplified version is shown in Figure 1. What follows is a summary of the main features, eliminating some of the detail.

Whether he was aware of it or not, a newly unemployed person entered the system by making a choice either to attend an Unemployment Benefit Office or a Jobcentre. If he went to the Unemployment Benefit Office, the clerk he saw would complete a form and arrange for the claimant to return each fortnight on a given day to 'sign on', that is, to declare that he had not worked in the interim period and was then available for work — availability for work being a pre-condition of receipt of benefit. He would also be given a 'transit card' and told to go and fulfil a further pre-condition for receipt of benefit, namely, registration at a Jobcentre. He handed in his transit card there, and Jobcentre staff sent another card back to the Unemployment Benefit Office acknowledging the registration. If the newly unemployed person went first to the Jobcentre a reverse process operated. In either case, the claimant had to go to both offices.

The next task for benefit staff was to establish whether the claimant had adequate National Insurance contributions in the relevant year to justify payment of benefit. In almost all offices, details of the claim were transmitted to one of two Unemployment Benefit computers,

FIGURE 1: *A Governmental 'Spaghetti Junction'*

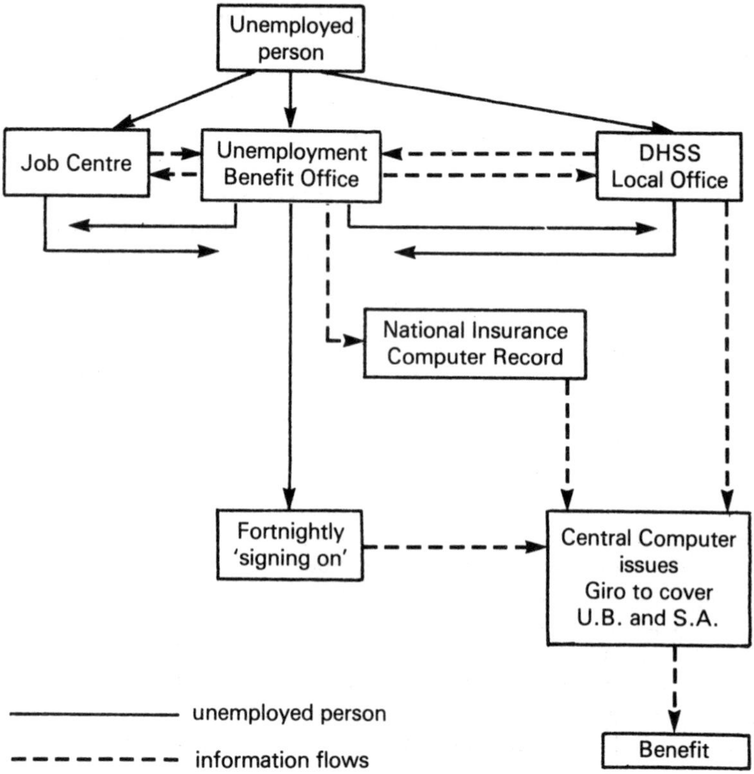

which then tapped into the main Department of Health and Social Security central record computers in Newcastle to check the claimant's contributions. If these were sufficient, the Unemployment Benefit computer would produce a Girocheque to be posted to the claimant's home address, and a form for the local office for the claimant to sign on his next fortnightly visit. Only when that form was signed and fed back into the computer would the next Giro be paid. So far, so simple.

Unemployment benefit was not available for the first six weeks to those who voluntarily left work or who were sacked for misconduct. New claimants were asked for their reasons for leaving work and a form was sent to their previous employers asking for their version of events. If the clerk believed that benefit ought to be stopped, he submitted the issue to a superior officer, who, acting as insurance officer, made a decision — subject to appeal ultimately to the National Insurance Tribunal. Payment each fortnight was a week in arrears and a week in advance. When a claimant found work and ceased to claim, the office had to find out whether work started during the second week when the claimant was receiving advance payments, and if so, had to take steps to recover the money. During a period of claiming, the Unemployment Benefit Office would perform a number of random checks on claimants to try to ensure that their claim was valid.

At the time of the scrutiny, only about half the claimants received unemployment benefit alone. In 1979/80, 4.3 million claims for unemployment benefit and 3.4 million claims for supplementary allowance were made by unemployed people. On average during that year, 1.3 million people were registered as unemployed at any one time with 1.2 million claiming unemployment benefit and 0.6 million claiming supplementary allowance instead or as well. The scrutineers calculated that once current policy changes, such as the abolition of earnings-related unemployment benefit, had worked through, 66 per cent of all unemployed people would claim supplementary allowance.

Hence, after making a claim for unemployment benefit, two out of three claimants headed off in the direction of their third government office, the Department of Health and Social Security, taking a form from the Unemployment Benefit Office. This was the Integrated Local Office (ILO — 'integration' referring to the fact that the Department of Health and Social Security deals with some insured benefits, such as sickness benefit, in the same building as non-insured, means-tested benefits). The claimant there made an appointment to return for an interview by a clerk who would assess his needs, taking into account his income, including any unemployment benefit and any savings above a certain limit.

Supplementary allowance was paid via the same Unemployment Benefit computer as paid the insured benefit. The Integrated Local Office sent another form to the Unemployment Benefit Office informing them of the amount due, and the computer included both unemployment benefit and supplementary allowance, if both were due, on the same Girocheque to the claimant. The claimant did not need to attend the Integrated Local Office again, but he would not get a further payment of either benefit unless he triggered payment by 'signing on'. Supplementary allowance was paid two weeks in advance. Sometimes needs were too pressing to wait for the computer system to be set up, and Girocheques were drawn up locally. The Integrated Local Office then had to communicate that information to the Unemployment Benefit Office to ensure that no double payment took place.

Further flows of information related to the six weeks' stop on unemployment benefit for people who had made themselves voluntarily unemployed. Supplementary allowance was also reduced in those circumstances by up to 40 per cent. The Unemployment Benefit Office had to inform the Integrated Local Office if benefit had been stopped, although the Integrated Local Office might contact the former employer itself. Checks on the validity of claims were performed by a number of different Department of Health and Social Security officers. Claimants were to be visited in their own homes about six months after they first claimed. They were also called into the office after three months to see an employment review officer who tried to sort out any problems concerning work, and who then might see the claimant as often as he thought appropriate in a particular case. The Department of Health and Social Security also had fraud officers called 'special investigators' who looked into cases where fraud was thought to be likely — perhaps because of staff suspicions, or a 'tip-off' from a member of the public, or because an individual was in an occupation where there was no shortage of jobs, but had still not found work.

Those are the key features of the system, dealing in 1979/80 with a changing population averaging 1.3 million claimants.

Diagnosis and Recommendations

The scrutineers found a system under pressure from rapidly increasing numbers of unemployed, unable to cope owing to three major factors:

i. The involvement of so many groups in the systems — the three networks of local offices, the three operational commands at headquarters, and the many policy divisions.
ii. The existence of two benefits — one designed to meet need and the other an insurance benefit designed partially to replace earnings.
iii. The complex legislation and detailed codes for the two benefits which Parliament, ministers and administrators had developed piecemeal over a long period in response to many differing pressures. (Department of Employment, Department of Health and Social Security, 1981)

One serious weakness was in the application of benefit controls. Although Unemployment Benefit Offices and Jobcentres both had the job of ensuring that a claimant was available for work and willing to take suitable employment, such control seemed to have been given a low priority, particularly in Jobcentres where the main emphasis was placed on serving the needs of employers (and thereby the labour market) by finding them good staff, rather than on their subsidiary function as part of the control of benefit system. High and rising unemployment made this particular requirement increasingly unrealistic. The survey of claimants found that only 3 per cent said they felt any pressure from the Jobcentre to find work. The survey based on eight areas, two of which (Harrow and Hounslow) were in areas where jobs were still relatively plentiful. The response there was only slightly higher, at 5 per cent.

There were many examples of duplication in the system. All three offices required the same personal details. Both Unemployment Benefit Office and Integrated Local Office often contacted former employers about the reasons for a claimant's leaving work. All three offices carried out reviews, test-checks and home visits to check on home circumstances and availability for work. These checks were not coordinated and the information gained was not pooled. The structure was anything but simple, the staff anything but lean.

The two benefit offices also added to the complications. The benefits were complex, particularly the means-tested ones, and it was rare for the junior staff to understand any part of the process outside their own immediate responsibility. Wrong advice to claimants was not infrequent because of that, and a great deal of time was spent in communication between the two offices. The scrutineers observed Department of Health and Social Security assessment clerks making four telephone calls to an Unemployment Benefit Office over the assessment of one claim. This lack of understanding led to over-payments and delays. The two offices also add to the inconvenience and expense incurred by claimants. 39 per cent of callers at Integrated Local Offices had to travel more than one mile from the Unemploy-ment Benefit Office — and some were even in different towns. The system was not close to the customer.

One Benefit? One Office?

The diagnosis of an overloaded system undertaking tasks of a scale and complexity for which it was not designed is one with which few would disagree. Recommendations for change, however, did not meet with such general agreement. The scrutineers believed that an ideal solution would be one benefit for all unemployed people, since a declining minority of claimants are entitled to unemployment benefit alone. One way of doing this would be to phase out unemployment benefit altogether and put everyone on supplementary allowance. However, this would disentitle some people who had made national insurance contributions, notably married and cohabiting women, whom the supplementary allowance system assumes to be supported by their husbands and partners. In addition, the scrutineers felt that the stigma still attached to means-tested benefits made this solution politically unacceptable. An alternative was to offer all who had been working, regardless of their contribution record, a flat rate benefit for a year before then applying a means test. While this would have reduced the number of staff in the system by 10,000, it would have raised the cost from £50 million to £150 million more per year in public expenditure, and so was ruled out. Given that 'one benefit' was out of the question, there were more minor modifications that could be made to make the benefits more compatible. Aligning the pay periods and smoothing the transition between sickness and unemployment benefit formed part of the team's recommendations.

Their key recommendations, however, lay in the proposals for one benefit office. Their view of the part played in the system by registration at Jobcentres has already been made clear. They had no hesitation in recommending removing registration as a condition of benefit. 'Voluntary registration' euphemistically described the proposal to cut the links. Only volunteers would henceforth use the services of the Jobcentre. The scrutineers claim that in fact only those who were keen to be placed in employment currently got a full service, because Jobcentre staff did not want to damage their good reputation with employers by sending 'hard-to-place' people for interview. So, in effect, this was no loss to the unwilling or the diffident.

One office down, one to go:

> On the basis of what we have seen in the scrutiny we are in no doubt that the taking of claims, assessment of benefit due and payment of both Unemployment Benefit and Supplementary Allowance should be administered from one office . . . that office would also provide all review and control functions. (Department of Employment, Department of Health and Social Security, 1981)

Which office should absorb the other's work was a delicate question of interdepartmental politics. Middle managers on courses at the Civil Service College very frequently presented a 'one-office' solution when asked to diagnose the problem and almost invariably proposed shifting responsibility from Unemployment Benefit Offices and concentrating work in the Department of Health and Social Security Integrated Local Office network. Their reasoning was that policy and executive responsibility should not be separated, and that supplementary allowance was the more complicated benefit and responsibility should be concentrated where there was existing expertise in running it.

This was not the choice of the scrutineers, however. They considered the costs and savings in staff and premises involved in such a change. Because of the cutting out of duplication, 2300 person-years would be saved, a reduction of £14 million in running costs. The changes to premises involved in merging the disparate office systems would have been considerable, and assessing their cost was extremely difficult because of the inadequate information available about property assets. However, operational researchers in the Department of Health and Social Security produced a model based on one region's property which provided figures by extrapolation for overall capital investment and annual running costs.

A further complicating factor in the situation was the significant overcrowding that existed in offices, particularly the Integrated Local Offices. This was a violation of a third Peters and Waterman principle, productivity through people. The Property Services Agency, which was responsible for all office accommodation, had only a small amount of its budget available for the relief of overcrowding, but it advised that it was not possible to add extra accommodation on to a new office and leave the original staff in overcrowded conditions. The scrutineers did not feel that the full costs of dealing with existing overcrowding should be included in their investment appraisal, so they produced two sets of figures comparing the options.

Option 1: combining work in the Unemployment Benefit Offices of the Department of Employment
(a) including correcting overcrowding: capital costs £80−£90 million; annual non-staff running costs increase by £8 million;
(b) excluding correcting overcrowding: capital cost £4−£50 million; annual non-staff running costs increase by £2 million.
Option 2: combining work in the Integrated Local Offices
(a) including correcting overcrowding: capital costs £70−£130 million; annual non-staff running costs increase by £1 million;
(b) excluding correcting overcrowding: capital costs £55−£100 million; annual non-staff running costs decrease by £1 million.

Using the Treasury's test discount rate of 7 per cent to assess the viability of investing the capital in order to save recurrent expenditure, options 1(b) and 2(b) are viable, also option 1(a). Option 2(a) is viable except at the highest estimates of cost. This quantitatively based investment option analysis tends to lead to the choice of the Unemployment Benefit Office as the basis of the new system. That choice was supported by further non-quantitative evidence cited by the scrutineers. Perhaps they were influenced by the rough ride they were given by the trade unions in the Department of Health and Social Security, but they very much gained the impression that Unemployment Benefit Offices were easier to manage. They are on average only a fifth of the size, in staffing terms, of Integrated Local Offices. What little evidence there is about comparative performance of small and large Integrated Local Offices tends to suggest that large size reduces efficiency. Unemployment Benefit Office staff had been less willing to take industrial action, and Department of Health and Social Security staff had negotiated special higher payments for staff on benefit work. Their management structure was also more highly graded than that of the Department of Employment. All of these factors combined to leave the impression that 'innovation, experiment and work measurement' were harder to achieve in the Department of Health and Social Security. Since they believed it was essential for the two benefits to be dealt with by the same clerk, major change in the work practice of junior officials was necessary, and this was more likely to be achieved in the Department of Employment.

The scrutineers did not accept the counter-arguments that: (1) separating policy-making from administration and (2) having two elements of supplementary allowance run by separate departments were inappropriate developments. The evidence of the existing unemployment benefit system, run by one department with policy responsibility resting in another, was cited as evidence. There was no indication that policy-makers in the Department of Health and Social Security were any more out of touch with the realities of life in Unemployment Benefit Offices than those in Integrated Local Offices. Their proposal for one office, and one clerk, dealing with both benefits left policy responsibility for supplementary allowance for unemployed people with the Department of Health and Social Security.

While the heart of the scrutineers' recommendations centres on the 'one-office concept', there were 81 recommendations in all, many of which were valid independently of a decision about the amalgamation of local offices. A major area of concern was the detection of fraud. The scrutineers proposed eliminating Jobcentres from their role in detecting fraud, but in return called for more fraud staff, closer working between the departments on this issue, and an increase in staff. Other suggestions included simplifying forms and creating multi-purpose forms, improving computer procedures, cutting out redundant processes and so on.

Implementation

The report was surrounded by publicity because of the very large savings and job losses involved. The scrutineers gave a report to Cabinet in person and were apparently given an enthusiastic hearing. One Cabinet minister is said to have remarked, 'This is what we came into government to do.' Full acceptance of the scrutineers' proposals would have ultimately yielded savings of 5000 jobs and £75–£80 million a year, and further would have improved the service to claimants in non-quantifiable ways. By June 1984, 34 of the 81 recommendations had been fully implemented at an annual saving of

£31 million; 14 recommendations which would have brought a further £23 million were subsumed under other changes made for other reasons, bringing parallel or greater savings; 18 recommendations had been rejected; and 15 were still under consideration. For a more detailed account, see the National Audit Office report on the Unemployment Benefit Service (National Audit Office, 1985).

It is not our purpose to go into the detail of what happened, but the outcome of the main proposals reveals much that is interesting about the politics of management reform. Changes at the level recommended by the scrutiny team involve coordinated action by a number of departments in order to realize potential benefits, and thus call into question the departmentalist tendencies that are a prevalent feature of the 'culture of Whitehall'. Second, the realization of savings and improvements in management is essentially a long-term process contingent on the investment of considerable resources. The scrutiny therefore provides a test of acceptability for the 'spend to save' principle. While improvements in efficiency can sometimes be achieved simply by direct reductions in inputs, substantial savings over the long term often involve strategic investments in administrative reorganization, staff training and improved management. In this case, attempts to improve administrative performance ran counter to established expectations and implicit assumptions, which are more closely geared to the maintenance of an existing system than to planned management change. Whereas a small-scale scrutiny falling within the scope of a single department may proceed to implementation in a relatively straighforward way after the recommendations have received ministerial acceptance, implementation of the payment of benefits scrutiny was bound to be more complex on account of its size and the multiplicity of departmental interests involved.

The main recommendations of the report were accepted in principle by ministers, and the process of implementation began. At the technical level there was more detailed consideration of the precise implications of the recommendations and an attempt to identify and evaluate alternative ways of putting them into effect. At this level the process of implementation can be seen as a continuation of the scrutiny process itself. At the political level, interdepartmental negotiations began to establish the acceptability of proposed changes and ensure their feasibility by securing the allocation of the resources required. To resolve the technical issues arising in the process of implementation the One Office Concept Working Group was formed.

This group developed and considered alternative options alongside the proposals in the report for transferring all supplementary allowance work to Unemployment Benefit Offices. Each of these was consistent with the one-office concept but they had different implications for administrative responsibility, for the need to transfer staff between the Department of Health and Social Security and the Department of Employment, and also for accountability. The One Office Concept group estimated that 30 per cent of staff savings identified in the report could be made independently of any proposals for reorganization that they made. Savings dependent on reorganization could not be fully achieved until four years after reorganization began. Most of the manpower savings projected would not actually come on stream until after the April 1984 deadline for the achievement of a 100,000 cut in staff to meet the target of 630,000 civil servants, a very significant date in the civil service calendar. The working group did not come to an agreed conclusion. It confined itself to the technical task of laying out options and evaluating them. None of the options was cheap, and since each of them involved reorganization on a considerable scale the transitional period would be long and the costs of reorganization substantial.

At the political level, implementation had to run the gauntlet of interdepartmental negotiation. In addition to the departments directly involved in the scrutiny, other interests were involved, bringing different perspectives to bear and introducing constraints that the scrutiny team had not been required to consider. In a number of respects the process of negotiation over the implementation of the one-office concept reveals the differences in attitude and assumption between what Rayner had called 'the culture of Whitehall' and the requirements of large-scale management reform. Realization of the one-office concept required sustained effort to win consent and cooperation within the machinery of government from a wider circle of interests than those directly involved in managing the system for paying benefits to unemployed people. The process of change required the consent and participation of other departments. One way of looking at the politics of implementation is as a coalition-building process. The scrutineers' report constituted an integrated set of proposals which required the agreement of various organizations for whom this particular scrutiny was tangential to their main interests.

Three examples will serve to illustrate the obstacles that have to be overcome in the course of making changes of this kind in a highly complicated system. First of all, the change from compulsory to voluntary registration at Jobcentres required new legislation, and therefore a share of parliamentary time in an already overburdened legislative programme. Fighting to secure a place in the parliamentary timetable was one essential task in the strategy for change. Sir Derek Rayner's access to 'political clout' enabled him to remove obstacles in this area. Because the one-office concept depended on a substantial office reorganization, the Property Services Agency also had to be included in the coalition to implement change. Although the Property Services Agency was later to be put on a repayment basis, at this time it had its own funds which it used as it judged best, and it did not welcome diverting its resources to accommodate a particular scrutiny. The Property Services Agency was willing to see additional accommodation provided if it was funded from the budgets of the two main departments, even though some of the resources were required because of the need to bring existing offices up to standard, and were nothing to do with the scrutiny. Rayner himself was truly appalled at the working conditions of staff in some benefit offices. He believed that the quality and quantity of work would be increased by improving the standard of accommodation, for both staff and clients.

This raised the whole issue of whether additional resources were to be made available to ensure the implementation of the scrutiny recommendations, or whether implementation should be achieved by reallocating resources already committed to departments. Failing interdepartmental agreement on the reallocation of existing resources, additional resources had to be sought from the Treasury. The Treasury's attitude to this request was that, while the savings of £5 million achieved by immediate implementation of some recommendations was welcomed and accepted, the Treasury was not willing to regard this as having any bearing on the question of whether additional resources should be committed to achieving the much larger long-term savings forecast by the scrutiny team. In the Treasury view, short-term economy had priority over long-term improvements in efficiency and effectiveness. Rayner challenged the Treasury on the grounds that the scrutiny recommendations were not a series of isolated proposals but a package which had to be seen as a whole. The objectives of the scrutiny would be defeated if only the short-term savings were agreed and accepted while the longer-term savings that were dependent on investment in reorganization were rejected.

The Treasury has the twin roles of controlling the overall volume of public expenditure in order to fulfil its task of managing the economy, and also securing value for money in the resources that are expended. It would be easier if those two roles were never in conflict, and some Treasury officials like to believe that is the case. This scrutiny presents a classic example to counter that belief. The scrutineers' calculations put the expected rate of return on the investment proposed well within the Treasury's own target figures — even taking account of dealing with the overcrowding in offices which was, strictly speaking, another issue. However, the early 1980s was a time of very great political pressure to reduce public expenditure, since the public sector borrowing requirement was regarded as the prime cause of inflation. In those circumstances, Treasury instincts to reduce expenditure —

reinforced as they were by the experience of losing control of the rise in public expenditure in the 1970s — were given free rein. The Treasury orthodoxy was well summed up in a speech by Sir Leo Pliatsky to the Public Administration Committee Conference at York in 1985: 'In the last analysis, if you have to save money, it doesn't matter how you save it.' Sir Derek Rayner's plea fell on deaf ears.

The Treasury stance was helped by the position of the Department of Health and Social Security. It appears that the Rayner principle of gaining and retaining high-level support for the scrutiny from within the department was not fully operational here. Perhaps top officials and ministers believed that the one-office concept could not possibly work anywhere but in the Department of Health and Social Security, so the alternative option was not seriously considered. At any rate, departmental energies were mobilized to fight back. On the other hand, the Department of Employment's vital interests were also involved. Employment benefit staff made up a very high proportion of total staff and the loss of this function would have left a small rump of a department. At a time when the Secretary of State for Employment believed in keeping out of industrial negotiations, there would have been little to justify his separate Cabinet existence. It may be this practical, political reality that informed the calculations of the scrutineers (who were after all meant to have the political antennae of good civil servants) — the calculation that a department fighting for its very existence would fight harder.

Conclusions

The scrutiny report on the system for paying benefit to the unemployed presents a picture of a system in disarray. Unlike the system described in the last chapter, where some tightening up was required, here we are presented with the need for a major reorganization of an increasingly obsolete system thrown into crisis by events in a rapidly changing environment. In other words, the problems to be tackled through the scrutiny process are infinitely more intractable, and this attempt to solve them certainly failed. The reasons for that failure indicate clearly some of the major obstacles to better management in government.

Rayner asserted the principle of going with the grain of departmentalism. The scrutiny approach was designed to secure high-level departmental support and retain it from the development of recommendations through to their implementation. Problems like the payment of benefits to unemployed people straddle departmental boundaries. Not all problems are located within one department; indeed, in a departmentalist culture, the most pervasive and untackled problems will be in the interstices between departments. Rayner tried to provide a pressure towards interdepartmental cooperation, in this case partly by reasoned argument and partly by the use of political clout. Knocking heads together may solve some problems, but it is not an adequate response to a situation that can be improved only through the development of concepts of management which take on board interdepartmental relationships, and the need for cooperation. Civil servants tend to take the design of their organizations, and their relationship with others, as a given, as something outside their control, as a politician's decision. Only when concepts of strategic management develop which include the capacity to acknowledge the need for interdepartmental working will there be an appropriate context for dealing with the problems raised by this scrutiny. Only when the culture of Whitehall has changed will there be a chance of resolving such issues, which challenge that culture at a very fundamental level.

The capacity to think about organizational design will develop as civil servants take on a strategic management orientation. Strategic management also implies a capacity to adopt a longer-term perspective. Civil servants often complain that ministers are incapable of thinking beyond the next election, and that, as an election approaches, time perspectives get shorter and shorter. In the past, the civil service response has been to echo that, and adopt a similarly short-term perspective. This view is seen at its most extreme in the Treasury, ever wary of demands on the public purse that are heavy in the short term and may or may not produce benefits in the long term — which may be after the next general election. The failure to provide the resources for the one-office concept is a good demonstration of that characteristic. Recognition of the damaging results of that short-term perspective is one step on the road to better public management.

Both the interdepartmental relations issue and the issue of investing in managerial improvement call for the centre of government to adopt a new perspective. The Efficiency Unit provided one voice at the centre calling for a more strategic approach, but this particular battle was lost. Even though some recommendations were put into effect, the main proposals were not pursued. Had the exercise been carried out today, the outcome would probably have been the same. Although many managerial improvements have been made since this scrutiny, they have stressed intra-departmental matters, and not come to grips with system-wide issues.

A new management role for the centre must be defined if the fragmentation that is at the heart of this particular problem is not to persist. The creation of successful inter-organizational relationships is a vital part of improved public management. It is a responsibility that has been shirked by the central departments but cannot be shrugged off much longer if public management is to continue to develop. At the time of writing there are some indications that this weakness at the centre is being recognized and the Efficiency Unit is acquiring a role in situations where problems span departmental boundaries. This is an advance on leaving departments to sort things out themselves, but, given the very limited resources of the Efficiency Unit, it cannot be a complete solution.

6
The Review of the Government Statistical Service: a Profession in Government

While Raynerism is most clearly associated in the public mind with the 'one-off' scrutiny, dealing with a particular problem in a particular department, the task of improving the efficiency of the civil service is too large to be dealt with entirely in this way. At first it was assumed that certain recurring themes would emerge and be applicable elsewhere, but while one or two scrutinies struck a chord — for example, the Joubert cost-centre proposals and the MINIS report, both of which were carried out in the Department of the Environment — there was no easy means of spreading the message to other departments. One way of coping with this problem was to review common functions across the whole, or part of, the civil service. The possibility of interdepartmental comparison offered the Efficiency Unit the opportunity of making a greater impact than was possible with the one-off scrutiny. As the Efficiency Strategy evolved, multi-departmental reviews came to play a prominent role, which is discussed in Chapter 7.

The forerunner of the multi-departmental review programme was the review of the Government Statistical Service, on which Rayner reported to the Prime Minister in December 1980 (Rayner, 1980). As a major exercise in comparison, it provided important lessons for improving public management. It also attracted a great deal of publicity at the time, and affected the image of Raynerism not only with the general public but also, and perhaps more importantly, within the civil service. In addition, the review was significant in offering up large savings in money and manpower: £17 million and 20 per cent of the manpower employed on statistical work were at stake.

A feature of the review on which there was little comment at the time was that it touched on the problems of managing professional groups in government, an important aspect of managing the civil service, and it opened up again the issue of the relationship between specialists and generalists raised by the Fulton Report (Fulton, 1968). The management of professionals is a major issue in public management and has figured prominently in other parts of the public sector, through, for example, the Griffiths Report on the National Health Service, and the Jarratt Report on universities (Griffiths, 1983; Jarratt, 1985).

The background to the exercise is discussed first, followed by an account of the conduct of the review; we then develop the methodological implications of the review for the Efficiency Strategy, before moving on to consider its importance for statisticians as professionals in government, and their relationship with generalist administrators.

Background to the Review

The Central Statistical Office had been set up in 1941 to coordinate and clarify the statistical issues that came before Cabinet. Churchill insisted that Cabinet discussion should not be handicapped by disagreement over factual matters. In the years following, a rudimentary professional statistical service became established, and played its part in the policy process. In 1966, the House of Commons Estimates Committee reported on the Government Statistical Service, making a series of recommendations which were designed to improve the quality of the statistical services (House of Commons, 1966). Since this report was the last major discussion of statistical services before Rayner, and therefore established the framework of ideas within which the Government Statistical Service worked until Rayner, it is worth noting something of what it said.

The report called for an expansion and development of the Government Statistical Service, in order to improve the quality of policy work in government and to provide information that would be of benefit to potential users outside government, such as research institutes, private companies and so on. It recommended a stronger coordinating role for the Central Statistical Office, to ensure that statistics collected for one department's purposes might be usable more generally. It also recommended that the status of statisticians within government be raised, by making the head of profession a permanent secretary, by improving the career prospects of statisticians and by encouraging their continued involvement with the profession outside government. All of this was designed to enable them to play a fuller part in the policy process. The report came at a time when it was widely believed in parliamentary and civil service circles that, if only the economic and social planning mechanisms were modernized, the relative economic decline that Britain was suffering could be reversed. The Fulton Report itself was another manifestation of this view. The difference between this approach and that of the Rayner review, only fourteen years later, is instructive.

When Sir Claus Moser became permanent secretary head of the Government Statistical Service and the Central Statistical Office in 1967, the process of expansion and development began. The number of statisticians in government rose from 159 in 1966 to 540 by 1979, and the number of clerical and executive support staff, mostly collecting and processing data, rose from 4075 to 8310, with the cost of the system doubling in real terms to £100 million at 1979 prices. The Government Statistical Service grew in size and in professionalism, developing a higher profile in the policy process, just as government intervention in economic and social life was growing.

The prospect of Sir Claus Moser's retirement in 1978 prompted a process of reflection on the changes of the previous decade. Moser himself made preliminary soundings about a review of the service, and a pilot study of economic and statistical services in the Department of Trade and Industry in 1979 recommended cuts of 14 per cent. There had also been a Programme Analysis and Review (PAR) exercise on the use of statistics in social policy. Programme Analysis and Review, introduced in 1971 by Edward Heath as part of a package of reforms of the policy process, was designed to ask some of the fundamental questions about the continuing need for the provision of particular services that were later asked by Rayner. In the early 1970s, there was prime ministerial backing for Programme Analysis and Review — the same kind of political clout as for the Rayner programme — but the attention moved elsewhere after a year or two, and the momentum slowed down (Gray and Jenkins, 1982). In common with many similar exercises, the examination of social statistics produced no actual changes.

The Civil Service Department had a programme of multi-departmental reviews as part of its own efficiency work, and when the Government Statistical Service was added to their list Sir Ian Bancroft asked Rayner to carry out the review. He accepted, although it was done under the aegis of the Efficiency Unit rather than for the Civil Service Department. The review had an immediate appeal to those who thought that government collected too many statistics and burdened the private sector with demands for form-filling and information. Eliminating burdens was a very attractive political slogan (Department of Trade and Industry, 1985).

The review began in January 1980. It appeared to give scope for moving in a direction that was politically very appealing. Comparisons with 1966 have already been made; the emphasis then was on increasing the resources going into policy-making in order to improve the planning process, both directly in government and other parts of the public sector, and in the planning of commercial enterprises, by making available to them information that ought to be of use. The link between providing more resources and improving the policy process was assumed to be relatively direct and unproblematical: more money spent led to better policy planning. The prevailing view in 1979 was very different. Instead of emphasizing the service to industry offered by government, government was said to indulge in too much paperwork and to be a burden on private sector firms which were legally required to submit returns for inclusion in government statistics. There was also the belief that increasing expenditure on administration did not necessarily lead to a better outcome in policy terms: that relationship was one to be established after empirical investigation, rather than by a prior assumption. The review of the Government Statistical Service offered the opportunity of satisfying both the prevailing political ideology — it was a good opportunity to 'roll back the frontiers of the state' — and more sophisticated scepticism about the utility of existing planning mechanisms.

Conduct of the Review

Nineteen departments were involved in the review. In most cases, the scrutiny officer was an administrator, not a specialist statistician, but all had access to their chief statistician and many had a professional statistician available to them for full consultation and discussion. The responsibility for looking at the Central Statistical Office, and at all interdepartmental aspects of the review, fell to a team of three: an assistant secretary from the Civil Service Department, a chief statistician from the Central Statistical Office (Ian Beesley, who later joined the Efficiency Unit) and a consultant seconded from the National Westminster Bank. Separate reports were produced for all 19 departments, with the Central Statistical Office scrutiny team providing the coordination.

The review resulted in 700 recommendations throughout the service, offering savings of £19.4 million. Ninety per cent of these recommendations were accepted by ministers and £17 million of savings either have been made or are expected to be made. Recommendations for change covered a wide range of issues, such as improvements in methods and procedures, computerization, asking hard questions about government's real need for data, reducing the form-filling demands on business, substituting sample for census-type surveys, decreasing sample sizes, increasing the involvement of professional statisticians in the management of data collection and processing and shifting away from purely analytical work, charging for publications, and cutting international obligations for statistical information to the minimum.

While these particular recommendations are important in themselves, perhaps more important in the longer term are the changes recommended in the management of the statistical services. Rayner called for the assertion of managerial values, and in particular for the development of cost-consciousness among both statisticians and administrators in the collection and use of statistical services. There was evidence that the organizational framework within which statisticians worked was not conducive to good management. Traditionally, specialists and generalists worked in parallel hierarchies, with specialists responsible to line managers who were fellow professionals (Judge, 1981). The senior professional in a department would be directly responsible to top management in the department, but would have a 'dotted line' relationship on professional issues with the head of profession, who is usually, but not always, located in one of the central departments.

Parallel lines never meet and parallel hierarchies imposed a structured separation which meant that there were unclear managerial lines of responsibility. Departmental management had not, on the whole, kept as close an eye as it ought to have done on how much it was spending and what it was getting for its money in the statistics area. This is probably a reflection of the gulf that still exists between specialists and generalists — statisticians have often just been left to 'do their own thing' — as well as of the wider 'culture of Whitehall' issues which are central to the Efficiency Strategy.

One way of creating greater managerial responsibility for statistics would be to establish firmer lines of managerial control by the head of profession. Alternatively, the existing department arrangement could be improved. Given the Rayner view of working with the grain of departmentalism, it is not surprising that the latter solution was adopted. In accordance with principles that were later to be spelt out in greater detail in the Financial Management Initiative, it was decided that responsibility for the costs of the statistics service should be borne by those best placed to control them, namely, those who were closest to the activity. For this reason statistical divisions should remain with departments and departments should become more aware of the costs of the statistical work that went into their part of the policy process. Departments are not, of course, the sole clients for statistics and not necessarily the surest guardians of the interests of other clients.

Rayner recommended an annual departmental statistical budgetary system which would bring this work to the attention of top management, laying before them costs and options for change, so as to enable them to make informed decisions about how resources should be used. In return, chief statisticians were to be quite clear that they were accountable to departmental management for the resources they commanded, and they ought, therefore, to ensure that those making demands on their services did so in a cost conscious way.

In Chapter 2, we discussed the relationship between allocative efficiency and X-efficiency. Allocative efficiency is about the optimal distribution of resources among producing units, while X-efficiency is about the managerial utilization of resources. Allocative efficiency is a more highly developed conceptual field; and making organizational units trade within a market place, even a market place that is a creation of the internal accounting system, was preferred to the alternative of developing management as a way of improving efficiency.

Where feasible — where it did not make 'bureaucratic nonsense', in Rayner's words — the costs of statistical work were to be met on a repayment basis and not as a common service. This would be most appropriate in the cases where a department collected statistics on behalf of other departments — for example, Customs and Excise for Department of Trade policy divisions — but was also an appropriate strategy for intra-departmental arrangements. A 'customer–contractor' relationship between statistics-producers and statistics-users would force each side to examine its own needs and lead to a tauter, more cost-effective, service. But it failed to address the public goods problem where no immediate customer existed who was willing to meet the costs (Public Money, 1981; Thomas, 1984).

The use of the term 'customer–contractor relationship' reveals assumptions about the role of statisticians which are worth elucidating, and calls to mind the old retailing proverb, 'the customer is always right'. Those in receipt of services or products are not always customers. Sometimes alternative terms are appropriate. Professionals have clients, commercial businesses have customers; to call the departmental policy-makers 'customers' is to imply a particular type of relationship. It implies that statisticians should simply provide the service demanded — not a role that recognizes the full potential of their professional contribution (Flaxen, 1983). One of the great challenges of public management is to look beyond reducing the consumption of resources, and to harness professional talents in a creative way to the task at hand: long-term diagnosis of needs rather than just meeting short-term demands. Rayner was not unaware of this. He was anxious to apply the customer–contractor principle in a flexible way that did not lead to bureaucratic nonsense. He believed that the free flow of information in the policy process was vital if officials were to incorporate an awareness of the environment in their policy advice, and that an overvigorous application of commercial-type principles should not be allowed to disrupt this.

Indeed, Rayner was as concerned to improve the strategic capacity of government as he was to cut costs. Even with a government committed to withdrawing the state from many areas of activity, there was still a need for a vast range of information. Any strategic capacity needs an intelligence-gathering and -processing faculty, covering a range of issues from the most immediately important and central to the more speculative. It is tempting to cut the speculative aspects, but there is no way of knowing when they will become significant. Tunnel vision threatens strategic capacity.

The proposals for managing the Government Statistical Service were meant to compel decision-makers to use their strategic resources in a more considered way. In fact, cuts did occur which proved damaging in the longer term. For example, government's capacity for evaluating regional policy suffered through the reduction of surveys of trade. Perhaps the most ironic example was the awarding of the Nobel Prize for economics to Sir Richard Stone in 1984, for his work on international economic comparisons based on figures that Britain had just ceased to collect.

A further tactic in the effort to assert this concept of managerial values involved altering the remit of the head of the Government Statistical Service. The role of head of the profession has been interpreted in the past as being concerned above all with maintaining the integrity of the statistical services, ensuring that data were collected, analysed and presented in a way that fairly reflected reality. Coordination of interdepartmental statistical matters was a further major aspect. The report recommended that the head should also be the source of advice for top management on questions of efficiency in statistics, and this was accepted. Ambivalence from the head of profession was something Rayner sought to avoid, and this recommendation was a way of incorporating him in the process of change.

Management Issues
In a management operation such as multiple retail store, where there is a great deal of similarity between the activities carried out at all the separate branches, it is likely that changes that improve the operation of one branch will have an obvious and immediate application in other branches. It will be possible to 'read across' from one branch to the others, in the jargon of Marks and Spencer. The civil service consists of a vast collection of different kinds of management units carrying out some similar and many very different functions. Initially, it was hoped that the lessons provided by the early scrutinies would somehow be read across to other departments, but it soon became clear that this needed to be boosted by dealing explicitly with the same function simultaneously in a number of separate departments — in other words, through multi-departmental reviews.

Comparative methodology appears to have much to offer in the search for greater efficiency; it helps a review officer to see the world as it might be, if he has before him examples of how similar things are done differently, and maybe better, elsewhere. Examples of good practice by other civil servants will carry more weight than private sector examples, since civil servants tend to stress the uniqueness of their organizational context. But any social scientist knows the pitfalls of the comparative approach, particularly those connected with conceptual clarity and comparability. To get the full benefit of the comparative approach depends on ensuring that like is compared with like, regardless of what labels are attached in the two or more systems in the comparison. All of this called for strong and active coordination at the centre, particularly when the actual fieldwork was carried out by a multiplicity of fieldwork officers.

These are the technical dimensions of comparative work which have to be dealt with by whoever is running the project; but there are also management dimensions which must be addressed. What strategy should be adopted for getting the best out of the individual scrutineers? Two alternative lines are possible. One is to regard them as a project team which, with assistance from the centre, might form a mutually supportive network which would encourage inter-organizational learning and development. The role of the centre in that strategy is to foster the relationships and keep track of the development of ideas that emerge. The alternative line is to regard the centre as the repository of all learning and to provide strong central guidance to the scrutineers. It is the second line that more accurately describes the intention of the Efficiency Unit in the Statistics review. However, it was not so easy to match practice to managerial precept. In this forerunner of the multi-departmental reviews, the degree of central direction was rather limited. The scrutiny approach imposes counter-pressures, since one of its guiding principles is departmental choice. Multi-departmental reviews inevitably meant moving away from this principle to some extent.

One reason for limited direction from the centre in the Statistics review was the sheer impossibility of watching closely over 19 separate scrutinies. The decision to include such a large number of departments in the review appears to contradict another principle of Raynerism: do not try to put everything right at once; be selective. Later multi-departmental reviews covered far fewer departments. In fact, the term 'multi-departmental review' is one that post-dated this case. The review of the Government Statistical Service was at the time called a 'service-wide scrutiny', a term that reflected a much more ambitious approach, and probably also reflected its origins as a Civil Service Department, rather than a Rayner, project. The civil service tradition of thoroughness and equity seems to have prevailed over the more commercial ethos of biting incisiveness.

The consequence was considerable disparities among departments. The Office of Population Censuses and Surveys produced an initial review which recommended savings of only 4 per cent in the department with the third largest statistics budget (£12.8 million in 1980–1), while across departments the range of proposed cuts was from 4 to 33 per cent. Since the Office of Population Censuses and Surveys was one of the most visible centres of statistical work in government, this did not meet expectations. The scrutineer in the department had failed to come up with the goods. The team reviewing the Central Statistical Office, which also had the remit to look at interdepartmental issues, went over the scrutiny and recommended much greater savings than had initially been proposed, including cuts of nearly 50 per cent in the Social Survey Division, contracting out as much ad hoc survey work as possible, introducing repayment by departments for survey work, and reducing the frequency of the continuous surveys.

The redoing of a departmental review by central intervention is a messy way of effecting change. It would have been better if the problems identified had been picked up at an earlier stage. The fact that this did not happen suggests that the central unit did not have the capacity to manage this large review effectively. The Office of Population Censuses and Surveys was the one that got away — initially. The costs to the image of the Efficiency Unit of publicly going over the same ground again were considerable. It was easier to cast them in the role of imposers of swingeing cuts, rather than coordinators of departmental change, and the opposition of the professional network was all the more heated. At this stage the Efficiency Unit had not learned enough about how to manage such an exercise and did not have the resources to cope with it fully. All the later multi-departmental reviews, discussed in the following chapter, covered more manageable numbers of departments.

An important public management issue concerns how open the review process in cases of this kind should be. Reports produced for Rayner exercises were reports to ministers, or to the Prime Minister, and were considered to be draft reports until they received ministerial acceptance. One reason why the Government Statistical Service review was so unwieldly was that this convention imposed an extended period of non-disclosure of information. Not until each departmental minister had accepted this report, and the interdepartmental aspects had been picked up and reproduced for the central report to the Prime Minister, could reports be published.

Meanwhile, rumours abounded. Given the well-developed, professional network of the statisticians, it was not surprising that word began to get around about what was to be proposed. Separate items of information were pieced together to make a more or less accurate picture of what was happening. The convention about proposals being made first to ministers may have some justification if it is possible to keep control of that information but, if not, the situation rapidly becomes farcical. In order to avoid that, the Efficiency Unit eventually gave the trade union side a summary of the proposals. In doing this, a realistic strategy for disclosure is required, which is appropriate to the particular case. Slavish adherence to a constitutional doctrine made no managerial sense. Control of information is a two-edged sword, and the rumour generated in the absence of accurate information may do the process of change more harm than disclosure. In this case, the

Efficiency Unit was controlled by events rather than the other way round, and had no chance of winning the presentation game. The press publicity surrounding this review helped to spread incipient panic among statisticians and fuelled their opposition; but the way to deal with this problem is to supply more information and justification.

A further strand in this scrutiny concerns the conflicting roles of the professional head of the Government Statistical Service. In a situation like this, anyone filling this position is bound to have an unhappy time. As a permanent secretary, he is part of top management and must be committed to the collective policy of that management. Efficiency in government was clearly high on the list of priorities. On the other hand, unlike other permanent secretaries, the head of profession had the kind of affinity with those being scrutinized that compelled him to take their views and expectations seriously. Statisticians across the whole of the civil service looked to him to defend the integrity of their profession against government cutbacks. It was hard to be catapulted from a relatively uncontroversial obscurity into a very uncomfortable limelight, especially as professional statisticians have not served the apprenticeship in organizational infighting of their administrative colleagues.

And yet, in a sense, his position was strong. No one was in a better position to know the views of all concerned, and for both sides on the issue the head of the profession was a crucial ally. Statisticians hoping to resist the proposals for a reduced service would have the ground cut from under them if their professional leader did not go along with their views. Similarly, top management would find it difficult to impose positive change on a professional group without cooperation. If the recommendations for improved performance were to be properly implemented, cooperation was needed. While top management can decide unilaterally that some action must cease, it can only influence people to change, or improve the way they do their jobs. In order for the positive aspects of the proposals to be effectively implemented, it was necessary for the head of the Government Statistical Service to persuade his professional peers that they ought to cooperate in the change. The importance of his cooperation was given symbolic recognition in the reduced level of cuts made among his immediate staff: 19 per cent savings in posts in the Central Statistical Office was on the low side of the mean.

A Profession in Government

Although this review was the subject of a lot of press comment, none of it centred on what may be the single most significant feature: that it dealt with the management of a professional group within the civil service. It is important that the concept of management used in government reflects the complexity and diversity of the tasks of government. Civil servants who know very little about management in business often assume that it is more straightforward than is actually the case. They then import those 'simple' principles of management and complain that they do not fit the complex reality of work in government. Management is always and everywhere a complex task, and one aspect of that is how to deal with those who possess a specialist skill which the organization needs to use (Abrahamson, 1967). Anyone who hopes to understand the problems of management in government must come to grips with this issue.

Many professional codes carry statements about the public interest which may conflict with the main stream of legitimacy that flows from the electoral process. These issues are not confined to management in central government. Throughout the public sector, the question of relationships between professionals and general managers is a live one. Local government confronted these issues through the corporate management movement of the 1970s. More recently, two major reports have attempted to shift the balance of power. The Griffiths Report on the National Health Service is the most obvious example, addressing the difficulties experienced by general managers in an organization dominated by the medical profession. The Jarratt Report on the universities also proposed the injection of managerial values into the self-regulating professional world of the academic community.

The major differences between the civil service and these other parts of the public sector is that the civil service generalist is the dominant partner. Prestige and status lie with the administrator. Almost all top positions are held by generalist administrators, and few specialists reach senior management other than as representatives and leaders of their professional group. This influences the culture. Questions about how to get the best out of professionals in government are perceived differently from elsewhere in the public sector.

Much has been written about professional bodies, and much more about bureaucratic organizations, but the task here is to examine the role of a professional body of people who work within a bureaucratic hierarchy. In Whitehall language, it is to examine the relationship between specialists and generalists as it emerges from the review of statistical services. It is appropriate to start this by contrasting certain aspects of the internal organization of the two types of group, and in particular to specify what we mean by the word 'professional'. One survey of the literature found the following usages:

Expertise. Professionals possess expertise, that is, specialized training in a body of abstract knowledge.
Ethics. Professionals maintain codes of ethics requiring that they behave towards clients with neutrality and without emotional involvement, and by

applying universalistic standards.

Collegial maintenance of standards. Professionals believe that they alone have the technical competence and ethics necessary to police their speciality and to assure quality service.

Autonomy. To a greater degree than non-professionals, professionals demand self-control over both decisions and work activities. Autonomy is sought concerning innovation, individual responsibility, and free communication.

Commitment to calling. Professionals feel a strong sense of calling to their fields, careers and work and believe that their professions perform valuable, even indispensable, services to society.

Identification with profession. Professionals feel a strong identification with their chosen profession. . . . They typically maintain stronger commitments . . . to their professional subculture than to their employing organizations. (Schriesheim, von Glinow and Kerr, 1977)

While no particular group of professionals in all circumstances adheres to this description, it is a useful way of unpacking some of the many meanings of the word. The contrasts between professionals and generalists are instructive.

One essential element of a professional group is that it consists of people who are in important senses peers; while there are degrees of seniority, all who have undergone the apprenticeship and gained admission to the group, are regarded as of equal worth. The 'apprenticeship', or training, that is a passport to group membership not only provides an understanding of the appropriate skills and knowledge, but also imparts a set of professional values which must be accepted by the trainee — indeed, prior acceptance of the professional culture is usually a prerequisite for admission to training. Group members internalize the values of the profession, and since a consensus exists there is a very limited need for supervision or control. A non-hierarchical ethos prevails. As discussed in Chapter 2, accountability is through standards generated within the professional peer group.

A bureaucratic organization, on the other hand, seeks to achieve highly complex objectives by a specialization of labour which involves breaking up the task into small parts, which are coordinated and controlled through a hierarchy. Organizational members do many different kinds of jobs which involve different training (or no training at all). They derive their authority and legitimacy from above and are accountable not to their peers but to hierarchical superiors.

This analysis of alternative bases of power and forms of accountability directs attention to the stresses and strains inherent in the relationship between civil service professionals and generalists in a wider organizational setting dominated by the latter group. The 'ideal' member of a bureaucratic organization is committed to the organization, but not to any particular goal, such as providing a service or activity. If decisions about changing priorities are made at the top of the office — for example, that a certain service should be provided at a diminished level — the bureaucrat is expected to comply willingly. In practice, he or she might be unwilling to do so, but outright opposition would go against the grain, leaving the individual concerned isolated, with no legitimate outside body on whom to call for support. One of the reasons for moving administrators from post to post at frequent intervals is to avoid identification with a particular activity; in a phrase characteristic of the culture of Whitehall, to prevent them 'going native'.

In addition to conforming to the wishes of superiors which is stressed in the occupational culture, generalist administrators do not usually have the choice — except in the most existential sense — of working outside their organization. Most do not have transferable skills, or qualifications that prove their level of competence. Their future careers rest fairly and squarely in the hands of departmental management. This bind afflicts middle management most. In mid-career they have much more to lose than someone at a more junior level, and yet in most cases they do not have the market power of senior managers, who may have the contacts and influence that provide them with a way out of the service if they need it.

The typology of professional characteristics quoted above shows that professional groups tend to have a different kind of loyalty. Depending on how close to the ideal type they are, they will have more or less commitment to the prevailing values of the profession. All professionals who work within an organization, rather than as independent practitioners, will have had to temper their values to some extent — to exchange some independence for the resources required to exercise their skills, at the very least. If they are to be regarded as professionals at all, however, there must be a point beyond which they will not go. In the case of government statisticians, there is strong support for the view that they must present data that accurately and objectively reflect the reality of the world, both in the quality of the data collected and analysed and in the range of issues covered. Any attempt to interfere with this central tenet of the culture would be resisted if the word 'profession' had any meaning for the people concerned. There is much scope for conflict between this professional commitment and the notion of ministerial responsibility which constitutional convention posits as the organizing principle of administrators.

If conflict does arise, the greatest strength professionals have is that, far from being isolated individuals with no call on legitimate groups to represent them, the profession is by definition a group of peers who will be in relatively good communication with each other both inside and outside the government — through learned societies, professional journals, personal networks based on friendships made during the training period and so on. In the case of government statisticians, their professional communication network was vastly superior to the administrative system of interdepartmental communication, which, given the departmentalism of British government, is not particularly quick off the mark. The Efficiency Unit, charged with coordinating the nineteen departmental scrutinies, did not anticipate the speed with which the profession would piece together bits of information from separate sources to provide it with a fairly accurate picture of what was going on: the First Division Association Statistician Branch network was used for this purpose.

In addition, government statisticians were less dependent. As a professional group, they have skills that are marketable. Admittedly, at a time of recession, their opportunities were somewhat limited. Nevertheless, they are not quite such prisoners of the system as most generalist administrators, and their market power is reflected in the vehemence with which they sought to defend their position. This vehemence was also a function of the timing of the scrutiny. It began during the first year of Mrs Thatcher's government, at a time when the civil service was in a state of shock over announcements about staff cuts, and was having to adjust to the fact that life was going to be different from then on. Expectations are important in determining behaviour, and the Government Statistical Service review coincided with the beginning of a revolution of falling expectations. Two or three years later, the review might not have had the impact on statisticians that it had, but to be singled out as the first major group to fall victim to the cuts hit them very hard. The press publicity that attended the process both reflected and exacerbated their anxiety.

As this shows, the process of change is more difficult to manage when it involves cutting back professional groups than when it involves administrators alone, particularly when that change consists of the assertion of a managerial ethos which may not be subtle enough to appreciate fully the contribution of the professional group. In this instance, whether that appreciation was there or not, most statisticians believed that it was not. The process of change was more difficult because the professionals felt their essential values under attack, and they had resources such as group solidarity, good communications networks and the confidence that marketable skills brought to enable them to resist change.

So far, the discussion has been related to the culture of the profession, and contrasts have been drawn with some abstraction of a bureaucracy. But the term 'culture' has now entered the language of civil servants in another context — that of the culture of Whitehall, the denigration of management values and the elevation of activities 'close' to ministers which Rayner would argue has been so disastrous for good management in government.

The culture of the profession could be said to be a sub-culture of the culture of Whitehall. For professional statisticians, analytic or creative statistical work has high status and management of resources low status. Professional workers in large organizations — be they teachers, social workers, museum professionals or whatever — often face up to relinquishing the exercise of their own professional skills in favour of managing other more junior staff, who in turn are still doing professional work. The culture of the profession will influence whether that shift in the pattern of work is sought after or resisted. Since such a move is associated with increased status within the organization, it will usually be sought after, and the professional task abandoned with more or less regret. Government statisticians, however, operated in a sphere where tasks such as controlling resources and managing staff have not been highly valued. In fact, 'the culture of Whitehall' denotes an attitude among administrators that policy advice to ministers — arguably, exercising the professional skills of senior generalist administrators — takes precedence over resource management. If administrators do not value management, why should professional statisticians?

During the review of the Government Statistical Service, as it became clear that there would be a call for greater cost-consciousness in departmental statistical divisions, and a greater participation by professional statisticians in managing the support staff who work on the processing of data, doubts were cast by statisticians on the possibility of attracting good new recruits to the service if the work changed in the recommended direction. This is just another way of saying that no self-respecting statistician should be spending his valuable time supervising data processing staff.

It is an interesting reflection on changing attitudes in the civil service to costs (and perhaps more widely to the British economy) that the term 'Rolls-Royce', used adjectivally (as in 'Rolls-Royce system'), has undergone a change of meaning. Whereas once it was used to denote something that was a by-word for excellence in design and workmanship, it has now come to have unfavourable connotations, implying that what is so described is unrealistic and out-of-keeping with the needs of the modern world. The Government Statistical Service was described by the review team as providing a Rolls-Royce service — shorthand for saying that statisticians were not conscious enough of the cost of their activities, were overconcerned with quality, and were unused to relating costs and benefits in a systematic manner. In their turn, members of the Government Statistical Service felt the quality of statistics reflected on their professional integrity, that wider issues of the public interest were involved in the quality of statistical work undertaken, and that statisticians were ultimately the only people qualified to judge this.

Instead of professional autonomy on statistical decisions, the review team argued for the principle of customer sovereignty — that the statistical service should be in closer harmony with the immediate customer (the policy division in departments), and that ministers, through them, should decide on the best way of serving the public interest. If policy divisions do not require a particular service or quality of service, and if no outside paying customer required it either, then the service ought to be thoroughly examined with a view to cutting it out. If there were wider public interest issues at stake, they should be addressed openly within the policy network rather than being under the protection of professional statisticians. This constitutes a clawback of some of the autonomy which they, as a professional group, had acquired and dilutes their claim to professional status.

The mechanism of clawback was to create a market framework within which statisticians had to sell their services. 'Customer orientation' is a phrase that has been buzzing round the civil service for some time. An examination of what the phrase means, however, usually reveals imagery about the relationship between suppliers and users of products or services which bears a remarkable similarity to the relationship prevailing in the retail world. Within a predefined range of products, the supplier sells the customer what he wants. He does not try to define what the customer's unacknowledged needs are, or lay claim to a special expertise to which the customer should submit himself. Other types of market framework, such as the trade in professional services such as architectural services, produce different images of the relationship between supplier and user, one that involves a negotiation between their views of appropriate outcomes. A 'client orientation' better describes that arrangement. The rhetorical richness of the 'customer orientation' has served to disguise the diminishing of professional status.

If improved management sprang from limiting the professional autonomy of particular groups within an organization, then a market framework dominated by 'customers' might be the right way to go about it. Indeed, many generalists do believe that keeping professionals in line with organizational objectives is the primary management task. Professionals are sometimes seen as a nuisance who get in the way of good management. However, when quality matters — the quality of health diagnosis, the design of a building, the design of a social survey to reveal reliable information — the value of the professional shows. It is professional training and the commitment to professional values that lead to a good survey design, and those values do not sit easily with a culture devoted to short-term responsiveness to ministerial wishes. It may be possible for those two value systems to co-exist, but the management movement has brought them to a head-on clash.

In that clash, the dual hierarchy that exists in government has not served professionals well. This hierarchy involves professional and managerial hierarchies working in parallel up to a certain level before they come together under some broader generalist grouping, with a dotted-line relationship to a head of profession. The problem comes from the gulf in understanding that exists in the space between, and from the inequality of power of the two hierarchies. Decisions about resources are actually made within the managerial line, and an understanding of the contribution of professionals is inadequately developed there. Some commentators (Schriesheim, von Glinow and Kerr, 1977) recommend a triple hierarchy, a proposal unlikely to find favour in the current management climate, but one that none the less is a means of bridging the gulf between managerial and professional cultures in a way that does justice to both. It would entail the career development of a special group who would undertake that bridging role, and who would be able to speak the languages of both the generalist and the professional. This could come about only if there were a recognition that professionals make a contribution to the organization that is of vital importance, and an acknowledgement that the major management problem in the professional field is how to get the best out of them, rather than how to get them to toe the line.

Conclusions

The review of the Government Statistical Service demonstrates a number of lessons which are important either in the tactics of management change or in the strategy for improving public management. Some of the tactical issues are developed in the next chapter, on multi-departmental reviews, so we will not dwell on them here. As the first multi-departmental review conducted by the Efficiency Unit, however, this example demonstrates the problems of holding together a large, collective, comparative exercise when capacities at the centre — in the Efficiency Unit — are stretched to and beyond the limit. The Statistics review convincingly makes the case for limiting the scale and scope of comparative exercises, to ensure that comparison, which is the primary purpose of the activity, actually takes place.

This case also demonstrates very clearly the importance of managing the presentation of policies to civil servants as well as to the general public. Rigid adherence to formal rules and ministerial etiquette about non-disclosure of information was counter-productive. The problem of rumour in the management of change is acknowledged. A coherent strategy for managing change requires a communications policy that is likely to diminish opposition and persuade people of the need to change. Many elements of Raynerism acknowledge the importance of communications — the guidance to scrutineers requires them to talk directly to those carrying out particular operations. Later dealing between the Efficiency Unit and the press indicated that the presentation lessons of this review had been taken to heart.

It is for the strategic issues of managing professionals, however, that this review is really worthy of note, and the lessons to be learned are negative ones. There is insufficient recognition that managing professionals is different from managing generalist administrators. Reading between the lines of the reports, it is possible to observe an attitude that regards professional statisticians as 'other-worldly', academic (invariably an insult in the culture of Whitehall), and out on a limb. The problem of management was defined as how to pull them into line and get them to work for departmental objectives.

The mechanism for this purpose, the establishment of the 'customer–contractor' principle, relies on the customer independently having clear ideas of his needs. When the customer does not have such a clear idea, he may end up relying more on the supplier to define his requirements, in which case 'client–contractor' is more accurate than 'consumer sovereignty'. New ways of fostering a partnership between professionals and generalists in the civil service are needed if the two groups are to work effectively together. More people are needed who span the two cultures and can translate the languages.

The danger of defining the relationship as customer–contractor only is illustrated by the current controversy about the treatment of employment statistics. Since 1979, the Thatcher government has changed the methods of collecting or calculating the number of people unemployed no less than eighteen times. The government appears to be riding roughshod over professional standards when they find they conflict with their political interests. Behind this there is a larger public management issue. The client for government statistics is not just the government but the public at large which has an interest in evaluating the effectiveness of public policies and needs the figures on which to base a judgement. Statistics are the basis of public policy information systems, and there is a clear and sharp contradiction between the positive attitude to management information systems as a means of assessing performance within departments — exemplified by MINIS — and the negative attitude to statistics — characterizing them as an unnecessary burden of form-filling and paper work — when statistics provide the public with the information on which government policies can be assessed.

7
The Efficiency of the Efficiency Strategy: the Role of the Multi-departmental Reviews

Previous chapters examined individual scrutinies and initiatives not only as cases in their own right, but also as illustrations of general principles and problems of public management. Scrutinies in the areas of management information systems, decentralization, interdepartmental coordination and so on addressed general problems. Because officials involved in the Efficiency Strategy were aware of their generality, they began to consider how far it would be possible to capitalize on the results of early investigations in two ways:
1. to generalize from individual cases and avoid the wasteful process of reinventing the wheel; and
2. to disseminate the findings from particular cases and make the lessons learned more widely available.

If the lessons learned in the course of one investigation could be generalized and made available more widely, there would be a real chance of building on successes and avoiding known pitfalls. An investment of time and effort is needed to realize these benefits. As we saw in Chapter 3, the diffusion of organizational innovations does not operate with a high degree of automaticity. Slippage or breakdown can occur at any stage in the five-phase process of agenda-setting, matching, redefining, structuring and interconnecting (Rogers and Kim, 1985). The probability of speedy improvement is reduced further when the innovation process is inter-organizational and not just intra-organizational. There is some justice in the 'not invented here' mentality. Departments differ substantially. Solutions that work well in one department may well be inappropriate in another. Exhorting departments to imitate solutions to problems developed in other departments may well be misconceived. In addition, as earlier chapters have illustrated, process is important for the successful management of change. The right answer wrongly introduced can arouse resistance to change that would be avoided by more sensitive handling. The problems of interdepartmental innovation are worth dwelling on, because the programme of individual departmental scrutinies is not geared to the tasks of catalysing general changes across departments. MINIS was the exception rather than the rule. The impact of scrutiny findings and recommendations tends to be localized. Departments can argue quite plausibly that they have enough on their plates implementing their own scrutinies without being drawn into the process of reinterpreting the findings of all the scrutinies that other departments are conducting to see if they are relevant. The Efficiency Unit, for its part, operates with very slender resources and has neither the capability nor the desire to take on these functions itself.

Nevertheless, if the Efficiency Strategy relied solely on the one-off scrutiny, its rate of progress would be severely constrained. This chapter examines the use of multi-departmental reviews as one way of circumventing these constraints and thereby increasing the efficiency of the Efficiency Strategy. The purpose is to examine the role of multi-departmental reviews as a method of transcending the limitations of the one-off scrutiny and facilitating the process of innovation at the interdepartmental level. Applying basic Rayner questions to the Efficiency Strategy itself, we are asking what value is added by linking individual scrutinies across departments and what costs are incurred by doing so? Do multi-departmental reviews provide an efficient means of generalizing the impact of scrutiny investigations? They may do so by facilitating the process of sharing experience of common problems, amplifying the influence of recommendations within participating departments, and broadcasting the messages more widely to departments not participating in a particular review. Against these benefits, such reviews are more complicated and costly to manage. There is, therefore, a question of whether they represent value for money.

The Origins of Multi-departmental Reviews

Although they do not appear to have been a part of the original concept, multi-departmental reviews evolved as an element of the Efficiency Strategy soon after it began. Their development as a distinct approach to improving public management was foreshadowed in the Government Statistical Service Review. Their emergence was no accident, even if, to start with the topics chosen for investigation were empirical responses to particular opportunities rather than part of a preconceived plan. As the Efficiency Strategy has evolved, multi-departmental reviews have consolidated their position and could well play a greater role in the future. But, obtaining full value from them depends on taking full account of their distinctive features and the managerial problems they present. To avoid continued use of ponderous terms, they will be called 'reviews' as distinct from 'one-off scrutinies' so long as no ambiguity results from doing so.

The growing importance of reviews as a component of the Efficiency Strategy is attributable to a combination of factors. First, they are a valuable means of building on the platform created by scrutinies. Scrutinies played an important role in launching the

Efficiency Strategy and establishing its credibility. Their initial demonstration effect was helped by concentrating on individual cases. But problems that fit the scrutiny format are not inexhaustible. Simply looking around for yet another topic for a scrutiny could easily mean that important targets might be missed. Departments would start to look for problems to fit the method and satisfy prime ministerial expectations rather than choosing more significant problems that did not fit the scrutiny format.

Second, most departments now use the scrutiny process, or something like it, on their own initiative rather than waiting to be prompted by the Efficiency Unit. This is a not unexpected development. The general scrutiny approach is consonant with that of departmental management services and internal audit functions. As we indicated previously, the political clout behind the Efficiency Strategy gave both a badly needed boost. What the Efficiency Strategy really changed was top management awareness of methods that had been underutilized in the past. The question 'should we do a "Rayner" on this?' has become a question that departments can ask themselves when top management sees a need for an incisive analysis of a particular area.

Third, the development of reviews occurred because the scrutiny programme itself did not generate 'read-across' spontaneously. Initially there were expectations that the findings and recommendations of early scrutinies would be widely applicable. These expectations were not fulfilled. It became clear that, even with sustained prime ministerial backing, the rate of progress of the Efficiency Strategy would be slow and somewhat piecemeal if it continued to depend almost entirely on individual scrutinies. To accelerate progress and increase the efficiency of the Efficiency Strategy a more powerful tool was required, a method designed to enable departments to draw upon and learn from each other's experience. A deliberately planned approach to generating and using interdepartmental comparisons was needed. This meant creating an agenda of topics that were of interest to several departments and would lend themselves to investigation on a comparative basis. It also entailed developing a framework within which such investigations could be conducted fruitfully.

These requirements for an interdepartmental agenda and framework for improving management raised sensitive issues that the scrutiny programme had justifiably avoided to begin with. In order to ensure a quick and effective start, the Efficiency Strategy deliberately went with the grain of departmentalism. Departments, always jealous of their own autonomy, were allowed a large measure of discretion in deciding how and where to seek savings and effect improvements. But at some stage, the quest for better performance was bound to challenge the restrictive assumptions of the culture of Whitehall and go against the grain of departmentalism. It was also likely to raise latent issues about the role of the central departments which the scrutiny programme had not.

The Role of the Centre
The role of central departments had been a subject of muffled controversy for a decade before Mrs Thatcher's government assumed office in 1979. During the lifetime of the Civil Service Department, which had the formal central responsibility for improving management throughout government, there was no satisfactory resolution of the problem of defining a role that was accepted as legitimate by other departments. Attitudes and perceptions polarized in defence of departmental interests. The options were cast in either—or terms — departmental autonomy versus central control — along the lines of the conventional debate about centralization and decentralization, but pitched at the interdepartmental level. The dominant assumption of spending departments was that central control would be rigid, uniform and insensitive to significant departmental differences. Since the Civil Service Department was responsible for administering some service-wide controls which departments found irksome, there were some grounds for these fears. Even if the Civil Service Department wanted to develop different relationships, it was stuck with what one of its senior officials described as an unresolved identity crisis.

The Civil Service Department was a child of the Fulton Report. It ceased to exist after the civil service strike in 1981 when, in dramatic circumstances, its permanent secretary, the head of the Civil Service Sir Ian Bancroft and his deputy Sir John Herbecq, who was responsible for industrial relations, were summarily retired. After this ritual bloodletting the Prime Minister made a new allocation of central functions. Responsibility for civil service pay and industrial relations was transferred to the Treasury along with some other functions. The remaining personnel and management responsibilities were assigned to the newly created Management and Personnel Office within the Cabinet Office.

The Civil Service Department's contribution to progress in improving departmental management was limited and patchy. As Richard Wilding, one of those closely involved, noted, most progress was made in the quasi-commercial and manufacturing operations of government such as Royal Ordnance Factories and the Royal Mint and in the large executive operations, for example the huge machine bureaucracies in the social security field and the revenue departments, where the repetitive nature of the work and the need for close attention to detail in handling numerous individual cases favoured the use of work measurement and related techniques. One of the undesirable and unintended consequences of this was that it reinforced belief in the impoverished concept of management. In the eyes of policy-oriented senior civil servants, it confirmed their assumption that management only meant running routine operations.

Behind the poor record of the Civil Service Department lay persistent problems about the scope and legitimacy of central initiative in the management field and ambivalence about the respective roles of the Civil Service Department and the Treasury:

> the former CSD launched the development of internal audit, management accounting and management information systems more generally. Again, creditable things were done. But looking back it is difficult to escape the conclusion that progress was too slow and the impetus insufficiently sustained. Lack of a sustained ministerial interest was surely one reason for that. But having been personally involved in this area for some years, I am convinced that the division of functions between the Treasury and CSD was another. To put it crudely again, while finance was the responsibility of the Treasury and management was the responsibility of the CSD, financial management was apt to fall down the crack between the two. (Wilding, 1982b)

This quotation anticipates questions about financial management which are the main focus of the Chapter 9, but it is relevant here because it points up a chronic structural weakness in British public administration: the lack of credible and well-defined central competence for improving management. Despite the outward impression of strong unified government, the reality has been that departments have resisted central encroachment on their managerial prerogatives. By stereotyping central initiative as attacks on their independence, departments reserved the right to give as much or as little attention to management as they thought fit.

It is worth considering the programme of multi-departmental reviews as the precursor of a more constructive and productive partnership between the centre and other departments. It creates an opportunity for the centre to play a facilitating role in improving public management which has been lacking in the past. Whether it really is a new start depends on whether the centre can persuade departments that reviews have comparative advantage over individual scrutinies. But perhaps it is better to begin at a more mundane level. The minimalist justification for multi-departmental reviews is administrative convenience. Conducting parallel investigations in different departments on a common theme economizes on the use of staff at the centre. Multi-departmental reviews simplify the task of the

Efficiency Unit in coping with a larger workload. Given the severely restricted staff resources of the Efficiency Unit, this is by no means an irrelevant consideration. By the same token, it hardly amounts to a great leap forward in redefining the role of the centre. To a very large extent, it would mean continuing to go with the grain of departmentalism. It would also imply greater routinization and standardization of the work of the Efficiency Unit, almost reducing it to the role of a secretariat without powers of initiative.

Taking the opposite view, it is worth asking what potential for improving the efficiency of the Efficiency Strategy multi-departmental reviews offer, and how best their potential can be realized. There is a delicate balance to be struck. Any attempt to exert central authority in order to impose changes would foment departmental resistance and produce limited results. Moreover, it would run counter to efforts to encourage decentralization and greater delegation which lie at the heart of the Efficiency Strategy. The main justification for multi-departmental reviews is that collaborative effort by departments will have more impact and produce superior results to those that would emerge from separate scrutinies. The constructive contribution of the centre is more in facilitating the process than in controlling the outcomes. Indeed, given the background of strong departmental loyalties, attempts by the centre to arrogate more responsibility would be self-defeating. Any real contribution to improving public management that the centre might make in this field would come from developing a distinctive competence in aiding interdepartmental collaboration and mutual learning. If this increases the authority of the centre, the increase should be based on acknowledged expertise rather than grudging acceptance of hierarchical prerogative. It should be a professional–client relationship and not a superior–subordinate one. This will be considered further after discussing the origins and evolution of the programme of multi-departmental reviews.

Statistics and Forms
The initial agenda of efficiency work included two subjects, statistics and forms, which have long been causes of complaint about government — and probably always will be. Complaints about both go right across the board and are not specific to this or that department. As a source of generalized grumbles about government, statistics runs a close second to grouses about the number and incomprehensibility of the forms that constitute the staple diet of government bureaucracies. Statistics and forms are not unrelated. Generating basic data for public policy purposes imposes burdens on the private individuals and organizations that are obliged to submit

returns. There is no need to labour once again the criticisms that have already been considered in the previous chapter on the Government Statistical Service review. Forms are a necessary evil. Government needs standardized information for many purposes, statistical and otherwise. Forms are used throughout government for regularizing the process of receiving and disbursing money as taxes, charges, grants, benefits and so on. Forms are also used for many internal administrative purposes. As the analysis of the Payment of Benefits scrutiny and the Regional Development Grants scrutiny illustrated, they are not necessarily as efficient in conveying information as they might be.

A multi-departmental review of forms revealed a very unsatisfactory situation. Of 14,000 forms examined, many were unnecessary and others, to a greater or lesser degree, were incomprehensible. More than 25 per cent of them have been abolished and a similar proportion has been significantly redesigned. The review of forms has been followed up by a continuing campaign to simplify and clarify the forms essential to the efficient conduct of government business. This campaign serves the two objectives of easing the burden on those who have to complete forms and simplifying the task of officials who have to decipher completed forms, check them and, where necessary, ensure that errors and omissions are attended to.

Because both statistics and forms are across-the-board subjects they were obvious candidates for an interdepartmental approach. In each case a group, representing different departments, was brought together to carry out the work. These investigations were the forerunners of the programme of multi-departmental reviews. However, it is not clear that at the time they were carried out the concept of multi-departmental reviews had crystallized. The main elements were present, but the idea of forming a group that was more than just the sum of its parts had not taken on a definite shape.

The Mechanics of Multi-departmental Reviews

One sign that multi-departmental reviews were not independently conceived is that they share many procedural features with one-off departmental scrutinies. Scrutineers are selected as individuals or small teams from departments. They are appointed and assigned tasks on a departmental basis. They carry out investigations within their departments. They submit their reports to their own departmental ministers. After consultation with the Efficiency Unit, departments are responsible for overseeing implementation. In procedural terms, the difference between multi-departmental reviews and individual scrutinies is that, in addition to the departmental reports, there is a central report written by a central team which identifies common problems and draws out general lessons and recommendations. The central team is formed on an ad hoc basis for each review. It is composed of individuals drawn from the Efficiency Unit, the Management and Personnel Office, and the participating departments. The central report is presented to the prime minister. At a minimum, the central report could be little more than an abstract; summarizing findings and highlighting general themes that might be relevant more widely to departments that had not taken part in the review.

The mechanics of the process are illustrated by the review of research and development support services. This review, which was one of the earliest, scrutinized support services in nineteen research and development establishments in six departments. Research and development establishments themselves are widely regarded as being off the beaten track of departmental activity. This is often literally the case geographically as well as in organizational terms. The administrative back-up for the work of their scientific and professional staffs has not been of burning interest to top departmental management. The kinds of support functions the scrutineers had to investigate included domestic services such as security, catering, transport and maintenance, estate management and accommodation services, personnel management from recruitment through all aspects of career development, clerical support such as filing, typing and messenger services, financial services such as purchasing, monitoring of costs, stores and stock control, and other internal and external financial management functions. They also included highly technical and specific services such as calibrating equipment, monitoring trials, providing high-quality photography, fabricating test equipment and prototypes relevant to the work of an establishment dealing with, say, roads or building research. These services are, by definition, auxiliary to the main tasks of the establishments. Nevertheless, support services alone accounted for £100 million in expenditure and 8000 posts at the time of the review.

One of the key contributions of the central team at the start of this review was to provide scrutineers with a central study plan, a set of questions that provided common themes for their investigations. In addition, each of the participating departments was asked to provide their scrutineers with a 'starting brief' based on the central study plan, setting out the main facts about the objectives and resources of establishments and how they were related to the functions of the department. Unintentionally, this provided a great deal of evidence of disparities among management systems. A member of the central team described what happened:

> Most examining officers soon arrived in my room looking glum and clutching either a four-inch thick computer print-out answering all the questions plus many others, or a few sheets of A4 listing the questions and answering most

with 'not known' or 'not understood'. Our briefing request turned out to be a crude diagnostic instrument for the health of establishments' costing systems. (Payne, 1982: 243)

Crude or not, it pointed the way to one of the important advantages — and major problems — of multi-departmental reviews, namely, the use of comparisons among similar functions in different situations to generate criteria for evaluation and uncover ways of improving performance. Comparing their starting briefs quickly made scrutineers aware of departmental differences in the practice and performance of similar functions.

One of the findings of this review, the £30 rat, has already been mentioned. The story of the £30 rat attracted a good deal of popular press comment. At a superficial level, it showed up bureaucratic waste and inefficiency. At a deeper level, it illustrated the advantages of making systematic interdepartmental comparisons. Collating the findings from several departments not only showed up failures of control that had long gone undetected but also offered practical solutions that were already in use in some departments and could be applied in others. In this case, the Ministry of Defence provides a best-practice model that the Ministry of Agriculture could use. The disparities in cost-accounting systems were so obvious that the message was clear.

The crucial new element in reviews is systematic in-depth comparison among departments. Given that read-across from department to department did not emerge spontaneously out of the scrutiny programme, these reviews provided a means to achieve planned read-across. As the £30 rat story illustrates, the initial outcome of these reviews is not a direct comparison of results and outcomes so much as an awareness of the unevenness and variability of departmental competence. The point of departure is several steps back from a position in which a well-developed set of concepts and well-organized body of information allows detailed quantitative interdepartmental comparisons. In many reviews, the first task of the scrutineers has been to piece together basic data about their own departments. In order to make effective use of these data, the centre has to put the information on a consistent basis and establish a coherent framework for evaluation and comparison of findings.

The Programme of Multi-departmental Reviews

Since the pioneering scrutinies of statistics, forms and support services, multi-departmental reviews have become an established feature of the annual scrutiny programme. By 1986, fourteen had been completed. Table 1 lists the scrutinies by name and indicates their date of completion and also the participating departments. Statistics stands out

TABLE 1: The Programme of Multi-Departmental Reviews

	1980	1981	1981	1982	1982	1982	1983	1983	1984	1984	1984	1985	1986	1986
	Statistics	Forms	R&D Support	Personnel Work	Running Costs	Resource Control	Admin. Support Services	Contracts and Procurement	Consultancy Inspection and Review	Internal Talent	Office Accommodation	Burdens on Business	Using Private Enterprise in Government	Delegated Budgeting
MAFF	X	X	X	X									X	
CSO	X													
C&E	X	X		X			X	X		X	X	X	X	X
MoD	X		X			X			X	X				X
DES	X	X			X									X
DE				X	X		X			X	X	X		
DEn	X	X			X						X	X		
DoE	X		X		X		X			X	X		X	
FCO	X		X					X						
HSE	X													
DHSS	X	X		X				X	X	X	X	X		X
HMSO								X						
HO	X	X		X			X	X				X	X	
IR	X	X		X		X			X			X		X
LCD	X			X			X				X			
MPO	X						X			X	X			
NIO	X			X	X	X		X	X	X				
OPCS	X													
PSA						X			X	X				
SO	X			X		X			X	X			X	
DTI	X		X	X	X	X			X	X	X	X	X	X
DTp			X					X		X	X			
HMT					X	X		X						
WO	X													
MSC														X
Total	19	7	6	10	7	7	6	9	7	11	9	7	6	7

Ministry of Agriculture Fisheries and Food
Central Statistical Office
Customs and Excise
Ministry of Defence
Department of Education and Science
Department of Employment
Department of Energy
Department of the Environment
Foreign and Commonwealth Office
Health and Safety Executive
Department of Health and Social Security
Her Majesty's Stationery Office
Home Office
Inland Revenue

Lord Chancellor's Department
Management and Personnel Office
Northern Ireland Office
Office of Population Censuses and Surveys
Property Services Agency
Scottish Office
Department of Trade and Industry
Department of Transport
Her Majesty's Treasury
Welsh Office
Manpower Services Commission

as an exceptionally wide-ranging review covering nineteen departments. The others have covered between six and eleven departments and most have only involved six or seven. This reflects the managerial difficulties of reaping benefits from interdepartmental comparisons without making the whole process too cumbersome and long drawn out. The early experience with statistics taught a clear lesson that participation should normally be limited to fewer departments. In the statistics review, the scale of participation was mitigated by the cohesiveness of the professional group under investigation.

It is too early to be definitive about the role that multi-departmental review will play, but the subjects chosen so far are not just a random and unrelated selection that happen to have been caught in the multi-departmental review net. There appears to be a pattern emerging within the programme as it has evolved so far. Three overlapping themes are in evidence. One is the management of professionals and specialists who have an operational management function, as for example in the statistics, personnel, contracts and procurement reviews. A second is the application of expertise to improve organizational performance — the consultancy inspection and review capabilities, forms, running costs and resource control, internal talent and, again, personnel reviews. These reviews cast specialists in the role of assisting line management rather than having direct responsibility. The third is in one sense a miscellaneous category and in another sense a group of subjects which, while peripheral to the main objectives of departments, are important in their own right when looked at from the standpoint of government as a whole. They are subjects in which the centre has a special interest and they include research and development support services, administrative support services, accommodation, burdens on business, competitive tendering and contracting, and budgeting. These three categories — the management of professionals, improving organizational performance and central interest in peripheral topics — are each considered briefly below.

The Management of Professionals

Government employs professionals and specialists in large numbers and great variety. Often they work in highly technical areas in establishments remote from Whitehall. Nevertheless, their work should be organized and managed to ensure that it contributes to policy objectives. As discussed in Chapter 7, managing professionals well depends on recognizing the points of tension and potential conflict between generalist administrators and professionals so as to create structures and develop management styles that accommodate the concerns of both. Managing professionals should take account of the distinctive orientations and values of people with substantial training and expectations of autonomy in the exercise of the skills they have acquired. The old specialist–generalist debate, which was such a prominent theme of Fulton, only scratches the surface of this subject. The Rothschild customer–contractor principle, intended to make professionals more responsive and less inward-looking, misdefined the relationship by approximating it to a market relationship. Often, the problem for professionals is that, instead of having customers who know what they want, they have clients who cannot formulate their needs clearly in advance of professionals being called upon to meet them. A supplier–customer relationship is appropriate when customers know their preferences and can specify what they want; a professional–client relationship is appropriate when clients' needs are ill-defined and the prior tasks of formulating problems and devising ways of solving them must be undertaken.

In recent years efforts have been made to remove barriers between different grades and categories of staff within the civil service. Some of the more absurd rigidities are disappearing, but old attitudes linger on. The management of professionals is one area where change is needed. Specialists of all kinds and levels are still liable to be labelled in what are negative terms from the standpoint of the culture of Whitehall as perfectionist, enthusiastic, politically naive, expert and therefore blinkered. It is possible that multi-departmental reviews will accelerate the process of developing greater understanding of the distinctive requirements for managing professionals. But there is much still to do.

Improving Departmental Performance

As well as the management of professionals as such, reviews have addressed the task of using professional and specialist expertise to improve departmental performance. In these circumstances the client is departmental management. Although government departments have employed large numbers of specialists, ostensibly to fulfil this function, their use has been hedged about with assumptions and practices that have seriously limited their effectiveness. The review of consultancy, inspection and review capabilities (Jenkins et al., 1984) investigated the use of full-time services in departments: staff inspection, management services and internal audit, whose primary function is to improve the internal administration of departments; the use of operational researchers, computer specialists, economists, statisticians and accountants, who advise on the effectiveness of operations and programmes; the contribution of task forces for tackling specific problems; and the use of external consultants. The review showed that these services employed about 5000 staff in total, and at the time of the review cost about £100 million per year. The findings from the six departments investigated showed a number of common weaknesses; overlaps, different services covering the same ground; gaps, selective attention to a rather narrow range of in-house problems with little contribution to programme review or assessment of the work of sponsored bodies. Linked to this, and reflecting the traditional fragmentation of responsibility, was a lack of clarity on the part of line managers about what specialist advice was available and how to use it. Instead of a professional–client relationship supplementing their efforts to improve performance, many line managers saw specialists as agents of the centre evaluating and imposing controls. Some feared that calling in specialists might be perceived as a threat or as implied criticism.It might upset staff who were working beyond the call of duty, or reflect badly on their own ability as managers.

There is another practical issue. Organizational differences affect the extent and the ways in which it is appropriate to use specialists to improve performance. Government departments differ in form and function. A department like Health and Social Security has different needs from the Property Services Agency or the Treasury, each of which took part in the review. Identifying the differences systematically would provide a basis for defining appropriate roles for specialists. As in other areas of human resource management, enabling staff to give of their best involves the adaptation of personnel policies to circumstances.

Central Interest in Peripheral Topics
The third category of multi-departmental reviews is less clear-cut in substantive terms but not less important. It embraces topics that are unlikely to excite departmental interest because they are peripheral to departmental policy objectives but which in aggregate are of significance because of the way in which they impinge on the quality of service to clients or because of the resources involved. The forms review is an example of the former and the review of accommodation costs is an example of the latter. The way in which accommodation has been costed and allocated in the past did not give departments any incentive to economize on the office space they were using or even to consider it as a significant part of their management of resources. More recently, the scrutiny of competitive tendering and contracting and the scrutiny of budgeting conducted in conjunction with the Treasury and the head of the Government Accounting Service have introduced a new element. Both, in different ways, reinforce subthemes of the Efficiency Strategy to be examined in the following chapters. They assess progress and identify avenues for improvement by examining delegated budgeting and introducing market approaches in public management.

Interdepartmental Comparison and Departmental Learning

What distinguishes multi-departmental reviews from one-off scrutinies is the deliberate use of comparisons among similar functions in different departmental contexts to guide and stimulate the quest for improvements in public management. Government departments constitute a set of organizations that display similarities and differences which in principle provide opportunities for learning from each other's experience. But, at least from a management stand-point, they constitute a weakly articulated set. Whereas in a business environment there are often competitive incentives for companies to pay attention to what their rivals are doing, so as to respond to any advance in management methods or to innovate themselves to strengthen their market position, in government these pressures are absent or inadequate. The problem is how to increase the visibility and mutual awareness among government departments of relevant similarities and differences in management practice that can provide a basis for upgrading their performance. Where external pressures for improving performance are weak, internally generated incentives acquire greater importance. Interdepartmental comparisons can be used to aid and accelerate departmental learning.

The use of comparisons to facilitate performance improvement is selective in two senses. First, it is based on selecting a group of departments on grounds of relevance and willingness to participate, criteria that do not always go easily together. Reviews avoid the standard criticism of the centre by departments, that it is seeking to impose a universalistic blanket approach. Nevertheless, selectivity opens up scope for argument and negotiation about who should and should not be included in a particular review which may be quite protracted. It is not unknown for departmental scrutineers to be pitchforked into a review team at very short notice after their department has lost a rearguard action to stay out of a review.

Second, the review approach is selective in the sense of choosing specific topics. It is not an effort at holistic comparison of departmental organization. This has the advantage that review teams have not bitten off more than they could chew. Equally important, it has given a cue to the selection of members for scrutiny teams with some direct knowledge and expertise in the area under investigation. Possibly also, it has led to the choice of people with a longer-term career interest in the development of a particular aspect of management.

Creating a framework for comparison is vital to the success of a multi-departmental review. It aids cross-fertilization and an exchange of ideas in the course of a review and assists cross-checking of analyses and recommendations at the end. Without a comparative framework, scrutineers, who in any case spend most of their time working in their own departments, are unlikely to be able to benefit from the experiences and perspectives of others. Comparison is more important than tightly defined objectives. Objectives are liable to undergo review and modification as a review progresses. The requirements of useful comparison must be clearly understood. There is little to be gained from simply putting different departmental experiences side by side. While this is a marginal improvement on individual scrutinies, it is unlikely to achieve a break with the traditional culture of Whitehall hostility to comparison. The 'we are different' appeal to departmental uniqueness easily becomes a rationalization for rejecting any and all attempts to draw interdepartmental comparisons. Denying the possibility of useful comparison is an element of the Whitehall disbelief system which rests on the assumptions that comparison is possible only between identical cases and the transfer of ideas is a process of imitation. Underlying this is a deeply entrenched reluctance to take theory — in this case, organization and management theory — at all seriously. But, as two of the major figures in the development of ideas about organizational learning have argued, one of the essential elements in the learning process is recognizing that a theory-in-use always guides administrative practice. Modifying practice in a significant way involves reviewing and revising the strategic variables and values of the theory-in-use (Argyris and Schon, 1974).

A distinctive feature of multi-departmental reviews is that they are exercises in interorganizational learning. This has advantages and disadvantages. The disadvantages stem from the fact that more time and effort are needed to build an information base, and to ensure that participants in the learning process have a common perspective. The advantages stem from the fact that the diversity of departmental experience offers a greater variety of models and approaches than would be generated by purely intra-organizational processes. Contrary to the 'culture of Whitehall' assumption, variety and dissimilarity, not identity, form the basis for fruitful comparison and interdepartmental learning. The real challenge in reviews is to develop intervening concepts and theory that facilitate the process of abstracting from different cases and then applying what is learned more widely and systematically. Intervening theory demands more work by the review team to pool and organize their findings. The gain from this effort is that it provides much greater flexibility in identifying ways of improving management and performance. A number of forms of comparisons are possible and provide a basis for strategic choices by review teams.

Strategies for Organizational Learning

At the simplest level, one department participating in a review may stand out as a best-practice model from which others can learn. To take a pertinent example, a department may have invested considerable time and resources to develop management accounting systems to keep track of expenditure and regulate costs. Such a best-practice model provides a ready-made standard of reference. Other departments can easily see the inadequacy of their own systems and have clear guidelines for levelling-up. Of course, it is important not to overlook the extent to which such a best-practice model rests on established accounting theory which provides the medium through which transfers of knowledge and experience can be made. It is not a process of direct imitation.

Often, such a paragon of virtue is lacking. No department provides a ready-made model. It may be that several departments can claim superiority in particular respects, or that investigations reveal common deficiencies for which no department has the answer. This gives the review team the additional task of combining a number of elements to construct a model that does not correspond to practice in any department. The review team then faces the task of establishing a new set of general standards that all departments should aim at. This means that not all departments do the same thing, but that they work out solutions appropriate to their own circumstances in line with common principles. An example of the process is the effort to shift staff reporting systems from assessing the qualities of personnel to assessing their performance. This is not the place to go into the considerable difficulties that are involved in implementing this change, but is simply an illustration of the way in which new standards may emerge from the review process.

A further level of complexity is introduced when the diagnosis of problems and circumstances indicates that departments differ substantially. The problem is not so much to synthesize a new set of common standards but to establish a basis for prescribing different responses in different contexts. This does not mean an ad hoc approach based on the flaccid formula of treating each case on its merits without spelling out how the merits of the case are to be assessed. In effect, what is required here is a contingency approach of the kind that has become common in the management field for matching organizational structures to different technologies or to different sets of environmental constraints, going back at least to the classic studies of Joan Woodward (1965) and Lawrence and Lorsch (1965).

The review of consultancy, inspection and review capabilities is an example of this kind of situation. Traditionally, the provision of these capabilities has followed a rather uniform pattern since it served predominantly the needs of the centre to monitor compliance with given standards. Shifting the focus from compliance to performance improvement necessitates establishing a clearer relationship between the kinds of capabilities provided and the needs of line management in different departments. A horses-for-courses approach is needed.

Mintzberg (1983) outlined a schema for matching technical expertise devoted to improving performance to the needs of managers in different organizational settings. For instance, he emphasized the greater scope for standardizing work processes by using work study analysts and operations researchers in what he termed machine bureaucracies with complex but rather stable structures. Large parts of the Department of Health and Social Security exemplify this. In what Mintzberg termed a professional bureaucracy, it is skills rather than processes that need to be standardized, hence personnel specialists have a relatively more important role. The Property Services Agency employs a wide range of professionals and specialists and while where is certainly scope for standardization of work processes, standardization of skills should have greater priority. In a conglomerate department like the Scottish Office there is a clear need to look closely at the specific organizational characteristics and requirements of each area.

Each of the ways of using comparisons discussed above assumes a cross-sectional perspective — looking at differences and similarities among departments. The perspective is appropriate within a single review where the topic is narrowly defined. Clearly, the centre has a special responsibility for ensuring that the potential benefits of interdepartmental learning are actually realized, and this involves providing a strong lead in establishing a framework for organizing and interpreting departmental experiences. In addition, shifting from a cross-sectional to a longitudinal perspective, the centre has a unique responsibility for building up expertise in managing multi-departmental reviews. The benefits of hindsight are often lost because most people are not repeatedly faced with the problems of participating in or managing reviews. But over a period of time, as the number of reviews increases there is an opportunity for the centre to act as a repository for experience and a source of expertise. This requires evaluation of successes and failures, identification of key choices and options and acknowledgement of failures and missed opportunities. In multi-departmental learning, the centre has a special responsibility for learning to learn.

The Management of Multi-departmental Reviews
The management of multi-departmental reviews is a significant determinant of their contribution to raising the efficiency of the

Efficiency Strategy. As indicated earlier, there would be an administrative saving in simply conducting parallel scrutinies on the same topic, but few benefits of the kinds discussed in the previous section are likely to accrue if this minimalist strategy is adopted. On the other hand, and prompting comparison, building a common framework for analysis and facilitating interdepartmental learning require a greater and more intensive management input to create a collective commitment and to overcome the difficulties and conflicts that arise.

The procedural similarities between reviews and individual scrutinies have already been mentioned. They are similar in relying on giving scrutineers freedom from departmental constraints, encouraging them to go for direct knowledge of what is happening and requiring them to form an independent view of what is being done and what should be done. As with individual scrutinies, the bulk of the work starts from the bottom with scrutineers working in their own departments. These are valuable, perhaps indispensable, elements of the review process, but they are not enough to ensure that multi-departmental reviews achieve their full potential. The similarities between reviews and scrutinies should not be allowed to obscure important differences. There is a real danger that too little account is taken of the extra management burden that coordination of multi-departmental reviews entails.

In assessing this burden, it is important to recall to mind two sets of factors. First, there is the structural context. Reviews are, by definition, conducted at the interdepartmental level. They are attempts to manage change and improve the standards of public management through inter-organizational processes. By contrast, much, though not all, private sector experience is based on intra-organizational change processes. Multi-departmental reviews go against the grain of departmentalism and are therefore likely to succeed only if the managerial investment in them overcomes the centrifugal tendencies of inter-organizational relations. Second, there is the choice of topics. The agenda of multi-departmental reviews consists of subjects which to a greater or lesser degree run counter to the assumptions and precepts of the culture of Whitehall. The management of professionals, use of expertise to improve performance and emphasis on topics peripheral to departmental concerns all call for a greater effort to modify attitudes and raise consciousness than is the case with departmentally selected topics. For these reasons, there is a need to rethink the management of multi-departmental reviews; to treat them as an addition to the management tools of government in their own right rather than simply an extension of the one-off scrutiny.

One of the distinguishing features of public management is getting things done through other organizations. Multi-departmental reviews exemplify this. Not only is the centre working with and through other departments, but departments themselves are put in a position of learning from each other's experience. A model of management is needed which reflects the complexities of this task and the structural context.

Fortunately, reviews are not *sui generis*. Their management requirements can be usefully analysed from a project management standpoint. Project management differs from operational management in being concerned with seeing a particular task through from its inception to completion. The project is a finite task and not a continuous function. A project management exercise starts, at least in principle, with a set of clearly defined objectives, limited resources and a definite time-frame. The key to success in project management is the ability of project managers to create a team to complete the project by welding together disparate elements to serve a common purpose. Seen from a project management perspective, the management requirements of multi-departmental reviews are neither unique nor new to the public sector. There are many areas of governmental activity where project management skills and competences are used regularly. Road construction programmes are familiar examples and, for obvious reasons, project management has close associations with all types of construction activity. Within departments, new ventures such as the introduction of computers and new information technology illustrate ways in which project management is an integral part of making organizational changes. Thus, there is some relevant experience and some training resources on which to draw in considering how best to manage reviews.

However, these similarities should not detract from significant differences between project management in substantive areas where the outcomes have a concrete end-product (sometimes literally) and the less tangible outcomes of management reform where the purpose is to make organizational changes that will have indirect and long-term effects on performance. As a management concept, project management is in the management-by-objectives (MBO) tradition. But, in practice, it is employed much more widely to deal with genuine management problems and not just with control problems.

Multi-departmental reviews share the perennial problems of project management, the start-up and team-building problems, the definition and maintenance of objectives and the dangers of cost and time overruns. The qualities most needed for success in project management are skills in integration (Galbraith, 1973). In essence, the task of integration is to ensure that the whole group that forms a project management team achieves more than the separate activities of the participants would achieve if they worked on their own. In making the whole greater than the sum of its parts, the integrating manager can depend less on formal authority than the line manager and therefore relies much more on building networks, assembling information and establishing confidence and mutual trust among groups and organizations that would normally go their own way.

Project Management and the Role of the Centre

The main responsibility for ensuring that integrative capabilities are provided lies with the centre, that is, with the Efficiency Unit and the Management and Personnel Office. It is up to the centre to give a lead and ensure that the task of building a comparative framework for the effective exchange of ideas is successfully carried through, and that the resulting conclusions are used to good effect. However, this does not mean that the centre is the fountainhead of all ideas, or that it should operate in a heavy-handed way. Effective integrative leadership in project management is primarily effectiveness in team-building. Team-building is needed to ensure that the energies of participants are used to further the objectives of a review and are not dissipated because of failures of communication, divergences of objectives and unresolved conflicts. As Beckhard (1972) pointed out, optimizing team-building efforts calls for interventions which serve the needs of the group rather than reflecting the priorities of those making the interventions. In multi-departmental reviews this involves addressing issues to do with objectives, with defining the work programmes that follow from the objectives, with building a team spirit among the participants.

What has emerged from research and experience on project management is a chronic tendency to underestimate the investment of management resources required to assure timely and cost-effective completion. For political reasons, over-optimistic assumptions are made. But the course of project management never runs smooth. Without adequate preparation and planning at the initial stages, there is every chance that efforts and energy will be wasted. Team-building is a continuing responsibility. Hence, to regard reviews as a means of easing the burden on the Efficiency Unit is mistaken. Undermanaged reviews are false economy. More rather than fewer management resources are needed to ensure value for money. Reviews are a sphere in which the 'spend to save' principle applies.

This is particularly so because, if anything, reviews pose a more difficult test of management competences than conventional project management. One complicating factor is the conflicting loyalties of departmental review team members. They do not join a review team and, for the duration, sever their connections with their home department. Instead, their scrutiny work takes place in their departmental environment at the same time as they are taking part in the process of establishing new reference points and criteria for evaluation in the review team. There is a built-in tension which may or may not be creative, depending on how it is managed. Genuinely integrative management has to search for solutions which place individual cases in a comparative perspective that takes account of similarities and differences.

At the interdepartmental level, there is a related leadership problem maintaining the momentum for change without losing support and commitment. This calls for skills in conflict management because divergences of view and interest are sure to arise. The idea that conflict should not arise if objectives are clearly defined at the outset is simplistic. It does not always apply within departments, and at the interdepartmental level it is an implausible assumption. Frequently, objectives are only sketched in, in a tentative way, at the beginning of a review. In the course of a review, departmental diversity and a revision of ideas are almost certain to lead to unforeseen differences and to create some conflicts. To some degree at least, the centre has an interest in promoting competitive conflict between departments to force up standards and expose issues that are normally submerged below the surface of interdepartmental dialogue. But the primary task of the centre as an agent of interdepartmental learning is to uncover areas where conflict can promote a higher degree of cooperation. Exposing differences can deepen understanding of problems and prepare the ground for resolving them by encouraging critical evaluation of the feasibility and acceptability of alternative solutions. It is no accident that studies of Japanese organizations stress the amount of time spent in examining differences and resolving conflicts at early stages in the policy formulation process. This gives the appearance of slowness and indecision but actually resolves many ambiguities that otherwise emerge later to disrupt implementation. Time lost on the policy formulation swings is more than regained on the implementation roundabouts. Conversely, suppressing conflict breeds defensiveness and mistrust, which, in an inter-organizational context, lead to superficial contributions and token involvement. Time and effort go into papering over cracks, and finding acceptable forms of words to mask disagreements and avoid clear commitment.

Devoting time and management resources to integration and conflict management goes against well-established Whitehall assumptions and the assumptions of the scrutiny programme. In both cases there is an assumption that the way to manage change is to have an individual or small group working quickly to produce strong, positive recommendations. There are situations where this approach to managing change does produce results; there are many other situations where it does not, and it is highly debatable whether it is the right strategy for multi-departmental reviews. Its main weakness is that it does little or nothing to prepare the ground for implementation, the Achilles heel of so many ventures in planned change. It usually rests on the convenient assumption that it is enough to have top management commitment to ensure implementation. In an inter-organizational context this is an even more shaky assumption than it is in the context of a single organization. Commitment is needed from several top management groups, and in addition there is a need to build strong links from the review teams back into their departments. Involving team members in implementation is one element in this, but it is far from being a complete answer.

Given these inescapable complexities, it might seem advisable for reviews to concentrate on simple problems. But this advice is easier to give than to take. After years of neglect, government is not in a position to pick and choose its management problems. Nor is it easy for government to divest itself of responsibilities in the way that businesses can. In this respect multi-departmental reviews present some of the challenges to innovation in public management that Nelson (1973) neatly summarized in his analysis of the 'Moon-Ghetto Metaphor': 'If we can send men to the moon why can't we solve the problem of the ghetto?' Sending men to the moon was a major challenge to project management. The technical problems to be overcome were certainly immense. Even so, going to the moon was not a voyage of discovery for public management in the way that ghetto-type problems are. It was a process of implementing a solution to problems that were stable and well defined. The objectives were clear at the start, and the criterion of success was unambiguous. Money was no object. Solving ghetto-type problems means initiating projects which may be technically simpler but are politically much more complex. The problems of inner-city areas are as difficult to define as they are to solve. Instead of well-defined criteria of effectiveness, there are great difficulties in formulating problems. Instead of a controllable process of implementation, widespread support has to be mobilized and maintained. Resources are not abundant. Problems, objectives and resources may all vary during the course of the project.

Reform in public management may not have all the difficulties associated with problems of this complexity, but it would be wrong to assume that the techniques and skills required to carry out a continuing series of multi-departmental reviews are readily available. In all probability, this is an area where government will have to innovate and pioneer new approaches to project management in order to deal with the problems it faces.

Conclusions

As the Efficiency Strategy moves into uncharted territory and seeks to bring about lasting reforms, it will need to rely more extensively on more sophisticated methods than the one-off scrutiny. Multi-departmental reviews offer the prospect of more focused and more concerted action to deal with problems common to several departments. They provide an opportunity for departments to learn from each other and level up standards of managerial competence. They cast the centre in the role of providing the context for specialist project teams, devoted to a particular task, to cooperate by pooling ideas, reformulating problems and developing best-practice standards.

The dynamics of multi-departmental reviews involve stimulating competition as well as promoting cooperation. In the first instance, competition among scrutineers as members of review teams prompts an identification of ways of making savings, reducing costs and improving standards of management. More fundamentally, perhaps, by generating common standards they can assist the process of making comparisons among departments on a continuing basis. Again, there is a role for the centre in ensuring that interdepartmental communication channels are kept open so that departments have an incentive to assess and evaluate their own performance against what others are doing.

In addition to providing a framework for public management improvement more general than that of individual scrutinies, reviews contribute to broadening the agenda of efficiency work, extending it into areas where scrutinies would not produce such good results. A dozen or so cases is a small sample from which to draw generalizations, but the emerging patterns suggests that these reviews are able to address topics that departments, left to themselves, would not choose. In part, at least, reviews represent a way of overcoming the institutional and cultural constraints built into established administrative practice. They go against the grain of departmentalism, and they also cut across long-held assumptions of the culture of Whitehall — notably, in relation to the roles of professionals.

Managing at the interdepartmental level presents the centre with an opportunity to play a constructive role which does not pose a direct challenge to departmental prerogatives. As the principal agent for facilitating interdepartmental learning, the centre not only must develop project management competences to facilitate building comparative frameworks but also must handle the interdepartmental political problems of establishing sufficient autonomy for project teams to function effectively without the members losing touch with their respective departments. Good relations with departments are important before and especially during the implementation stage. Moreover, since reviews typically cover only a few departments, it.is up to the centre to devise ways of ensuring diffusion of innovations and defining a strategy for implementation on a wider front.

Since it is the centre that provides continuity in the programme of reviews, it is especially important that it makes good use of the experience acquired in managing successive reviews. Reviews in themselves involve interdepartmental learning processes: the distinctive role of the centre in improving the efficiency of this process is in learning how to learn at the interdepartmental level. Existing ideas about project management provide the appropriate starting-point for this learning-to-learn process. However, there is much that needs to be done in adapting and developing the concept of project management to address more complex problems.

The resource implications of managing multi-departmental reviews should not be ignored. It is clear that realizing the potential benefits demands more managerial input than has been made or can be made at the moment. Reviews present difficult management problems if they are to be done well. If they are to be done better by learning from experience through an analysis of successes and failures, the management resource requirements will be heavier. The Management and Personnel Office will need to play a larger role in the conduct of reviews, including following up implementation and capitalizing on the experience gained as the programme evolves. Improving public management is not a free good. It raises 'spend to save' issues and requires political courage to defend additional management resource inputs against criticisms that frequently appear to start from 'Health Farm' assumptions. The conduct of reviews requires an investment in the training and the development of the human resources upon which the skilful management of change depends.

8
Market Approaches to Public Management

Modernization of public organizations is often portrayed as nothing more or less than the substitution of up-to-date business management methods for old-fashioned public administration practices. In a literal sense, the way to make government more businesslike is to make it more like business. This assertion implies that management concepts, methods and techniques that have withstood the test of the market can and should be deployed in government. It also implies that there are benefits in terms of efficiency and effectiveness in exposing public sector activities to market pressures and using markets to serve public purposes.

Business experience does have a good deal to offer. Where business has developed solutions to specific management problems, there is a compelling case for government's avoiding the process of reinventing the wheel. Government can learn from business even where there are contextual differences between public and private sectors which mean that business practice does not provide ready-made answers to all public management problems. In the past, governments have been slow to take advantage of the fact that management is better understood and developed in business. Proposals for selective application of particular methods tended to be swamped by generalized scepticism about the possibility of valid comparison and overstatement of the difficulties of introducing changes. The disbelief system of the culture of Whitehall reinforced these prejudices. Senior officials and less senior aspirants to top civil service jobs were reluctant to identify with the role of manager.

The opposite is the case in business. In contrast with the impoverished concept of management as dull, low-level routine, business managers are at home with the idea that they are part of a larger process of management and their responsibilities and perspectives widen in scope as they ascend from lower to higher levels. This breeds a more positive attitude to innovation and change. Under pressure of competition businesses have evolved new techniques, methods and concepts of management. The increasing complexity of business operations has forced businesses to develop new concepts and practices. Current emphasis on organizational culture is only the most recent phase of a continuing process of responding to new challenges by management innovation. No doubt, there is an element of fashion, but there is also a serious contribution to increasing the capacity to reorganize and respond flexibly to rapid environmental change.

For these reasons, there is a strong case for making use of relevant private sector experience. From the beginning of the scrutiny programme, scrutineers were encouraged to examine private sector practice relevant to the problems they were investigating and to consider whether it provided useful guidelines. Scrutineers were not required to apply private sector practice automatically. Comparisons showed up differences as well as similarities. Rayner himself is on record as emphasizing both the complexity of public management and the real differences that exist between it and business management:

> There is no risk whatsoever of my assuming that running government is like running Marks and Spencer either in content or execution. Government has to provide services which no sane business would undertake and whether it is more or less of government that the nation needs, a government will have to deal with those issues which private enterprise and voluntary activities cannot handle. (Rayner, 1983: 3)

Hence, government must develop its own approach and use private sector practice in a selective and discriminating way, guided by a concept of public management. This qualified and conditional position prompts a closer examination of an issue that tends to be viewed in all-or-nothing ideological terms. The Efficiency Strategy has evolved in a context in which political attitudes have polarized sharply. Conformity with ideological convictions has been a stronger factor in the advocacy of particular forms of public organization and styles of public management than empirical evidence of their relationship to efficiency and effectiveness. Indeed, there almost appears to be an inverse relationship between the strength of feeling engendered and the amount of evidence available.

Ideological polarization is symptomatic of marked changes of attitude towards government which go far beyond the Efficiency Strategy or indeed British politics. 'Thatcherism' has become the well-established term of adulation or abuse which identifies a general shift from reliance on hierarchical forms of public organization to greater reliance on the market. A similar tendency towards greater reliance on market approaches is apparent elsewhere. Governments in most advanced countries are in process of reconsidering or revising basic assumptions about the boundaries between public and private sectors, the scope of regulation and the opportunities for deregulation.

Privatization
Much of this movement is subsumed under the general label of 'privatiz-ation'. Privatization lumps together several different policy themes, including deregulation, charging for public services, contracting out, adopting commercial management methods in government, and trans-

ferring ownership of assets from the public to the private sector. Privatization is a two-way street. It serves to export public management responsibilities and also to import private management ideas and practices (Heald, 1983; Kay and Silberston, 1984; Young, 1986). As this indicates, the Efficiency Strategy is not an isolated phenomenon. It is part of a broader vision of economy and society. It is an integral component of a radical strategy of institutional and cultural change designed to give a freer rein to private initiative, widen the scope of individual choice, increase the efficiency of market forces, and place greater reliance on voluntary effort as against the mollycoddling of the 'nanny-state'. It is interesting to place this change in a comparative and historical perspective. King, writing in 1974, compared the extent of public ownership in the UK, the USA, Canada, France and the Federal Republic of Germany and observed that there were clear differences. The USA made little use of public ownership, while the UK was close to France, which had the greatest spread of direct government involvement in industry. A similar survey now would show the UK in a different light as a result of the privatization programme conducted by the Conservative government since 1979.

From the standpoint of public management, it is King's interpretation of his cross-national comparison that is of particular interest. He argued that the differences among the five countries could not be accounted for by variations in the power of political elite, in public demands on government, on the strength of interest groups, or on institutional resistance to change. Instead, he suggested that the critical factors were in the realm of ideas, especially ideas about the appropriate role of government. What has been happening in the UK and elsewhere lends support to this emphasis on the importance of ideas in moulding political action. There has been a widespread shift in the climate of opinion against expanding the scope of public sector and towards reducing the interventionist role of the state. Whereas a few years ago it was fashionable to argue for the extension of government activity, citing in justification some variation on the theme of market failure, the tide of opinion has turned decisively. It is now government failure for which remedies are being sought. Some of these remedies directly and indirectly entail greater reliance on market mechanisms and commercial styles of management within government. This chapter assesses various ways of placing greater reliance on market approaches to public management and explores the implications of doing so.

Public and Private Choice

Market approaches to public management are strongly associated with values of individualism and draw their intellectual vitality from the exponents of public choice economics on the radical right. Their critiques of the performance of public organizations lead to prescriptions for reducing the role of the state and increasing the use of competitive processes to provide an effective framework of accountability. Substituting the values and ideals of individualism for those of collectivism is a major venture in social engineering — though its exponents would jib at the use of that label. They prefer to present it as deregulation — doing away with organizational frameworks and management structures, dismantling constraints, removing restrictions and breaking down barriers created by government to the free operation of the invisible hand of the market. In effect, they espouse an anti-Marxist version of the withering away of the state. However, free markets and competitive processes do not operate in the absence of an institutional framework. As Mueller, one of the foremost exponents of public choice theory, observed, 'Although often depicted as the perfect example of the beneficial outcome of purely private individualistic activity in the absence of government, the invisible hand theorem presumes a system of collective choice comparable in sophistication to the market system it governs' (Mueller, 1976: 397). The task is reregulation rather than deregulation. Private and public choice are interdependent elements of a total process, not alternatives. The real challenge for public management is to find more effective ways of combining them.

Portraying public and private choice as complements rather than substitutes has important implications for public management in general and privatization in particular. It provides a perspective from which to reconsider the assumptions underlying the increased use of market alternatives. Reliance on individualistic motivations and market methods does not do away with public management responsibilities. The interdependence of public and private choice transforms and redefines public management responsibilities in ways that put a premium on public managers' developing higher-level skills and particular expertise in designing and managing the framework within which operational management is carried out.

Business Practice in Government
The quest for a more market-oriented approach to public management is not just a matter of applying new techniques. It is an attempt to raise efficiency by subjecting public organizations to market conditions, by relying more on businesses that are subject to market forces to provide public goods and services, and by simulating market conditions within government to ensure tighter discipline in those areas that cannot be opened up to direct market pressure. None of these is entirely new to government, but each has undergone expansion and development since 1979. They will be considered below

under five main headings, each of which represents a sub-theme of the Efficiency Strategy, and each of which has figured throughout the scrutiny programme. The five categories are:

1. improving management accounting;
2. providing common services on a repayment basis within government;
3. charging for services provided to external customers;
4. contracting out the production of services;
5. buying in management.

Improving Management Accounting

More systematic management accounting is a sine qua non of any attempt to introduce commercial management practices into government. If a real move towards greater cost-consciousness is to take place, better financial information throughout government is essential. Financial control within the civil service betrays its nineteenth-century origins. The traditional system of vote-accounting was designed to satisfy parliamentary requirements rather than to act as a system of management accounting designed to aid planning and cost control. The vote-accounting system is primitive and serves only to keep track of cash payments to departments during the financial year. It takes no account of accruals or prepayments and does not differentiate between revenue and capital expenditure. The cost of allied or common services provided by one department to another, free of charge, has been accounted for by the supplying department and not the consuming department. This weakness is at the heart of a move towards repayment discussed below. In many departments more up-to-date accounting systems have been introduced alongside the formal-vote accounting system; but there was no consistent policy and no general pressure for improved accounting. It has been quite possible for officials at senior levels to have little information or serious concern about the substantial resources nominally under their command. Principal finance officers, the senior officials responsible for financial control, and permanent secretaries, as the accounting officers for departments, were not expected to have any special training or expertise in accounting or financial management.

The Efficiency Strategy and, more recently, the Financial Management Initiative (discussed in Chapter 9) have put this cavalier attitude beyond the pale. Anyone directly involved in financial management is now expected to have relevant training. All officials with management roles are now much more aware of their financial responsibilities. It is quite common to hear senior officials at conferences and meetings quote figures to indicate the extent of their budget responsibilities and the resources at their disposal. Not infrequently, they add the comment that until recently it would not have been possible to do so, because there was no means of assembling and presenting the relevant information. It is worth adding that management accounting in government may prompt accounting innovation rather than just involving the application of existing commercial techniques, concepts and conventions.

The deficiencies of government accounting were exacerbated by the small numbers of professional accountants in government and their limited role. In part, this is a legacy of long-standing civil service scepticism about the value of professionals and specialists in general. In part, it reflects the way trained accountants have been used. A high proportion of the government's accountants have been employed in the public purchasing field to deal with the commercial firms supplying to government departments rather than to provide financial and accounting information about the conduct of departmental business to departmental managers. Little progress to improve accounting was made during the 1970s despite the criticisms in the Melville and Burney report (1973: 202). Poor pay and career prospects are other factors limiting the role of accountants in government. Paradoxically, the civil service has a good record of training accountants, who rapidly find their way into the private sector once they qualify. As much as anything, it is economic recession that has enabled government to recruit accountants in larger numbers; otherwise many recent recruits would not have given the civil service a second thought.

There is no question about the strength of the case for upgrading and modernizing management accounting in government. However, the foregoing discussion of the intended consequences of better accounting for management is by no means all that there is to say on the subject. Accounting practices also have unintended, or at least unacknowledged, political and managerial consequences. These hidden side-effects mean that introducing new management accounting methods may also introduce new criteria and new values into decision-making and policy formulation. As with management information systems discussed earlier, accounting systems go well beyond a passive recording of what government does and the providing of purely neutral factual information about costs on which to base decisions.

As Hopwood (1983) pointed out, the values and perspectives that accountants bring to their work shape priorities and influence perceptions of problems as well as the desirability and feasibility of solutions. The accountants' 'value for money' slogan provides a rhetorical link between techniques and objectives of a particular kind. Accountancy flourishes in periods of economic restraint and puts a heavier emphasis on efficiency and economy than on effectiveness. Furthermore, accounting procedures provide symbols of accountability which enhance organizational legitimacy in the eyes of external reference groups. By defining which facts are significant, accounts can provide defences against external intrusion on managerial discretion. Accounts rationalize organizational activity in conformity with external expectations. 'The display of rational accounts may be oriented to those who ask questions of the organization and seek to probe into its affairs from without, rather than to those who determine from within the organization's course of events' (Hopwood, 1983: 183). The danger is that accountability processes lose real force as constraints or guides to decision-makers and become merely vehicles for public relations exercises and political window-dressing. Possibly the greater danger is that accounting reforms become no more than a bureaucratic routine which makes little or no contribution to higher-level management processes of strategic decision-making. If this is a recurrent problem in industry, it is likely to be even more of a problem in government where it is too easily assumed that management is about operational efficiency and not about strategic flexibility (Kaplan, 1983; Simmonds, 1983).

Improved accounting can and should make a significant contribution to improving public management, if only because there is so much ground to make up. The contribution it makes over the longer term will depend on recognizing that it is not just a technical tool to improve operating efficiency and increase cost-consciousness but that, at a higher level, it has implications for effectiveness, managerial discretion and the political values and priorities that shape the actions of public managers.

Providing Common Services on a Repayment Basis within Government

A second way in which market solutions can improve public management is by putting the provision of common services on a better footing. By tradition, some services have been provided across government by a specific department instead of each department making its own arrangements and acting independently. The provision of stationery, printing and publishing services by Her Majesty's Stationery Office is one of the most familiar examples. Another example is the Property Services Agency with its responsibilities for the provision of office equipment, accommodation services and estate management. A third example is the provision of service-wide training by the Civil Service College.

Before Rayner, it was established practice that these allied, or common, services should be provided free to the user. The costs of the service were borne on the budget of the providing agency. There were also bureaucratic restrictions on departments' freedom of choice in going elsewhere. Common services provided on this basis did not win the hearts of their clients. They were often a cause of resentment and frustration. In combination with the accounting weaknesses referred to above, the arrangements provided inadequate guidelines for effectiveness and few incentives for efficiency in provision or use. Hence a market approach, where recipients of services have to pay for and budget for what they consume and suppliers have to price their services in relation to costs, possibly under pressure from competitors, offers a way of encouraging more critical evaluation of what is needed on the demand side and what is provided on the supply side.

From the standpoint of economic efficiency, there are clear attractions in encouraging buying and supplying departments to negotiate and match what is wanted to what is provided. There are incentives on both sides to minimize costs. The incentives increase when there is competition from outside sources and where departments are not tied to a single intra-governmental source of supply. Experience may show that the case for common service provision is weak and departments should be allowed to go their own way. Alternatively, it may reveal that the managerial and resource costs to departments of assessing their own needs, evaluating alternative sources of supply and dealing direct with suppliers are greater than they anticipate. Free provision of common services obscures the extent to which suppliers actually absorb some of the managerial costs of handling customer–supplier relations. Repayment puts the onus on the customer department to manage the relationship with suppliers.

A simple illustration, which also illustrates accounting weaknesses, is the management of office accommodation by the Property Services Agency. Much government office accommodation is shabby and down-at-heel. It is also a significant element in departmental running costs. A scrutiny in 1985 estimated the costs of central government offices at £850 million. The report argued that costs could be reduced by £40–50 million within three years if departments themselves had clearer responsibilities and financial incentives to economize. The established system for charging notional rents to departments has been based simply on the area of office space and not on its location. Site values and the standard of offices have not been taken into account. Departments and line managers within them have had neither the information about costs nor the incentive to release surplus space or consider moving to less expensive and perhaps more suitable accommodation. A realistic pricing system could make departments more sensitive to the resources they consume.

There is no reason to suppose that there is a universal solution to the organization of common services. The argument for repayment on a strict commercial basis is clearer, though not unqualified, in the case of the Stationery Office and the Property Services Agency than in the case of the Civil Service College, for example. The appropriate model for the Civil Service College is not a business, but a business school providing post-experience professional education (Simon, 1967; Wildavsky, 1978). The major management issues are in the area of effectiveness rather than efficiency. Professional education poses more complex management problems than either discipline-based academic education or commercially provided training services aimed at a known and well-defined market. The appealingly simple idea that the Civil Service College should just provide what the departmental customer wants has frequently run up against the problem that departments have difficulty articulating their training needs. Hence, the definition of objectives and the generation of criteria of effectiveness are continuing elements in the tasks of management. There are analytical and path-finder roles to play in order to ensure effectiveness. Without rejecting the introduction of a commercial element, it is short-sighted to see the relationship between the Civil Service College and departments as one between a customer and a supplier. It is primarily a professional–client relationship, requiring a prior diagnosis of needs. Commercial criteria are secondary to this.

Focusing disciplinary inputs to meet the needs of client departments presents real management challenges. It can never reduce to a routine. The task of management is to ensure that relevance to clients is sustained through successive redefinitions of problems and progressive development of effective solutions. It is worth quoting Simon's observations on business schools as examples of professional education. He likened them to research and development organizations because their task is to make theory relevant to practice:

> Organizing a professional school or an R & D department is very much like mixing oil and water: it is easy to describe the finished product, less easy to produce it. And the task is not finished when the goal has been achieved. Left to themselves, the oil and water will separate again. So also will the disciplines and the profession. Organizing in these circumstances is not a once-for-all activity. It is a continuing administrative responsibility, vital for the sustained success of the enterprise. (Simon, 1967: 16)

The really difficult problems in professional education are to do with relevance and effectiveness. Financial self-sufficiency is secondary, though, at a time of cuts and restraint, the fact that the benefits are diffuse and long-term makes training vulnerable. Along with other forms of investment in human resources, it is easy to cut and the consequences of doing so are masked for some time. Financial criteria set limits to what can be done, but they do not define norms to guide what should be done. Particularly when the task is training for change, the effectiveness of the Civil Service College depends on the contribution it makes to developing the knowledge and skills they need for the future. Repayment may be a step on the way to achieving this, but market signals reflect current wants, not future needs. Repayment is a means to the end of better professional service, not an end in itself.

Charging for Services Provided to External Customers
There is nothing new in the idea of charging the public for government-provided services as a matter of deliberate policy. *Mutatis mutandis*, much the same issues arise as in the case of repayment. Indeed, charging external customers is simpler because there are actual market prices rather than artificial internal transfer prices to guide decision-making and action. However, the politics of charging are more complex and so are the managerial implications.

Charging the public in receipt of services rather than financing services out of general revenue can be politically controversial. One only has to recall the perennial controversy about National Health Service prescription charges. In that and other cases, the issue is not simply a matter of how to finance a service or how to ensure allocative efficiency: what is also at issue is the nature of the relationship between public and public organization. Controversy stems from prior questions of legitimacy rather than efficiency. It is not a matter of whether market criteria should apply, but whether market criteria should have priority over professional criteria. At this level the debate is primarily about the framework of accountability and only secondarily about management.

Putting on one side cases where the legitimacy and priority of qualitatively different definitions of relationships and forms of accountability are at issue, there are managerial questions associated with charging for services that are not straightforward to resolve. For a government committed to reducing the role of the state and the burden of government on the taxpayer, the motivations behind charging for services are obvious; to raise revenue from those who use services and reduce demand for services. The managerial implications of charging depend on the balance between these motives. There is an inbuilt tension that requires political decision. Reducing demand implies a reduced scale of provision and therefore lower levels of activity and associated public employment. Raising revenue implies an expansionary policy, meeting market demand where revenue more than offsets costs, and employing more civil servants to do so.

The trade-off between more revenue and fewer civil servants is a test of political priorities, which also has managerial implications. The more the emphasis is placed on seeking ways of increasing revenue, the more pressures there will be from those who are successful in doing so to expand existing activities and develop new ones. Such a process runs counter to well-entrenched civil service assumptions and attitudes. The civil service culture is not one that actively encourages people to look for ways of selling services. There are few specific organizational incentives, and the general bias of accountability systems is towards caution and risk-avoidance rather than risk-taking. Encouraging the exploitation of specialized markets and the development of tailor-made services, alongside those originally created to satisfy government's own needs, requires a more entrepreneurial culture. To some extent it is already happening. Examples include the production of specialized maps and cartographical services by the Ordnance Survey and customized weather forecasts produced by the Meteorological Office for farmers, fete organizers and sponsors of sports events.

Moves in this direction may be viewed as steps on the way to transfer to the private sector, though private sector businesses in related areas do not welcome public sector competition or the privatization of effective competitors. Moreover, responding to market demands can modify priorities and redefine decision-making criteria in ways that put valid public interests at risk. The argument that if people really want something they will be willing to pay for it assumes both the willingness and the ability to pay. If government continues producing and selling specific services, there is a more immediate set of public management issues that will force their way to the attention of policy-makers. First, making the most of the opportunities to meet market demands calls for a new breed of civil service managers and a new organizational framework for them to operate in. The rewards and incentives required to encourage managers to take risks are not a regular part of the civil service environment. Accommodating these requirements will mean greater organizational diversity and new personnel management problems, which would set up some strains in the system as career opportunities and rewards could be expected to diverge. If these problems were to be overcome, market-oriented areas could well become a training ground for the development of managerial talent that is in short supply.

The alternative scenario is one in which success leads to failure. Opportunities to expand and grow are blocked for political reasons. Experience in recent years is that the government's desire to limit the size of the civil service overrides its commitment to more entrepreneurial management. If it does, instead of being a training ground for public managers, commercial-style operations will simply be areas for good people to prove themselves and then move into the private sector where the financial rewards are greater and the frustrations less.

Contracting Out the Production of Services

Contracting out is often presented as the most important element of privatization. Instead of public organizations undertaking to produce and supply services entirely by themselves, using their own staff, they contract with private suppliers to do the job for them; government specifies what is required but contracts out the work on a commercial basis. This puts competitive market forces directly at the service of government.

There is nothing fundamentally new about contracting out. No organization, public or private, is totally self-sufficient. All organizations have to strike a balance between what they produce themselves and what they rely on others to produce for them. The make/buy decision is a strategic management issue which should be kept constantly under review. Precisely where the balance between making and buying should be struck is a decision to be made according to evidence rather than ideology. Efficiency, flexibility and security of supply are all relevant considerations in forming a judgement. At the moment there appears to be a belief that the balance has been tilted too far towards public provision and that too little use has been made of worthwhile opportunities to make economies by contracting out the supply of services to the private sector. Efforts are currently being made to widen the extent of contracting out, not only by central government but by local government and the National Health Service. However, belief in more contracting out is not universal. It is certainly not shared by public service unions, whose members' jobs are immediately at risk. For this reason alone, it probably ranks second to the sale of assets in public discussion and political controversy. At a time of exceptionally high unemployment, threats to jobs, security of employment, conditions of employment and living standards are not viewed with equanimity by those at risk. Nevertheless, contracting out has strong attractions for a government committed to reducing the number of civil servants and the volume of public spending.

At the very least, contracting out offers the certainty of reducing the number of civil servants simply because it transfers employment from the public to the private sector. Whether this also leads to a reduction in government claims on aggregate national resources is less clear. The arguments for greater efficiency through contracting out are based partly on the lack of incentives for efficiency and lack of cost control in government and partly on the greater competitive pressure on private firms to economize. Although there is strong advocacy of contracting out (Forsyth, 1983), real evidence about its efficacy is in short supply (Hartley, 1984). Determined and well-informed advocates are not deterred by inconclusive or conflicting evidence, however.

It is not our purpose to form a judgement on what has been done in this field so much as to highlight the lack of serious consideration of the managerial implications for government of contracting out. Government does not just hand over responsibility for all aspects of supply to the contractor. Whether it is functions like cleaning, security, maintenance, training, or even running prisons, the transfer of responsibility for supply does not absolve government from managerial responsibility. Though government ceases to perform production operations in-house, it retains managerial responsibility for planning and financing, deciding what should be provided and at what cost (Knipscheer, 1985).

Furthermore, as the customer, government has the responsibility for evaluating the product, deciding whether it meets the designated standards, and determining how to ensure satisfactory contract performance in the future. Given the controversy that contracting out arouses, there is a case for adding an extra public management responsibility to this list, making available comparative data about public and private performance to assist evaluation. These managerial responsibilities for planning, financing, monitoring and evaluating do not require the large workforces, operating on civil service terms and conditions of employment, that the production process requires, but they do require more high-level and highly trained management personnel.

Contracting out does not provide an automatic guarantee of greater efficiency. There is a series of choices and decisions to make once the basic decision to buy has been taken. Improved performance depends first on the appropriate choice of form of contract and then on effective contract management. Because of ideological polarization, the contractual options and managerial choices are frequently over-simplified. The extreme of efficient business working to tight specifications and strict cost limits is contrasted with slack bureaucracy; or, conversely, dedicated public service is contrasted with corner-cutting commercialism. It is all too easy to fall into the trap of considering only the limiting case of competitive tendering as the alternative to in-house provision. This option is only one of several alternatives. Under conditions of certainty about product and performance, competitive tendering offers a guarantee of identifying the least-cost supplier. Government can enter into a pure, arm's length sales contract (as opposed to an employment contract): in exchange for a specified payment, the chosen supplier provides 'a specified quantity of a completely specified commodity' (Simon, 1957). Where these strict conditions are met, the problems of contract management are virtually eliminated. Writing the contract solves the problem. Furthermore, the task of assuring public accountability is greatly simplified if reliance can be placed on the efficiency of competitive tendering to minimize costs.

However, these conditions are frequently not met in practice, and the quality of contract management may then make the difference between good performance and substandard performance. The more complex the task and the more uncertain the operating environment, the more contract management takes on the characteristics of an employment relationship with the customer exercising authority and playing a more active and extensive management role. Moreover, the image of the one-to-one customer−contractor relationship oversimplifies the problems of managing extensive networks of contractors and subcontractors. Instead of an environment approximating the conditions of a perfectly competitive market, the environment is an 'obligational market' which binds customers and suppliers in complex long-term relationships of interdependence; 'buyers who become dissatisfied with suppliers cannot easily relieve the situation by turning to alternative sources of supply' (Wachter and Williamson, 1978: 554). Effective performance depends not just on choosing the right suppliers but also on choosing the right forms of contract and on managing the contractual relationship effectively. In fact, many of the managerial problems that contracting out was supposed to remove through sloughing off the employment relation recur in an inter-organizational context in contract management. Even contracting out fits the concept of public management as getting things done through other organizations.

To moderate expectations about greater efficiency, it is as well to remember that contracting out is an extension of the range of public purchasing — a sphere in which government has not been notably competent. The thousand million pounds spent on GEC's Nimrod early warning radar system is a measure of the costs of error in this field. Although vast in scale, public purchasing has been something of an administrative backwater. The initiative to improve public purchasing, launched in 1981 by Sir Keith Joseph when he was Secretary of State for Industry, encountered both manpower and financial constraints. To do it well would have required more management resources and more financial resources in order to ensure better contract management and long-term value for money. Successful extension of contracting out depends on working on a 'spend to save' basis, rather than on looking for short-term savings. The government was not prepared to make significant increases in resources.

Pointing to the difficulties associated with contracting out does not imply a preference for in-house production. There is ample scope for improvement on both sides of the make/buy decision, and perhaps good reason for keeping the boundary between them fluid. Probably the most important action to take at present is to raise the all-round standard of management by evaluating the results of whatever balance is struck. Deciding arbitrarily that more or less contracting out is preferable and then refusing to evaluate the results lest they upset preconceptions will neither improve public management nor reduce the real level of public spending.

Buying in Management

In addition to contracting out work, government may introduce private sector management personnel in an effort to improve in-house performance. Perhaps the weakest way of doing this is through greater exchange of personnel between public and private sectors. Exchange schemes are common prescriptions for infusing government with a more positive managerial approach. Apart from the side-benefits of breaking down barriers between public and private sectors, exchange schemes rest on some optimistic assumptions. They assume that businessmen coming into government will rapidly make a positive impact, while returning civil servants will quickly apply the skills and techniques they learn in business. The results of exchange schemes rarely seem to live up to expectations. Managers from the private sector do not have time to make a significant impact in short secondments. Civil servants, on the other hand, seem to fare better in industry. Although there is a strong element of tokenism in exchange schemes, the benefits, such as they are, probably favour business. The costs are not high, but government is probably more likely to lose than gain competent managers in this way.

Recruiting top businessmen to take over and reshape some sector of government promises more than exchanges which introduce managers within an existing system. Yet there are more failures than successes. Rayner is the exception rather than the rule. The same seems to be true on the other side of the Atlantic (Allison, 1978). Businessmen find difficulty in adjusting to the political context of public management. How far this is due to inherent differences between public and private management and how far it is due to irksome and unnecessary administrative routines or simply obstructionism is not clear. Presumably there is some of each. Although not a central government example, the resignation of Victor Paige as chairman of the National Health Service management board in 1986, halfway through his three-year contract, fits the pattern of a private sector manager's being unable or unwilling to adapt to the different demands of the public sector. Importing top management from business may look like a quick solution to the problem of improving management, but the evidence suggests that individuals take time to understand the new environment, and even if they are in top jobs they are limited in what they can achieve by the organizational and political environment in which they work.

A more ambitious strategy is to buy in whole management teams. For example, in what remains of the naval dockyards, the government's intention is to retain ownership and responsibility but employ outside management to run them on commercial lines. There are some compelling strategic and security reasons why full privatization is not considered feasible in this case. Formally, buying in management is similar to contracting out. It presents problems of defining the terms on which a service, in this case management, is purchased. Government provides the public management framework within which private management works. Government sheds the work but not the worry. As with contracting out, this is an experiment that warrants careful evaluation. Bearing in mind that the dockyards resemble manufacturing operations more closely than they resemble the rest of government, it may not be easy to extrapolate to other spheres of government. Nevertheless it is a worthwhile move away from the notion that the organization for the dockyards should be modelled on Whitehall lines (Cooper, 1983).

Privatizing Ownership
The five elements of privatization discussed above offer useful options for the design and management of public organizations which warrant consideration when reorganizations take place or when new policies are introduced. They are not new in themselves, nor are they mutually exclusive. It is possible to see ways in which they can be combined with each other and with other patterns of management. However, to many on the political right they do not go far enough. They all assume that final responsibility for providing services rests with government. Whether government contracts out production or buys in management, it remains responsible for strategic decisions on the volume, standards and financing of services. There is still an interplay between public and private. Public management establishes the framework within which private management operates.

The more radical solution to the deficiencies of public management is to transfer assets and responsibilities from the public sector into the private sector. The political importance of asset sales is symbolized by the fact that the term 'privatization programme' specifically denotes the sales of industrial assets accomplished and planned. It is not the primary purpose of this book to discuss privatization in this sense.

Indeed, it might appear to be specifically excluded, since the main intention is to discontinue governmental involvement. However, privatization of ownership does raise some general public management issues which, for the sake of completeness, warrant brief consideration.

During the lifetime of the Thatcher government, privatization has become a much more important policy theme than almost anyone foresaw. The privatization programme has gathered momentum. Much has been done and a great deal more is in the pipeline. Sales of assets realized only £370 million in 1979/80 but the figure rose to £1142 million in 1983/4 (Kay and Thompson, 1986). Projected disposals of assets will produce substantial receipts if and when they are made. Early receipts came from sources such as sales of shares in British Petroleum and the leases of motorway service areas; but disposals of interests in Amersham International, Jaguar, Sealink and, of course, British Telecom and British Gas have all contributed to an increasing inflow to the government's coffers.

Expectations that the privatization programme would soon run out of steam were confounded; a combination of ideological commitment and hard cash has kept it going. Privatization has the double political benefit of advancing the cause of popular capitalism and at the same time reducing the public sector borrowing requirement. In addition, because of a quirk in the government accounting system, which counts receipts from sales of assets as negative expenditure rather than revenue, it also creates the appearance of reducing public spending.

However, as Kay and Thompson (1986) pointed out, there is a discernible change in the pattern of privatization as the scale of divestment has increased, which puts the rationale of privatization at issue. Prospective sales of the 'government's family silver', as Lord Stockton put it, include the British Airports Authority, and the regional water authorities. These, like British Telecom and British Gas, for various reasons, have substantial monopoly positions. Their potential market power gives rise to worries about the effects on economic efficiency of privatization, unless one is prepared to assume that the transfer of ownership on its own produces a managerial revolution.

It is worth dwelling on this point, because quite contradictory assumptions are often made about the significance of ownership. Advocates of privatization and nationalization both perceive sharp discontinuities in managerial conduct and organizational performance between public and private sectors, stemming from a close link between ownership and management. Although their analyses and evaluations are diametrically opposed, they are agreed that it is ownership that is the crucial determining influence on managerial behaviour and organizational performance. There is no denying that ownership makes some difference. Nationalized industries have long suffered from constraints on diversification, investment and pricing policy to satisfy Treasury financial objectives or the interests of the party in office. Often these objectives have been in conflict with each other and with commercial objectives, with damaging consequences for performance. Yet, these are not inherent features of public ownership: they are a product of a particular political culture and tradition. Other countries pay more respect to the integrity of management.

The belief that ownership is the critical factor is more an article of ideological faith than a generalization that is well grounded in empirical evidence. Nevertheless, it is a remarkably resilient belief, which has survived beyond the fiftieth anniversary of the publication of Berle and Meanes classic study of the separation of corporate ownership and management. Berlè and Meanes (1932) pointed to the shift of power from owners to managers and raised the question of potential disparities between the objectives and interests of the two. In the same vein, one may doubt the significance of changes of ownership if the private owners' influence on management is relatively weak. Other things being equal, why should anyone suppose that a public monopoly transformed into a private monopoly will undergo a dramatic transformation in conduct and performance? It is hard to see that ownership changes are either necessary or sufficient to bring about major improvements in performance.

> The political debate as between public and private ownership of organizations is even now based largely on the crude instrumental theory of administration which began to die out in the 1930s. There is no evidence based on observation as to what difference it makes whether an organization is titulary public or titulary private. The rules for organizational survival, the rules for individuals 'politicking' within organizations, seem to be much the same in both settings, and the old subjects of 'public administration' and 'business management' seem to have coalesced. Can anything be done to keep them apart? This seems a formal question; but the debate about capitalism and socialism will look pretty silly if we cannot give even a formal answer. (Mackenzie, 1967)

The process of coalescence and convergence has not proceeded as Mackenzie expected. At the political level, differences between public and private have acquired more significance than similarities. Nevertheless, the revival of the debate about public and private ownership has still to produce an explanation of how exactly a change of ownership results in changes in efficiency and effectiveness. It is simply taken as axiomatic that it does. But, if change of ownership is necessary to bring about organizational reform, importing private sector practice into the public sector will achieve little if anything.

There is an inconsistency in arguing that changes in ownership make a critical difference and at the same time arguing that private sector management practices can produce good results in government without a change of ownership. At the political level, where ownership is the issue, views are polarized. At the organizational level, where the issue is management, there is convergence. The tension between them cannot be resolved satisfactorily without reformulating the problems.

Contemporary organization theory offers ways of doing so by shifting attention from ownership to the constraints and opportunities generated by organizational environments. A benign, protective and stable environment applies little pressure for improvements in efficiency in the short term or stimuli to develop strategic capacities for long-term adaptation. A rapidly changing dynamic environment presents challenges that threaten the effectiveness and survival unless rapid and flexible responses are made. An organization accustomed to a sluggish environment may be thrown into crises from which it never recovers if sudden and unanticipated changes are imposed on it from outside. This does not seem to be a danger with privatization. Some of the worries about its consequences stem from the fact that newly privatized businesses will not be operating in highly competitive environments. Incumbent managements have been quite successful in negotiating terms that do not put them under great competitive pressure. Government may be throwing them into the shallow end rather than the deep end. Private monopolies have no greater incentive to efficiency than public monopolies.

Recalling the discussion in Chapter 2 of alternative forms and processes of accountability — external hierarchy, peer review, competitive market forces and internal membership accountability — privatization of ownership should be accompanied by explicit choice of accountability arrangements to match the characteristics of the newly created organization. Accountability arrangements are a major factor in defining the environment, the rules of the game within which all organizations, public or private, operate. Economists typically have a one-dimensional approach to this. More competition is the only solution they give serious and systematic consideration. Where competition is not possible or is inadequate, other sources of external pressure are needed to set performance standards and ensure accountability in relation to them. This design function cannot be privatized. It is inescapably a public management function — like others mentioned earlier — of choosing the framework within which private choices are made.

Hybrid Forms

An important reason for paying closer attention to the process of designing the environment in which newly privatized businesses operate is that, despite the all-or-nothing political rhetoric, the conduct of the privatization programme has been more pragmatic. When the details of privatization schemes are examined, doctrinal purity gives way to empirical diversity and a variety of hybrid forms. The belief that privatization means a complete shift from purely public to purely private ownership does not accord with the facts. Ownership is a continuum with varying mixtures of public and private participation, rather than a dichotomy. As Steel (1984) observed, the new ownership structures of privatized companies like British Aerospace and Cable and Wireless leave government with substantial shareholdings, and leave the companies with a trail of unanswered questions about their relationship with government. Too often, questions of organizational purpose and design are dismissed as of little importance. Present arrangements are perceived as merely temporary staging posts. However, a commitment to move from these hybrid forms to full privatization (or back to nationalization) may be difficult to implement and will in any case take time. More probably, future governments will have to come to terms with holding stakes in privatized companies and trying to develop constructive roles in relation to them. Hopefully, they will be more successful in doing so than governments in the past have been in defining effective and constructive roles in dealing with public enterprises.

One step in this direction would be to do what many other countries manage to do; that is, to face up to the characteristics and contexts of these businesses as they are, rather than dismissing them as unwelcome and temporary departures from pure private or public models. Politicians would have to treat the public management questions posed by hybrid forms of organization with less disdain. Civil servants would also have to become more expert in dealing with strategic problems which in the past they have regarded with Popish scepticism. Privatization, as a process, is not just selling assets and floating off companies that subsequently have no contact with government. It involves the exercise of two public management functions, which together create the framework for operational management. One is the organizational design function which establishes the structure of corporate governance (Tricker, 1983); the other is the regulatory function of shaping the environment and defining the accountability framework in which the newly created business operates. Government retains a responsibility for ensuring accountability. These two functions are a specialized part of the larger and poorly cultivated field of machinery of government questions. There is no evidence that they were given much forethought within the Conservative Party or within government before the privatization programme was under way. But they have a key part to play in improving performance.

A fruitful reformulation of the problems of designing and managing hybrid forms of organization could begin by considering whether it is ownership in a legal sense that matters or whether ownership is really a proxy for managerial responsibility. In other words, the motivational effects of privatization stem from managerial acceptance of responsibility for performance. Change of ownership is a psychological as well as a legal change. This is not a far-fetched idea. In organizational development, ownership is often interpreted as a psychological commitment and a sense of personal responsibility for seeing the job through, achieving results and solving problems. Building a sense of responsibility into an organization, whatever its formal status, is a problem of corporate governance which cannot be circumvented without causing considerable frustration and wasted effort. Unless the general issues of matching organizational purpose and capability are addressed in the design phase, ambiguity, confusion and conflict will result, as the history of nationalized industries attests. This is not the place to argue the specifics of what form of organization is appropriate here and whether the right choice was made there; the central point is that, whatever change is involved, privatization involves the continuing exercise of public management functions for design.

Conclusions

The Efficiency Strategy has, quite rightly, prompted civil servants to consider the applicability of private sector management methods to the tasks of government. The political appeal of opening up government to the pressures of the market place is obvious. Borrowing readily available methods can accelerate the process of improving public management, provided the assumptions and implications of doing so are fully taken into account. At the same time, private sector practice is not a universal panacea. A *Which?* consumer survey would put it in the category of 'worth considering' rather than awarding it the accolade of an assured 'best buy'.

Despite the strength of the ideological feeling that privatization generates, the amount of hard evidence one way or the other is limited. This chapter has sought to separate the wheat from the ideological chaff. There is a series of specific ways in which private sector management practices might be used to improve efficiency and effectiveness. To some extent they are in use already. Widening the range of organizational options available to government can be beneficial, provided the results of applying new approaches are carefully evaluated. The main themes of privatization are not in themselves new, systematic evaluation of their performance would be a big step forward.

The impression given by advocates of privatization in all its forms is that it offers an either/or choice — not just alternatives, but substitutes for public management. Reality is more complicated. Public and private management are often complementary. Even if government sheds blocks of work and direct production responsibilities, it retains higher-level public management responsibilities for defining the framework within which business methods are used. To do this properly, it is essential to encourage the development of higher-level management skills and capabilities within government. Paradoxically, privatization, which is supposed to shift management responsibilities out of government, requires at the same time the development of more sophisticated management skills for its successful implementation. This is a 'spend to save' issue. Investments in highly specialized managerial skills are needed. There are some obvious personnel management issues here — training, career development, organization design and remuneration. Government might find itself training highly skilled managers for business to poach if it fails to take them into account.

Interdependence of public and private activities applies equally to privatization with and without transfers of ownership. Where government does not retain any direct involvement in management — a rarer event than might be supposed — it still retains responsibility for managing the environment in which newly privatized businesses function. Liberalization involves reregulation rather than deregulation, and should stimulate and invigorate the rather moribund 'machinery of government' field where management and political concerns interact. This area should be a major source of innovation in the design of public organizations and the accountability frameworks appropriate to assuring their efficiency and effectiveness. There is no reason why it should be limited in scope to a consideration of market alternatives any more than that it should exclude them. There are many other types of organizations that should be deliberately investigated and evaluated. The paucity of evidence about the relative efficiency and effectiveness of different types of organization stands in sharp contrast to the firm ideological convictions that alternative proposals arouse. Perhaps the appropriate motto to satisfy proponents and opponents of privatization is '*caveat emptor*'.

9
The Financial Management Initiative: Changing the Rules of the Budgetary Game

The attitudes and actions of the Thatcher government have done much to change the terms of debate about public spending. Along with seeking better value for public money through scrutinies and reviews, there has been a continuing effort to reduce the overall level of public expenditure and an insistence that government should live within its means. In the period since 1979, reduced public spending has been sought not only as a necessary adjustment to poor national economic performance, but also as a political objective in its own right, and as a contribution to the government's macroeconomic objectives. However, it has proved exceedingly difficult to implement the political commitment to reduce the fiscal burden of government on industry and the taxpayer. Actual achievements in cutting public spending have fallen well short of what was hoped for. Cutbacks in some policy fields have been more than matched by unanticipated increases in others. The general trend of public expenditure since 1979 is up, rather than down.

Political optimism springs eternal but, if past experience is anything to go by, the prospects for success in constraining expenditure are not encouraging. The failings of previous governments and the impact of one-off events do not account for the obdurate upward trend. Likierman and Bloomfield (1986) concluded, from an analysis of the reasons for past failures to keep expenditure within planned totals, that governments are unlikely to be more successful in the future than they have been in the past. Recent overspending cannot be explained away by attributing it to non-recurrent and isolated events such as the Falklands war. The underlying forces maintaining upward pressures and the sources of uncertainty affecting current expenditure programmes are both pervasive and persistent. Planned growth in coming years is less than actual growth over the past six years in most areas of expenditure. However, closer analysis of spending programmes in the areas of defence, health and social security and education provides little assurance that targets will be met, particularly by a government approaching a general election (see Likierman and Bloomfield, 1986; and among others Heald, 1983; Levitt and Joyce, 1984).

Persistent failure to bring public spending into line with political intentions is symptomatic of underlying deficiencies in the way public expenditure is managed. Commenting on past disappointments, Pliatzky, who was second permanent secretary at the Treasury during the difficult period of the mid-1970s, compared the task of curbing public expenditure with that of Sisyphus in Greek mythology, who was condemned to roll a stone uphill but always to find it rolling down before reaching the summit, 'our Sisyphean task in reverse was to push public expenditure downhill only to find it roll back up again to an even higher point' (Pliatzky, 1982). Whether one believes that public expenditure should be greater or less than it is at present, reforms are urgently needed to increase the probability that actual budgetary outcomes correspond to those intended.

This chapter examines the progress and prospects of the Financial Management Initiative (FMI) as a major effort to bring about fundamental reforms in the management and control of public spending. On one widely held view, the FMI is simply an extension of the scrutiny programme on a broader front to achieve savings and raise efficiency relatively quickly. The alternative view is that it is the major embodiment of the other strand of the Efficiency Strategy — lasting reforms — and will take many years to come to fruition. It is the second perspective that has most relevance. The short-term impact of the FMI is bound to be limited. To judge its success by what is happening now or in the next two or three years is to underestimate the scale and complexity of the problem and perhaps to drop back into the outmoded view of administrative reform as a once-for-all change which is expected to produce quick, positive and virtually costless results. This is quite inappropriate. The FMI is, necessarily, a government-wide initiative. It is not just a narrowly based technical exercise in accounting and information systems, although both figure prominently within it. It is intended to have far-reaching effects on the whole style of management in government. In so far as there is a private sector analogue, it is the major initiatives in the field of corporate renewal forced upon large businesses by fast-changing and unpredictable environments. Changes in public management are likely to take even longer to come to fruition than corporate renewal in the private sector.

Any assessment of the FMI must begin from a recognition of the complexity of budgetary problems that modern governments have to deal with. In a comparative perspective, it is clear that British problems of curbing public spending are not unique. They are part of a more general pattern of fiscal overload and unmanageability that is common to advanced countries. Reform is overdue. But no government has yet found a long-term solution. Or if it has, it has not found a way of implementing it. As Tarschys (1985) observed, 'Nearly every OECD country has faced a scissors crisis in public finance since the world-wide depression of the mid-1970s; in slow growth economies public spending has been rising faster than tax revenues' (Tarschys, 1985: 23).

There are no signs of the scissors crisis abating in Britain. Demographic and economic factors are moving in directions that will increase the stress on the system. Moreover, the decline in North Sea oil revenues as reserves fall is bound to exert a considerable influence on what is affordable. It is hardly likely that in ten years' time people will look back on the 1980s as a golden age, but it is far from clear that the worst is over.

Budgetary behaviour has not adapted to much-changed circumstances. Cuts, in some form or other, have been governments' response to the scissors crisis. A wide variety of cutting devices has been brought into play including cash limits on spending, manpower reductions, reduced indexation rates, trimming services, tighter cash flow management, better monitoring of spending and public sector pay restraint. The impact of these measures has been patchy and short-lived. They treat the symptoms of uncontrolled expenditure growth without changing the underlying dynamics of the system that produces it. Instead of sticking-plaster solutions and cosmetic accounting, reforms are needed to change the rules of the budgetary game and the behaviour of the players in it. Effective reforms depend on a sound diagnosis of problems and the development and implementation of solutions appropriate to them.

It would be comforting if budgetary theory offered clear guidelines about what changes are required and how to introduce them. Regrettably, this is not so. There is neither a clear model of management to define what reformers should try to achieve nor a clear image of how to manage the changes required. The attempts to shrink public budgets in recent years have exposed the shrinkage of budgetary theory as a descriptive or prescriptive tool (Bozeman and Straussman, 1982). Orthodox budgetary theory, which still exerts a considerable influence on practice, presupposes a simpler and more benign environment than the harsh realities of the 1980s. In order to form a judgement about the FMI as a vehicle for reform, it is essential to consider what is necessary to manage public expenditure in the conditions that are likely to obtain in the future.

The Capacity to Budget

Government budgeting is a permanent problem without a permanent solution. Governments have to evolve new budgetary processes and methods of financial management as circumstances change. If they fail to do so, the political and administrative consequences are severe. Governments' capacity to budget is a key determinant of their capacity to govern effectively (OECD, 1982).

There are, of course, some enduring features of budgeting which derive from the basic purpose of making the best use of available resources. It is helpful to begin with a distinction between budgets and financial management. Budgets as financial plans set limits to available resources. Financial management is the process of making the best use of resources to achieve policy objectives. Budgets and financial management are the Yin and Yang of the budgetary process, the one setting external constraints, the other engendering internal commitment. The capacity to budget depends on maintaining a balance between these constraining and motivating processes. Unrealistic budgets and ineffectual financial management can both weaken the capacity to budget. When they combine successfully, the budgetary process creates a sense of challenge, a game spirit in response to the basic problem of 'How to live with budgetary standards and yet be motivated by them':

> Motivation through pressure from outside goes together with low job satisfaction; motivation from within goes together with higher job satisfaction. It also means that no energy will be spilt in fighting the system: in a game people accept the basic fact that there are rules. (Hofstede, 1967: 81)

Much of the discussion of budgetary reform disregards these conditions for effective budgeting and financial management. Reforms are almost always cast in terms of control rather than management. They underestimate the difficulty of the problems of balancing constraints and commitment. Efforts to impose control by tightening budgetary discipline are one-sided. They ignore the game-like qualities of budgeting as a system of multilateral bargaining and negotiation which combines elements of competition for resource allocations, cooperation in setting priorities and goals, and conflict resolution to settle differences between contending participants. The capacity to budget depends on increasing competences in each of these areas, not just on unilateral increases in control. Balanced development of the capacity to budget requires investments in organizational change and human resources that correspond with step-function changes in the complexity of budgeting.

As with any large-scale organizational change, the FMI involves 'spending to save'. Reform is a developmental process which is difficult to implement properly for political and organizational reasons. It is difficult politically because budgetary reforms in particular are expected to be parsimonious. Departments have been expected to absorb the not inconsiderable costs of implementing the FMI without receiving any additional resources. Organizationally, it is difficult because the positive side of budgetary reform involves changes in management styles that produce results only if they are much broader in their impact than financial management itself.

Implementing the FMI is tantamount to introducing a new public management ethos. To those who have adjusted to established ways of doing things, the changes involved are liable to seem either a chore, which contributes little to effectiveness, or a threat to fundamental values embodied in the status quo.

Incremental and Structural Change

Over and above the resistance to change associated with any reform there is a further complication associated with the FMI. The budgetary game has changed in ways that are not fully understood. The spirit has gone out of the game. New rules have been introduced in an *ad hoc* way rather than as part of an overall plan. Rekindling the game spirit depends on overcoming deep-seated scepticism about large-scale fundamental reform and developing a strategy for change which recognizes the particular difficulties of structural as distinct from incremental change. If an adequate capacity to budget could be developed step by step, an incremental reform strategy would gradually close the gap between existing competences and those that are needed to restore performance to acceptable levels. Within an incremental strategy, innovation in technique and methods of management are governed by the established framework of objectives and rules of the game. Improvement is cumulative, building on past experience.

Sometimes incremental reform strategies fail to close the gap. Disparities between actual and desired performance persist even if they are masked or fudged by reducing standards of service or lowering expectations. A dilemma of reform arises. Should something marginally different be tried? Or does the failure of successive incremental changes signal the deeper message that no workable solutions are available within the existing rules of the game? If the latter, structural reform is needed to change the rules of the game. It must be noted that structural reform is not the same as the conventional all-or-nothing reform efforts that have so often failed in the past. There are resemblances, but structural reforms give close attention to the management of change. By their nature, changes in the rules of the game are infrequent and discontinuous. They mark breaks with the past and can precipitate severe conflict. To some, the chance of a new start heralds radical improvements. To others, rejection of past achievements is a repudiation of basic values. Because they excite such different reactions, structural reforms are difficult to manage. The difficulties are compounded because they are infrequent, and managers accustomed to incremental change do not develop the experience and skills needed to manage these more fundamental changes.

Dunn (1971) drew an illuminating parallel between incremental and structural reform and Kuhn's (1962) distinction between normal problem-solving and paradigm shifts in scientific development. Normal problem-solving within an established paradigm works incrementally because the paradigm provides a framework of objectives and methods; it defines the problems that are solvable and worth solving. Problems are puzzles. With persistence and ingenuity, the pieces can be made to fit together. Paradigm shifts occur when problems turn out to be anomalies and not puzzles. They do not fit the normal pattern, and the creative process of developing a new pattern calls into question basic assumptions of the established paradigm. Because they challenge widely held beliefs, paradigm shifts encounter strong resistance from the scientific community.

What holds for scientific communities where innovation is a well established and prominent value is much more true of government, where the culture emphasizes values of continuity, stability and predictability rather than innovation. Public organizations and public managers are typically ill-prepared and ill-equipped to cope with structural change and are slow to respond to structural problems when the occur.

> They are frequently unanticipated by the management elite. The reorganization is defensive in character — that is, it is directed towards preserving and extending the life of the system in the face of change rather than taking the form of a directed self-transformation in pursuit of some higher order goal. (Dunn, 1971: 214)

This observation could stand as a general critique of contemporary government — fiddling while Rome burns. It has especial relevance to budgetary reform and particularly the evaluation of the FMI. For although, in certain respects, the FMI fits the pattern of incremental change, in other respects it requires structural changes for its full implementation. Hence in assessing the FMI we have to consider not only whether its practical prescriptions are appropriate to the objectives it seeks to achieve, but also whether the objectives themselves are attainable and appropriate for the budgetary context that governments will confront in the future. Even if the FMI is the right answer to the problem it is intended to solve, we must also consider whether it is addressed to the right questions. This is a tall order. It goes some way to account for the length of this chapter, which like public expenditure itself is large and complex and has proved difficult to cut. To ease the burden somewhat, the chapter is divided into three main parts. The first part describes the objectives, background and development of the FMI. The second part assesses the adequacy of the FMI's prescriptions in relation to its stated objectives. The third part considers whether its full implementation will create the capacity to budget that will be needed in the future. It gives particular attention to the question of structural change and its relationship to Rayner's theme of lasting reforms.

The FMI: Objectives and Developments

The Financial Management Initiative is the second exception to our rule of avoiding the esoteric initials and acronyms that pervade the language of Whitehall. Like MINIS, which was considered in Chapter 3, the FMI has achieved public prominence as a symbol of governmental commitment to lasting reforms of public management. It incorporates many of the specific prescriptions and principles that figured in earlier scrutinies, including a requirement that all departments should establish a top management information system equivalent to MINIS. Despite, or perhaps because of, its symbolic importance, the intentions behind the FMI are often interpreted in different ways. To some, it is the beginning of freedom to manage in government, an opportunity to remove the constraints and obstacles that have impeded decentralization of responsibility and obstructed coordinated management of resources within departments in the past. To others, decentralization appears to threaten the loss of the budgetary discipline which was one of the principal motivations of the Efficiency Strategy. It is perceived as giving too much discretion to spending departments at a time when the balance of budgetary power should favour the guardians of public money in the Treasury rather than the advocates of expenditure. Still others incline to the view that the FMI is one more bureaucratic chore tangential to their real tasks.

The Financial Management Initiative was launched in May 1982. Its announcement was part of the government's response to the publication of the Third Report of the Treasury and Civil Service Select Committee of the House of Commons on 'Efficiency and Effectiveness in the Civil Service'. The subsequent White Paper (Cmnd 8616), setting out its objectives, was published in September 1982 and specified three basic principles, to:

Promote in each department an organization and a system in which managers at all levels have:
(a) a clear view of their objectives, and means to assess and, wherever possible, measure outputs and performance in relation to those objectives;
(b) well-defined responsibility for making the best use of their resources, including a critical scrutiny of output and value for money; and
(c) the information (particularly about costs), the training and the access to expert advice that they need to exercise their responsibilities effectively.

The launching of the FMI was used as an occasion to emphasize the need for pervasive change in public management, in recognition of the indefinite continuance of tight budgetary constraints. There was a sustained campaign to increase awareness, throughout the civil service, of what the FMI sought to achieve, why it was needed, and how it would impinge on managers at all levels. Officials were encouraged to see the introduction of new systems and techniques as part of a process of changing long held and deeply entrenched attitudes to their work, especially their responsibility for seeking ways of improving performance from year to year. As we saw in Chapter 7, there has been a traditional division between managers with operational responsibilities and specialists concerned with improving performance. The FMI sought to shift responsibility for better resource utilization to line managers by increasing their discretion and instilling the motivation to improve performance.

The thirty-one largest central departments were given until January 1983 to assess their existing arrangements in the light of the three principles and to make proposals to bring practice into line with them. In addition to the personal backing of the Prime Minister, a Financial Management Unit was set up as a joint venture between the Treasury and the Management and Personnel Office. It consisted of about a dozen people drawn from within the civil service and outside consulting firms. Its role was to assist individual departments in developing their plans, to help the two central departments to steer the FMI as a whole, and to identify general issues and facilitate exchange of ideas among departments.

A White Paper (Cmnd 9297) issued in July 1984 reported on progress within individual departments and also outlined the more general issues emerging from the initial stages of the work. There has been a steady flow of more detailed reports on specific aspects of the FMI as it has evolved. Some of these reports are closely related to the three foci of the FMI, objectives, resources and information. Others, which were not foreshadowed in the original White Paper, have also emerged and are commented upon later.

The Background of the FMI

In any process of managing change, the complexity of the task depends not only on the objectives of change but also on the point of departure, the state of the system before changes are introduced. Some of the background of the FMI is general knowledge, but is worth summarizing it briefly to highlight the difficulty of the task. Before the FMI began, and before the Thatcher government came into office in 1979, major changes had taken place in the sphere of public budgeting. The 1970s saw a dramatic transformation in the practice and philosophy of managing public expenditure, a transformation summarized as a shift from planning to control (Wright, 1981). In the wake of a succession of economic and fiscal crises, governments were forced to introduce emergency measures for curbing the growth of spending. The system for planning and managing public expenditure, the Public Expenditure Survey, which developed in the 1960s following the Plowden Report, proved inadequate to the challenges of a difficult and sometimes turbulent environment for which it was never designed.

The Public Expenditure Survey is an annual exercise supervised by the Public Expenditure Survey Committee which is composed of departmental principal finance officers and chaired by the Treasury. Originally it was a mechanism for planning real resource commitments over the medium term. Within macroeconomic parameters drawn from Treasury forecasts of future economic performance, departments made submissions and claims for resources for coming years on the basis of unchanged policies. Negotiations built up to a report to ministers who, taking account of policy changes and available resources, settled aggregate public spending levels and allocation among programmes. Giving statutory force to the conclusions emerging from the Public Expenditure Survey system moved the budgetary process into the annual parliamentary ritual of estimates and votes. The process rolled forward each year.

Like many planning and budgeting systems in private business as well as the public sector, the Public Expenditure Survey was a creature of its time, with characteristic weaknesses and blind spots. It was built on growth assumptions — next year will be like this year only more so. Programmes could be rolled forward with only marginal adjustments of priorities and resources from year to year. Furthermore, the predominantly Keynesian economic philosophy encouraged a belief in the beneficial effects of growing public spending on economic performance. Since public spending per se was beneficial in macroeconomic terms, there was little interest in the efficiency or effectiveness of spending in achieving policy objectives at the micro-level. Improvements in management and efficiency were regarded as insignificant factors in macroeconomic policy-making. The failure of Keynesian policies and the switch to a monetarist economic philosophy reversed these assumptions about the virtues of public spending. In addition, the tax and public borrowing implications of expenditure plans were not treated as an integral part of the planning process. Because resources were costed in constant prices, the Public Expenditure Survey system disregarded inflation. The revenue implications of real resource commitments were indeterminate. With escalating inflation, these 'funny money' estimates became an increasing source of concern and public criticism. They were held up as evidence that public spending was not under control.

With the benefit of hindsight, the defects of the post-Plowden system are very clear. But its limitations were recognized only belatedly, and action to remedy them was slow to materialize. The rules of the game for managing public expenditure proved remarkably resistant to change. Failure to prevent public expenditure from rising even when adverse economic conditions persisted led to fears of continuing uncontrollable and unaffordable escalation. The public sector appeared insensitive to the plight of the private sector, suffering under the blows of high inflation and economic stagnation. Civil servants appeared to have succeeded in insulating themselves and their organizations from austerity afflicting the rest of society.

The British government was by no means unique in experiencing fiscal overload. The phenomenon was common to all democratic welfare states. The underlying factors pushing for increased public spending were deeply ingrained in the functioning of the system. Commitments and entitlements that were politically difficult to shed accumulated over time. Demographic changes increased the cost of health and welfare programmes. Economic recession restricted the pool of resources available and simultaneously increased demand-led claims upon them, through substantial rises in unemployment and social security benefits. Even so, the shock to the British system was more dramatic because the Public Expenditure Survey system that developed through the 1960s was well regarded. Aaron Wildavsky, one of the high priests of budgetary theory, acclaimed the system for managing public money as a unique British success:

> nowhere else in the world, to our knowledge, has the annual budget been replaced with an effective mechanism to control spending several years into the future. What we can learn from Great Britain's success in reform depends on understanding how and why PESC actually works. (Wildavsky, 1975: 336)

Hardly was this accolade bestowed than the serious flaws in the system became apparent. The virtues that provided stability in an era of relative affluence became obstacles to rapid and effective adaptation in the hard times of the 1970s.

Despite the introduction of the Financial Information System to monitor expenditure within financial years, cash limits to restrain departments, and the more general shift away from medium-term 'funny money' planning to short-term cash control, in 1981, Wildavsky described the operation of the system as 'disastrous'. Paradoxically, one of the reasons for its disastrous performance was that the politics of the budgetary process had changed very little. At least, they had not changed enough by 1981 to convince Heclo and Wildavsky that they should revise 'The Private Government of Public Money' which was published originally in 1974. 'Our point is simply that since our first edition very little has changed in the basic elements and culture of British central government' (Heclo and Wildavsky, 1981: xi). The FMI was launched the following year.

A Comprehensive Initiative

The FMI is much greater in scope than the individual scrutinies and multi-departmental reviews discussed previously. It is a comprehensive initiative in more than one sense. First of all, the general prescriptions for objectives, responsibility and information are intended to apply to all major central departments. Many of the Rayner themes discussed in earlier chapters information systems, decentralization, accountable management are subsumed under these headings. The inclusion of the requirement to establish MINIS-like top management information systems to serve the needs of senior officials and ministers has already been mentioned. Decentralization through delegated budgetary responsibility is a key feature of the FMI and was foreshadowed in the scrutiny programme. Given the brief to departments, the primary concern was increased delegation within departments. However, such changes also exerted pressure for true delegation at the interdepartmental level between spending departments and the Treasury; a shift from detailed case-by-case control to monitoring the effectiveness of departmental management systems. This is particularly important in the budgetary field. Accountable management is a third theme of the FMI. It appears in a number of guises, including more systematic use of management accounting, creation of cost or responsibility centres to clarify managerial tasks by establishing links between resources and objectives, and subdividing departmental activities into separate accountable units or businesses instead of basing organization on management functions.

The FMI is comprehensive in seeking to bring about changes in all facets of departmental management. An emphasis on strengthening the position of line management is associated with the shift to a new basis of organization. As a corollary of decentralization and account-able management, this deserves special mention. The culture and traditions of Whitehall have not favoured strong line management. On the contrary, fragmentation of responsibility for personnel, finance, policy and executive funcions necessitated time-consuming lateral coordination as well as reinforcing the centralizing pull of ministerial responsibility. Managers nominally responsible for a particular area of activity have had little real say in the resources allocated to them or very much flexibility in using them. This was not fertile soil in which to try to cultivate positive attitudes to accountable management. Furthermore, because civil service managers expect to move on to some quite different area of activity fairly rapidly, they have little incentive to invest time and effort in making changes that take years to bear fruit. They are much more likely to see their job as a maintenance function: 'keeping the show on the road', as one young under-secretary described it. The FMI seeks to change this by bringing performance improvement within the remit of much more coherent line management structures.

The Financial Management Unit and the Joint Management Unit
In the summer of 1982 a central Financial Management Unit was set up as a joint venture of the Management and Personnel Office and the Treasury to aid departments in developing their response to the FMI. It was a unit of six or seven people, a combination of civil servants and outside consultants, mostly with qualifications in accountancy, management, economics and operation research. The consultants had public as well as private sector experience. The Unit began by giving general guidance and subsequently moved on to assist with implementation on a selective basis with individual members working with departments and also providing a means of facilitating the exchange of experience and ideas among departments (see Russell, 1984, for more detail). The Unit focused its attention on three key areas: (1) the development of MINIS-type top management information systems, (2) delegated budgeting, and (3) the management of programme expenditure, the latter encompassing the inter-organizational dimension of public management by examining the linkages between departments and non-departmental bodies through which public services are delivered. The Unit was also closely involved in focusing discussion at the centre about how the FMI should be moved forward.

The work of the Financial Management Unit has been continued since 1985 by its successor the Joint Management Unit which has a similar status. The Joint Management Unit is smaller, with a professional staff of four (including one member located in the Treasury), but it can also draw on the resources of the expenditure divisions of the Treasury and the management and efficiency divisions of the Management and Personnel Office. In broad terms, its work follows the lines laid down earlier, establishing a professional–client relationship with departments and advising on or providing assistance with, the implementation of new systems. It is clearly not a means of imposing central direction on departments. The vast bulk of the work of planning and implementing the FMI in departments must be done by departments themselves. Nevertheless, this minuscule central capability seems quite inadequate in relation to the whole task, particularly when one bears in mind the comment of the former head of the Financial Management Unit on

> the importance of not underestimating the effort and time needed to effect the major changes envisaged in departments .... It has been helpful to have consultants point out that private sector organizations would regard the changes planned by departments as a very large-scale project indeed which would need to be planned and resourced accordingly (Russell, 1984).

The slender central resources are a reflection more of political sensitivity to potential criticism than a realistic contribution to the management of major structural change. With a political emphasis on cost-consciousness, those involved in improving public management are expected to be whiter than white. Operating on a shoestring budget will not achieve the desired results. We return later to consider the role of the centre in guiding structural change. Before doing so, however, the following sections examine the main thrust of the FMI proposals.

Something Old...
The basic principles and the thinking behind the FMI are familiar. It has often been said, especially by those centrally involved in promoting the FMI, that there is really nothing new about it. It just amounts to applying recognized principles and proven practices of good financial management. In short, the FMI involves doing systematically what some departments have been doing anyway and what all departments should have been doing. Interested outsiders have reflected the same attitude. 'There is nothing new in the FMI and work on many of the changes which might be required under it was already in hand in at least some departments before the Initiative commenced' (Peat, Marwick & Mitchell, 1984: 27).

The 'something old' theme runs together two strands of argument which need to be disentangled and considered separately. First, even if the statements of FMI objectives and principles and their subsequent elaboration are not new in themselves, it does not follow that their implementation is merely a routine process. Many of the ideas are familiar and there are few grounds for claiming them as original thoughts on how to manage. However, the challenges of innovation are real enough. Putting familiar ideas into practice calls for substantial changes in attitudes, behaviour, structures and styles of management simply because the point of departure is a fragmented and yet over-centralized pattern of organization. Furthermore, the diversity of governmental functions means that departments do have to work out their own solutions rather than implement off-the-peg solutions. The evolution of MINIS which was discussed in Chapter 3 illustrates these points very clearly.

Second, playing down the novelty of the FMI and emphasizing continuities with the past is a legitimate and necessary part of the tactics of implementation. Resistance to change may stem from a number of sources including a failure to communicate proposals in an understandable way. Lack of comprehension of the aims and methods of a proposed change can be a real obstacle to progress. Finding something old that gives proposals a recognizable shape may overcome this obstacle. The invocation of the fashionable 'Back to basics' cliché is often used to give a comforting sense that the FMI is a return to a former orthodoxy rather than an advance into a new and uncertain future. This kind of reassurance can be overdone. There are dangers in propagating the belief that there is nothing new in the FMI. If civil servants are encouraged to believe that they have seen it all before, they may conclude that it is doomed to failure. Real difficulties of implementation may be underestimated. On the most limited interpretation of its goals, the FMI requires considerable changes in methods of budgeting, accounting and reporting, as well as in Treasury control and the practice of audit, to assure greater emphasis on value for money. In addition, it involves changes in organization and management that go well beyond any definition of financial management. They include:

— changes in the way individual managers do their jobs, placing the emphasis on results and improving performance;
— changes in the discretion they are allowed in managing their resources, focusing authority on line management;
— changes in the way the parameters within which managers work are set, using budgets as a management tool;
— changes in the structure of departments, promoting decentralization and divisionalization;
— changes in the relations between spending departments and the Treasury, inter-organizational as well as intra-organizational delegations.

Completing this programme of reform is a task of daunting complexity. Even if none of the individual elements in the FMI considered in isolation were new, the programme considered as a whole is a quantum leap from the implementation problems associated with individual scrutinies and multi-departmental reviews. The FMI involves the management of change on a grand scale. Its success depends not only on political will and perseverance, but also on innovation in methods of managing change. As we have emphasized previously, one of the distinctive features of public management is that it is an inter-organizational process. The vast bulk of theory and practice in the management of change is concerned with change in single organizations. The FMI, therefore, is a major new departure in attempting to manage change at the inter-organizational level.

Something New . . .
Seen in these terms, the FMI is a significant step forward. Its scope is so wide that it attracts the scepticism and disbelief about the feasibility of large-scale administrative reform that are never very far from the surface of civil service thinking. Yet it does not fit into the classical model of preconceived blueprints for reform and all-or-nothing grand designs. As with the scrutiny programme, the emphasis from the beginning was on action; departments were given a strict timetable, but only general instructions to work to. There was a strong emphasis on a bottom-up approach to the development of new patterns of departmental organization within the requirement from the top that departments should initiate changes. The role of the Financial Management Unit at the centre was to assist developments at departmental level, not to impose a straitjacket on them.

One positive result of the combination of bottom-up and top-down elements is that the FMI is an example of adaptive rather than pro-grammed implementation (Bermann, 1979). Policies and problem definitions have been revised in the light of evidence generated and analysis conducted after the initiative was launched. An example of this is the management of programme expenditure. The FMI's objectives initially focused attention on management within departments. The main target for reform was intra-departmental organization to strengthen methods of controlling departments' administrative running costs. With the gradual realization that administrative overheads were only a fraction of the total costs of managing programmes, the spotlight switched to programme expenditure as a whole. As a result, the management of relations between departments, and the networks of non-departmental bodies through which public services are delivered, moved to centre stage. Managing programme expenditure efficiently and effectively depends on managing the inter-organizational network through which services are delivered. This is one of the major ways in which the FMI is bringing attention to bear on managing change at the inter-organizational level.

A similar process of redefining problems is apparent in the increased importance attached to policy management (FMU, 1984). Policy management is an expression that might have been dismissed as a contradiction in terms in the old culture of Whitehall (Richards, 1985). It supercedes the conventional wisdom of a clear discontinuity between policy and management. Contrary to custom and practice, government departments should not be designed with separate policy and executive divisions staffed by officials who have not only different functions but also different outlooks and career expectations. Sir Frank Cooper, the former permanent secretary of the Ministry of Defence, deplored what he termed the differentiation between gentlemen and players, with the gentlemen dealing with policy and advice to ministers, and the players, with executive functions and policy implementation (Cooper, 1983). The concept of policy management is intended to overcome the persistent tendency to attenuation of relationships between policy and executive functions. It demands closer integration of policy analysis into the management process and greater use of performance measurement to improve policy evaluation. The policy management lays responsibility for working out policy implementation requirements on those involved in policy-making. It requires policy-makers to recognize that they are managing inter-organizational networks. Practice does not appear to be following this precept. Instead of embracing all phases of implementation, policy management appears to be being redefined as policy evaluation alone, largely absolving policy-makers from responsibility for ensuring effective links between the different phases of the process and the organizations involved.

One of the main purposes of the FMI is to instigate a shift in the culture of Whitehall from standards based on static, business-as-usual performance levels to expectations of year-on-year improvements in performance. Achieving this will be a major cultural change, much more important than using a reform initiative as a shock to the system — an invigorating cold-shower effect — which hopefully produces a one-off improvement in performance. In contrast with the 'something old' image of the FMI, the assumption that departments should seek progressive improvements in performance, involves breaking new ground. Public managers will be under pressure to face up to the conceptual and practical problems of assessing performance and motivating improvement. In the past these problems of setting performance criteria, objectives and measuring results, have been ducked on the grounds that they are too complex to answer in government but lasting reforms cannot really take root without confronting the difficulties of establishing positive criteria of performance.

Something Borrowed...
From the beginning of the Efficiency Strategy, scrutineers were encouraged to consider the utility of existing best-practice business management concepts and methods. The FMI has followed the same

line, with the extensive borrowing of concepts from private sector financial management. Governments are always tempted to short-cut the process of evolving solutions to their own management problems by borrowing ready-made solutions from business, and enough has been said on this subject in Chapter 8 to indicate that a market approach is not a panacea. Nevertheless, there is a great temptation to reach for a model of management that is already available rather than embark on the laborious process of developing a new one. The ideas that underlie the FMI have drawn directly and indirectly from business as well as from previous attempts to reform public management. In this section we consider three of them: delegated budgets as management tools for controlling and improving performance, the multi-divisional form of organization and the assumption of loose-coupling or decomposability as a basis for designing public organizations.

The concept of budgets as a tool of management is at the core of the FMI. The value of budgets as a management tool is widely recognized outside government. However self-evident it may seem that the processes of resource allocation and resource utilization should be linked, government practice has not followed this precept in a consistent and systematic way. Lack of adequate management accounting is one reason for this — information about resource costs was often not available. When the formal system of vote-accounting was described during a Civil Service College course, one newly recruited accountant from the private sector exclaimed, 'My tennis club has more sophisticated accounts than this!' Another reason for poor coordination between resource allocation and utilization is fragmentation of responsibility for finance, personnel, policy and execution. Fragmentation contributed to overcentralization and militated against clear lines of managerial accountability and the growth of a sense of responsibility for effective resource management.

Viewed as a linked process of goal-setting and goal-achieving, budgeting requires and reinforces line management authority. It can establish conditions for control and for managing improvements in performance. However, realizing the potential of budgets as a management tool is far less simple than the bald statement of FMI objectives suggests. Research on the effective use of budgets as a management tool has identified a number of important behavioural variables: the impact of setting easy or difficult goals, involving subordinates in goalsetting or selecting a style of management in which goals are set without their participation, linking financial rewards to success in goal achievement, or relying on intrinsic satisfactions rather than extrinsic incentives to motivate performance (Dunbar, 1970, 1981). Although these issues are familiar in studies of motivation, leadership and budgetary behaviour in business management, there is no stock answer as to how budgets should be used most effectively as a management tool in government. Borrowing requires adaptation. So far, not enough has been done to adapt the basic ideas to the context of public management. Before budgets can perform the function of making the best of available resources, the opportunities and constraints of public organization need to be taken into account.

Another way in which the FMI has borrowed directly from business is by enjoining departments to move to a divisional form of organization. In the rhetoric of the FMI, departments are expected to move from structures based on centralized but separate responsibilities for finance, personnel, policy, executive operations and performance improvement towards structures that decentralize and cluster these responsibilities in 'businesses'. These 'businesses' then operate with a large degree of autonomy, subject to monitoring, supervision and steering by top management. Departments, in other words, should be divided into a number of relatively self-contained units, each with its own general management competence. The underlying concept is well known in business as the multi-divisional form of organization. Even if terminology is confusing — division is used in government as a synonym of function in business — the concept is clear enough. It can be traced back to the changes in business structure that followed and supported strategic changes in large US businesses such as General Motors and Sears Roebuck in the postwar period (Chandler, 1960). The multi-divisional form of organization provided a means of reserving strategic decision-making powers to top management while allowing divisional management the autonomy to use the resources allocated to them. Quite literally, what was good for General Motors in the 1950s is being prescribed as good for British central government in the 1980s and 1990s.

The multi-divisional form of organization has attractions as a means of streamlining management, reducing centralization, and clarifying lines of responsibility. As we mentioned in Chapter 4 it is appropriate to changing environments where functional organizations would respond to slowly. The correspondence between this model of organization and the use of budgets as a management tool is obvious. However, prescribing the multi-divisional form as a general solution, applicable across the board, makes assumptions about the tasks and responsibilities of public management that are ill-founded. The multi-divisional form is most appropriate in conglomerate businesses where different divisions can operate independently of each other (Hill 1985). Often, in these cases the only real link between the divisions and top management is the financial management system. It is highly debatable whether this degree of divisional autonomy is feasible in government. In a loose sense, government can be regarded as a gigantic conglomerate with very diverse interests. Many individual departments also carry out a variety of activities themselves. But, there are functional and political interrelationships within and between departments which call for coordination of activities and policies beyond what is needed to ensure central financial control. The effectiveness of one division depends on integrating what it does with what others are doing. If integration fails, performance suffers. In short, effectiveness in public management is often a result of joint effort, of managing interdependence rather than single-mindedly pursuing divisional objectives. The application of the multi-divisional form of organization should be based on an assessment of whether it is appropriate to the circumstances.

There is a more general but related point to consider. Prescriptions for accountable management — giving managers a clear sight of what is expected of them and the resources available to them — make assumptions about low interdependence similar to those that underlie the appropriate use of the multi-divisional form. The concept of cost centres or responsibility centres figured prominently in the discussions prior to the launching of the FMI. The debate was stimulated by the Joubert scrutiny of non-staff running costs in the Department of the Environment. That scrutiny revealed the inadequacies of the existing system, or lack of system, in the control of costs. Its findings were taken up and linked with ideas about accountable management borrowed by Fulton. These ideas bear a family resemblance to the widely used business concept of profit centres; and it was popularized by Schumacher (1973) in — be it noted — his writings on large-scale organizations under the slogan, 'Small is beautiful'. The model underlying these prescriptions for keeping public management simple has impressive academic support. There are several variations on the theme of designing organizations as loosely coupled systems, some of which focus on public rather than private organizations (Weick, 1976; Aldrich and Whetten, 1981). Simon (1962) defined precisely the requirements for the design of organizations as nearly decomposable systems, grouping together highly interdependent activities where interactions among the people involved are frequent, and separating them from groups with which they have infrequent dealings. Decomposing organizations into quasi-autonomous units minimizes the coordination load and helps establish an efficient match between tasks and operational capabilities. It is a recipe for specialization and incremental adaptation.

Looking After the Pennies: an apt slogan for management in loosely coupled or nearly decomposable organizations might be,

'Look after the pennies and the pounds will look after themselves.' As a guiding principle of financial management and budgetary control, this has an obvious appeal. It fits the ethos of Thatcherism and contradicts the argument that management improvements are insignificant small change in macroeconomic policy-making. But once again, the rider has to be added that it is not a general organizational solution: it works only when the level of interdependence is low and the rate of policy change is slow. It works when public managers are producers, pursuing well defined and stable objectives. At higher levels of interdependence, loose coupling can prejudice overall objectives by encouraging suboptimization, because the left hand neither knows nor cares what the right hand is doing. High interdependence requires substantial and deliberately planned coordination and integration of activities. The more interdependence increases, the more effective coordination depends on moving from control techniques to management. One of the classic organizational studies, by Lawrence and Lorsch (1967), identified different patterns of organization and management process associated with effectiveness in different environments. Organizations in more diversified and rapidly changing environments had to develop more sophisticated patterns of differentiation and integration to assure their effectiveness. There are parallel problems in public management. Public managers need skills, as integrators and boundary managers in order to cope effectively with more complex environments, and as innovators in order to formulate new responses to meet changing conditions. In recent years adapting to a rapidly and unpredictably changing environment has become a major focus of organizational analysis in business. Kanter (1983) pointed up the basic issue in her distinction between segmented and integrative organizations. Not enough attention has been paid to this in the public sector.

There are signs that the implementation of the FMI is bringing departments face to face with these issues. For example, the head of the Ministry of Agriculture, Fisheries and Food's Financial Management Team commented on the difficulties encountered in trying to decompose that department into separate units:

> A Department like MAFF cannot easily be broken down into separate accountable businesses in the way a commercial organization our size would normally break down its operations. . . . The issues we face are more like those which are often recognized in commercial organizations as the difficult cases like research and development and promotional costs. (Coates, 1985: 5)

This is a realistic judgement, and it is important that models of organization are developed that take higher levels of interdependence and uncertainty into account. Otherwise, inappropriate application of the multi-divisional form will justifiably reinforce civil service scepticism and disbelief about the utility of management concepts in government.

One of the main dangers of only looking after the pennies is that people are encouraged to believe that external change will not significantly affect their bit of the organization. They assume that the whole is just the sum of the parts. If this were true, it would greatly simplify the politics of administrative reform. Incremental reform efforts in different areas could proceed independently, localized successes would be retained, and failures in one area would not spill over and disrupt progress in other areas. Structural problems need never arise. Conversely, if this assumption of virtual independence is unwarranted, change in one area does affect what happens in others. Structural problems will occur and successful adaptation requires coordinated action. Failure to deal with larger structural problems can trigger chain reactions. The more interconnected different activities become, the more slipping on one banana skin increases the probability of slipping on others. But loosely coupled organizations predispose managers to underestimate the extent of their interdependence and to become too blinkered in outlook. Whatever the short-term gains from greater specialization, they may be wiped out by an inability to react promptly and efficiently to structural problems. The counter proverb to looking after the pennies is not being able to see the wood for the trees.

Thus, the main organizational prescriptions embodied in the FMI have limited validity. They do not cover the full spectrum of organizations and situations in which government operates. It is not sufficient to acknowledge these difficulties and merely suggest that principles should be applied with due allowance for particular circumstances. The limitations are built into the principles themselves. In addition to the multi-divisional form of organization, other organizational designs should be explored and greater attention should be given to the distinctively public management problems of inter-organizational design. Foremost among these is the redefinition of the role of the centre.

The Role of the Centre: although most of the discussion so far has concentrated on the departmental level, it has important implications for the role of Treasury Expenditure divisions. As the central department responsible for monitoring and controlling the way departments spend public money, the Treasury's response to the FMI is a key determinant of its success. Reluctance on the part of the Treasury to relax detailed controls over departmental expenditure would certainly vitiate efforts to increase delegation within departments. On the other hand, premature acceptance by the Treasury of the viability of new departmental management systems could easily result in serious failures of control. There are risks on both sides. Maintaining a balance between these two dangers presents a difficult problem of judging when and how to manage the transition from detailed case-by-case control to a pattern of oversight based on evaluating departmental management systems. Although the Treasury view might be that this is nothing new because it has always been a part of the Treasury's role in monitoring departmental performance, a significant change is involved. Treasury practice has lagged behind precept. The Treasury has never had the resources or skills to do the job. Adjustment to a new definition of the role of expenditure divisions depends on the Treasury's developing a credible competence in judging the quality of departmental management and spotting weaknesses in management systems rather than second-guessing particular decisions.

In order to perform this redefined role, staff in expenditure divisions need, among other things, to be well versed in management concepts and skilled in using them to assess new management systems and organizational designs. They need to know what the problems and the options are and in what circumstances particular designs are appropriate. Organizational design in this context concerns not just the design of structures and systems, but also the specification of patterns of accountability that correspond to particular functions and tasks. Expenditure divisions not only need to know which designs have been selected but also need to be able to ask the practical questions about the implications of organizational choices for objective setting, performance evaluation and accountability.

At a broader level, the centre — not just the Treasury — has a role in identifying circumstances where structural problems are emerging and where concerted action at the interdepartmental level is required. As we saw in Chapter 5, if government departments, including the Treasury in that case, simply fight their own corners, structural problems are not resolved and opportunities for fundamental reorganization are missed. The expenditure implications of failing to deal effectively with structural problems are hidden but they are likely to grow in importance.

As the following section argues, one of the major underlying causes of the continuing crisis of public spending is that the budgetary context is moving away from, rather than towards, the conditions in which a strategy of incremental reform will suffice. Structural problems, requiring a distinctly different approach at the inter-departmental level, will increasing overshadow problems of incremental change.

Something Blue: Reducing Public Expenditure
Reduced public spending is an aspiration dear to the heart of any true-blue Conservative. If strength of feeling and political resolution were sufficient to cut public spending, it would now be much lower than it is. Under Mrs Thatcher's government, public expenditure has continued its rise. Political clout has not been enough to guarantee the outcomes desired. The FMI was intended to strengthen the capacity to budget by bridging the management gap. On the evidence of recent years, it might be argued that it has failed. This judgement would satisfy cynics and traditionalists but it would also be hasty and uninformative. First, changes on the scale of the FMI take time to produce results. Expecting immediate improvements is unrealistic. It is premature to make a judgement on the basis of what has been happening to public expenditure in the last few years. Even if a judgement were possible, it would be necessary to disentangle issues on at least three levels: implementation, adequacy of prescriptions relative to objectives, and appropriateness of objectives to the problems.

A provisional judgement on implementation is that not enough has been done to meet the major problems of managing change that the FMI involves. Departments have been expected to draw on existing staff resources to push through implementation; the Financial Management Unit, like the Efficiency Unit, was understaffed from the start. Since implementation is by far the largest part of any modernization effort, the successful management of the transition from the old to the new requires its own temporary organization (Beckhard and Harris, 1977). The requirements of transition management, as in many other cases in the public management field, have been underestimated. This is not to denigrate the efforts of those involved in departments and at the centre: it is simply to stress the magnitude of the task and the timidity of politicians in putting money where their mouth is in the field of administrative reform.

Enough has been said already to indicate the limitation of the FMI's prescriptions in relation to its stated objectives. We now turn to the third theme of this chapter, the appropriateness of the objectives and general thrust of the FMI as a whole to the future problems of managing public expenditure. Would full implementation of current proposals achieve the desired result?

Financial Management and the Budgetary Context
The political priority given to reducing public spending creates a great danger of brushing aside arguments and evidence that cast doubt on the appropriateness of the FMI as it stands. However, financial

management reform cannot be realistically abstracted from the overall budgetary context. While the public image of the FMI is that of an initiative designed to improve economy and efficiency in resource utilization at the departmental level, some of the real problems are more general. Without reform of the functioning of the whole system of public expenditure management the gains at the department level may be smaller than anticipated or may even be wiped out. It is not sufficient to introduce new methods of financial management at the departmental level and treat the basic institutional framework as sacrosanct. The hand of history lies heavy on the management of public expenditure. Institutions and rituals of government accounting and financial control maintain deeply ingrained attitudes to the management of public money.

> [Accounting and financial procedures] were designed originally to give effect to the constitutional supremacy of the House of Commons in all financial matters, and to establish the especial sanctity of 'public money'. The financial supremacy of the House of Commons is now a myth rather than a reality: but it is a myth which affects practice. (Mackenzie and Grove, 1957)

The myth affects practice first by shaping the relationships between elected politicians and permanent officials throughout the budgetary cycle and second by structuring the relations between the Treasury as the agent of Parliament and the spending departments. The myth legitimizes Treasury control of expenditure. One Treasury official described it as 'delegated democracy'. 'Parliament is incapable of exercising its financial responsibilities. We must do it for them.' Departmental actors play out familiar and well defined roles within the cultural framework that this myth establishes. The standard operating procedures of the annual budget bring spending departments and the Treasury into negotiation in predictable ways. Established institutions are identified with central values of public accountability and democratic control. An inversion between culture and structure has taken place. Instead of institutions being regarded as means of serving values and being judged on their effectiveness, they are perceived as embodiments of values. Hence, proposals for change are perceived as threatening or subversive to those whose power and legitimacy derive from established constitutional practices. Changing the rules of the game arouses strong emotions because the guardians of public money are apt to see themselves as guardians of the myth that legitimizes their power. Structural reform raises fundamental constitutional issues about the justification of the right to manage public money and the framework of accountability within which authority over public spending is exercised.

In addition to constitutional and institutional rigidity, there are other obstacles to budgetary reform. Orthodox budgetary theory has pessimistic implications for reform. It limits the options to alternatives close to the status quo. It suggests that there are inherent limitations in budgetary behaviour that rule out radical reform. It assumes that the participants in budgetary politics are not capable of coping with anything other than incremental change. Their limited information processing capacities restrict the range of policy options that can be considered. Reinforcing these psychological constraints on change, there are political constraints on the rate at which changes can be made. The interdepartmental negotiating processes through which budgetary politics work preclude sharp changes in policy and resource allocation. The combination of these psychological and political constraints is not only thought to explain the inertia of the budgetary system but is often used to justify it. Familiarity breeds confidence — and a vested interest — in the status quo. The prospect of stepping out of roles and relationships that have long seemed part of the natural order of things induces a sense of insecurity and disorientation.

Such a doctrine of immutability in budgetary behaviour disregards the problem and discounts the possibility of structural change. The incremental patterns of budgetary behaviour, on this view, are facts of life to which everyone must adjust. This view of budgetary behaviour is a special case of the more general theory of incremental policy-making. It is possible to marshal a good deal of evidence in support of it. However, to show that certain patterns have recurred in the past is no guarantee that they are inevitable. Businesses have succeeded in inventing new methods of strategic management to cope with discontinuity and steer structural change.

It is particularly important to overcome the strongly entrenched disbelief in the possibility of structural reorganization in the public budgeting field. The stakes, in terms of enhanced efficiency and more important, effectiveness, are very high. The difficulties are correspondingly great. Changing the rules of the budgetary game is the management of change on a grand scale. It involves reform in interdepartmental relations as well as intra-departmental reform. It also involves the development of new management capabilities, in departments and especially at the centre, that were not needed in simpler and less demanding budgetary contexts in which incremental budgetary behaviour and theory evolved.

Playing the Budgetary Game in Different Contexts
A comparative perspective helps to clarify the managerial requirements of effective adaptation in different budgetary contexts. Since budgeting is the process par excellence of relating available inputs to desired outputs, it makes sense to look for ways in which differences on the input side place different demands on budgetary politics and financial management. This paves the way for a contingency approach to specify the capacity to budget. The analysis that follows is prescriptive. It outlines alternative patterns of public budgeting and financial management corresponding to the needs of well-defined type cases. The relationships between budgetary context and capacity to budget that are identified are not deterministic. If they were, reform would not be a problem.

Figure 1, drawing on Wildavsky's (1975) discussion of comparative budgeting, defines four distinc.ive budgetary contexts by dichotomizing two key input variables: resources, which may be growing or declining; and problems, which may be predictable or unpredictable. Crude as these distinctions are, they highlight basic differences in the requirements for managing public expenditure. This framework helps to isolate the strategic issues involved in assessing the appropriateness of the FMI to present and future budgetary problems.

The figure shows four significantly different ways of playing the budgetary game. The most obvious point is that the requirements for effective budgetary and financial management vary according to the characteristics of the budgetary context. The capacity to budget

FIGURE 1: *Budgetary Contexts*

PROBLEMS

	Predictable	Unpredictable
Growing	Incremental (1) Budgeting	Supplementary (2) Budgeting
RESOURCES		
Declining	Efficiency (3) Budgeting	Flexibility (4) Budgeting

means different things in different conditions. Each budgetary context makes different demands on public managers and requires different capabilities for coping with the various budgetary functions. The terms 'incremental', 'supplementary', 'efficiency' and 'flexibility' budgeting denote adaptive responses to qualitatively distinct budgetary contexts. Each response is discussed briefly below to bring out their different implications for financial management, budgetary politics and the role of the centre. There is a progression in complexity from the relatively easily manageable budgetary context (1) for which the familiar orthodox model of incremental budgeting is adequate through (2) and (3) to the much more difficult and demanding budgetary context (4) for which a new concept of flexibility budgeting is proposed.

1 Incremental Budgeting
The budgetary context created by growing resources and predictable problems is the easiest to describe from a theoretical standpoint and to deal with in practice. It comes closest to the incremental assumptions on which the Public Expenditure Survey system operated until the 1970s. Since resource allocations among departments can be made in broadly the same way from year to year, medium-term planning is geared to developing stable programmes of activity. Incremental budgeting is a low-stress budgetary game played for low stakes. Behaviourally, incremental budgeting gives rise to familiar budgetary tactics and strategies. The actors in budgetary politics seek to protect the base — the existing departmental share of available resources — and bid for at least a proportionate share of any additional resources. The scope of interdepartmental conflict is marginal: everyone can win, and everyone can have prizes. Even those who feel that they have lost in relative terms compared with the gains of other departments can look forward to recouping their losses in future years.

'Incremental budgeting' allows departmental activities to be programmed. It assumes the predictability of problems and the stability of departmental activity from year to year. The benign environment of incremental budgeting takes much of the heat out of budgetary politics and provides few, if any, incentives to improved managerial performance. There is little pressure on departments to improve administrative efficiency and effectiveness. In this budgetary context the focus is more likely to be on acquiring inputs than on improving outputs. Indeed, a reputation for efficiency may be a tactical disadvantage in interdepartmental negotiations where a case has to be made for increased resources. The budgetary process is a largely predictable ritual dance. The basic pattern of existing programmes and settled priorities gives little scope for an active central role. The role of the centre is little more than holding the ring and maintaining procedural conformity.

2 Supplementary Budgeting

More difficult problems arise when conditions depart from those to which incremental budgeting is an adaptive response. Consider first the context in which a government faces unpredictable demands but can still rely on increasing inputs of resources. Unpredictability means that problems cannot be forecast by extrapolating from past experience. New responses must be made. Supplementary budgeting is the adaptive response to this budgetary context. The budgetary system copes with uncertainty by throwing additional resources at unanticipated problems. At a minimum, supplementary budgeting means holding a contingency reserve, in departments or centrally, to provide leeway against unforeseeable events. Beyond this, it means appropriating a larger share of national economic resources for governmental purposes. Supplementary budgeting describes how governments cope with the overload problems of the 1970s.

Compared with incremental budgeting, there are some differences, but not dramatic differences, in budgetary politics and financial management under a supplementary budgeting regime. The central issue in budgetary politics shifts from marginal allocation among established programmes to promoting and authorizing the development of new programmes and providing for demand-led services. Budgetary politics under supplementary budgeting is driven by departmental empire-building and external pressures. Like incremental budgeting, it is predominantly a bottom-up process. But there is more at stake. Departments compete for additional responsibilities as well as additional resources.

Because the focus is on new initiatives and programmes undertaken with extra resources, supplementary budgeting does not create an environment in which the efficient use of resources receives much attention. The main concern is what is available to spend and what new projects it should be spent on. Whether public money is well-spent is very much a secondary issue. Potential conflicts among departments are avoided or mitigated by the soft option of consuming more resources rather than revising priorities and managing changes accordingly. Superficially, supplementary budgeting appears to be a positive sum game, but the budgetary process itself is conducted along similar lines to incremental budgeting. Extra resources rather than better management provide the capacity to budget. Skills in resource acquisition are more highly valued than a proven record for effective resource utilization.

In a supplementary budgeting context the centre can have a more active role in deciding which new departmental claims to meet and to what extent resource growth can substitute for conflict management. But so long as departments believe that claims for additional resources will be met, the centre is not in a strong position to press for improvements in financial management and departmental performance.

3 Efficiency Budgeting
The third budgetary context is one in which problems are predictable but the resource base is declining. The major budgetary problem at all levels is coping with the chronic shortfall in resources. The capacity to budget depends on increasing efficiency. In contrast with incremental and supplementary budgeting, this budgetary context creates strong pressures for improvements in departmental efficiency with a bias towards economy. An efficiency budgeting context has important consequences for financial management and general management within departments. Clarification of objectives and priorities, definition of responsibilities, and tight control of costs to squeeze as much as possible out of limited resources are the order of the day. Resource constraints put pressure on departments to apply techniques that ensure value for money and eradicate waste and duplication of effort. The watchword is 'cost-consciousness'. Resource constraints also mean that cut-back management may have to address politically sensitive problems of shedding functions or lowering standards. Efficiency budgeting puts a premium on achieving savings. Departments must run a tight ship internally and adopt hard bargaining postures externally. Fortunately, although times are hard, they are not unpredictable. There may be morale-sapping disappointments and frustrations, but there are few great surprises.

In an efficiency budgeting context, departments must compete vigorously to safeguard their positions in the pecking order by clarifying their own objectives and pressing their case for maintaining their existing allocation of resources or minimizing any cutback. Interdepartmental conflict over resource allocation is more visible and more important than in the contexts previously discussed. In this austere but predictable environment, departments know what they would do if resources were available. They are ready to pounce, with shopping lists of policies and projects if other departments fail to make a good case. Efficiency budgeting is a zero sum game: one department can gain only if others lose. The great stress on allocative issues has its problems. Increased interdepartmental competitiveness and defensiveness undermine interdepartmental cooperation and mutual trust. The scope for give and take is severely reduced if not eliminated altogether. To the extent that departments can go it alone, efficiency budgeting promotes better performance. To the extent that interdepartmental coordination is important, results may suffer.

This budgetary context strengthens the role of the centre in bilateral negotiations with spending departments. There is more scope for the development of a top-down approach to budgeting. Resource constraints and interdepartmental conflict cast the centre in the role of arbiter. The centre's discretion and power may be enlarged if it can apply divide-and-rule strategies. However, the centre is not restricted to a negative role of imposing cuts and scaling down aspirations. It may also seek to contribute actively to efforts to improve management and sponsor efforts to increase value for money. Efficiency budgeting corresponds closely with the theme of governing in hard times from which the Efficiency Strategy and FMI sprang.

4 Flexibility Budgeting

The fourth budgetary context describes the worst of all possible worlds for managing public expenditure. Declining resources and unpredictable problems combine to pose a severe test to managerial adaptability. For traditional civil service management, these conditions may go beyond what is manageable. They produce overload and persistent instability. The eruption of unexpected problems and the chronic shortfall of resources can stretch managerial capabilities to the limit and beyond. Where the capacity to budget is inadequate, these conditions give rise to repetitive, crisis budgeting. Budgets and resource allocations are adjusted frequently and erratically as circumstances and the balance of political forces change. The system lurches from crisis to crisis without really getting to grips with the underlying problems. Attempted solutions are rapidly overtaken by events. Policy failures undermine the credibility of subsequent efforts. Budget forecasts are falsified and plans are discredited, weakening the disciplines of financial management. Budgetary politics become a disorderly scramble for resources as departments struggle to safeguard their own interests without much regard for the consequences. Departments may well recognize that there is a general problem but in a disintegrating situation they perceive no realistic alternative to putting their own interests first. The result is stalemate and failure to adapt resource allocations to emerging needs.

Concentrating on the failure of budgeting in this context is understandable because the problems of adaptation are formidable. There is little practical experience of success from which to draw lessons. The complexity of the problems precludes the successful application of the general strategies that work in the other three budgetary contexts. Piecemeal incrementalism is ineffective. Supplementary budgeting is not an available option. Improving operational efficiency, precisely because it promotes specialization, also produces rigidity and hampers adjustment to change. Running faster, in order to stand still, is both exhausting and ineffective in achieving adaptation. The capacity to budget in this context depends on greater organizational flexibility at the level of individual departments and at the level of the budgetary system as a whole. Flexibility budgeting is a two-level process.

The distinction between this budgetary context and the other three is that successful adaptation to change, without additional resources, requires great flexibility. Furthermore, since change takes the form of a succession of structural problems as well as continuing incremental change, flexibility budgeting involves discriminating between the two and formulating responses which reflect their differences. Flexibility budgeting is a two-level process. At one level, primarily the micro level of the individual department, the need is for enhanced flexibility in coping with incremental change. The bulk of recent work on organizational learning has focused on ways in which organizations can widen their repertoire of responses to unpredictable and challenging environmental conditions. At the second level, primarily the macro level of the budgetary system as a whole, the need is for new capabilities specifically created for managing structural changes that normal interdepartmental negotiations would not resolve. This second level is a capacity for changing the rules of the game. Hardly any work has been done on this aspect of interorganizational learning.

But it is increasingly important because adaptability at the departmental level is not enough to cope with major structural change. Environmental change and shifts in political priorities put heavy pressure on interdepartmental coordination. At the interorganizational level it is very difficult to generate the positive commitment and mutual trust required to agree common lines of action. Especially when resources are scarce, inter-departmental competitive pressures are very strong. The situation is akin to a prisoner's dilemma game. Individual departments experience acute tension between the competitive and cooperative motives. Even if departments recognize their interdependence and perceive the need to cooperate in adjusting to change, they do not know how others will act. The uncertainties of the situation and the mistrust arising from previous interdepartmental conflict predispose them to select competitive strategies. But individually rational actions produce a collectively irrational outcome. Everyone is worse off than they would have been if the potential benefits of cooperation had been realized. Perversely, all take comfort in the fact that, even if they have suffered, they have conceded nothing to others.

The prisoner's dilemma game is one formulation of what is a key problem of public management, namely, recognizing situations in which independent action by separate groups, aiming to protect their own interests, blocks the realization of common or public interests. Its regressive outcome is a consequence of failing to take account of the different dynamics of incremental and structural change. Independent adaptation is adequate to cope with incremental change but it is ineffective, even counterproductive, in coping with structural change. Instead of combining adaptive capacities at the interdepartmental level, it pits departments against each other and reduces rather than increases flexibility to respond to change. Aggregating micro-solutions does not procedure a viable macro-solution. Coping with structural change requires interventions at the macro level to change the rules of the game (Metcalfe, 1974; Metcalfe and McQuillan, 1977). This casts the centre in the important role of orchestrating structural reorganizations that require intensive interdepartmental cooperation.

One of the important elements in this process is that it includes designing positive institutions of accountability to underpin organizational changes and provide new criteria of effectiveness not just impose *ex post* sanctions on poor performance.

Flexibility budgeting does not mean increased centralization in the conventional sense of tighter Treasury control. Successful structural change requires interventions and strategies for change that involve departments in the process of designing new rules of the game to govern their operation and guide performance. Flexibility budgeting, as a two-level process, gives public management a contingency reserve of flexibility by opening up options for innovation to make momentous choices (Dror 1984). It provides a design capability at the interdepartmental level which is not used on a day-to-day basis but comes into operation when normal interdepartmental negotiations cannot cope. The centre has a unique and vital role in this process. There are three crucial components: the renewal of the constitutional framework within which departmental management takes place; the redefinition of criteria of effectiveness; and the establishment of appropriate processes of accountability. Although there is a rough parallel with operational and strategic management in business, the requirements of managing structural change present a distinctive set of public management problems which have not really been addressed.

Changing the rules of the game requires concerted action to define a new framework for interdepartmental negotiation. It amounts to a deliberately managed process of constitutional change. In practice, the centre has often defined its role in diametrically opposing terms, shoring up an increasingly obsolete constitutional status quo and disregarding widening mismatches between forms of accountability and public management functions.

The FMI: an Appropriate Response?

The foregoing analysis provides criteria for assessing whether the FMI is an appropriate response to present and prospective budgetary problems. As originally conceived, the FMI is a formula for efficiency budgeting. It is a response to the third kind of budgetary context described above. With some marginal qualifications, its objectives and prescriptions address the problem of building lean, streamlined public organizations to serve well-defined and stable policy objectives. As we explained earlier, even if this assumption about the budgetary context were correct, the FMI proposals have certain limitations which would reduce its total impact even if fully implemented. However, the more serious question is whether the basic judgement about future budgetary conditions is correct.

Recalling the cost-consciousness-flexibility dilemma discussed in Chapter 2, it is evident that the FMI is based firmly on the belief that the principal requirement in strengthening public budgeting is the former. But even within the FMI itself, practitioners have found the need to consider ways of coping with interdependence and provide for flexibility. Moreover, the general assumption of predictable problems and stable policies in the future is suspect. Real-world conditions show strong signs of moving towards the fourth kind of budgetary context where adaptation depends on managing the interplay between frequent incremental change and intermittent structural change. It seems implausible to forecast stability and continuity in the fields of employment policy, the inner cities, law and order, social welfare provision and education, and a more or less unchanging allocation of resources among them and other policy fields.

Efficiency budgeting, as the term implies, gives top priority to improving performance in established directions. It takes existing objectives and institutional parameters for granted. This style of management, with a heavy emphasis on the producer roles, is clearly appropriate in times of austerity. But if austerity is accompanied by rapid change, efficiency budgeting may prove self-defeating. Instead of paring away at waste and inefficiency, it will be optimizing on the wrong curve. Policies and activities will become increasingly mismatched to changing problems. Instead of realizing significant savings, resources will be wasted on obsolescent projects that become memorials to past problems rather than solutions to future problems.

The more the emphasis is placed on flexibility budgeting, the more does strengthening the capacity to budget involve remodelling the role of the centre and redefining its relations with spending departments, so as to build the institutional capacity to cope with structural change. Managing structural change can never be the exclusive prerogative of the centre but the centre must play the leading role. Furthermore, since it is as much a matter of management as of finance, it points to an enlarged role for the Management and Personnel Office in promoting better interdepartmental coordination, and strengthening capabilities for organizational design — both of which are key requirements for managing structural change.

Finally, a shift from efficiency budgeting to flexibility budgeting brings out a paradox in Rayner's advocacy of lasting reforms. While the FMI has developed along different lines from many attempts at reform, it retains the old image of budgetary reform as a once-for-all change. It prescribes a new set of rules of the game to replace those made obsolete by the changes of recent years. This falls short of the requirements of flexibility budgeting. Flexibility budgeting requires a capacity to plan and manage an unending sequence of structural changes. The success of these changes in ensuring lasting improvements in efficiency and effectiveness, depends on their impermanence. Lasting reforms are a succession of temporary solutions. As we said earlier, public budgeting is a permanent problem without a permanent solution.

10
The Politics of Efficiency and the Management of Change

A framed quotation from Machiavelli's *The Prince* hangs in one of the offices of the Prime Minister's Efficiency Unit in the Cabinet Office. It reads as follows:

> . . . It must be considered that there is nothing more difficult to carry out, nor more doubtful of success, nor more dangerous to handle, than to initiate a new order of things. For the reformer has enemies in all those who profit by the older order, and only lukewarm defenders in all those who would profit by the new order. . . .

Machiavelli went on:

> . . . this lukewarmness arises partly from fear of their adversaries, who have the laws in their favour; and partly from the incredulity of mankind, who do not truly believe in anything new until they have had actual experience of it.

This quotation is a timeless comment on the uphill task reformers face and a clear statement of the institutional obstacles they must overcome. Management modernization is a political process and not merely the introduction of new techniques. As Machiavelli tells us, bringing about a new order of things depends on circumventing entrenched opposition and mobilizing positive support. The passage encapsulates the dual requirements of administrative innovation; effective handling of the politics of efficiency and careful attention to the management of change. Without the former, reform proposals do not survive. They succumb to the resistance and objections of those who profit from the old order. Without the latter, they cannot be translated into results. Successful management of change creates positive rewards to persuade doubters to lend their support to further efforts.

Whatever else may be said about it, the Efficiency Strategy was well designed, when it was inaugurated, to meet the requirements of the politics of efficiency and the management of change. Prime Ministerial political clout gave initial impetus. Commitments to cultural change gave long term direction. The Efficiency Unit was entrusted with the task of holding the strategy together by overseeing the development of the scrutiny programme and laying the foundations for lasting reforms. But now the Efficiency Strategy has outgrown its original format and our purpose in this final chapter is to make an assessment of its prospects. It is useful to take stock: looking back at what has been done and also looking forward to consider what the next steps should be.

Looking back, the Efficiency Strategy has achieved a good deal more than was expected at the start. Many people were prepared to write it off as an electoral fashion that would fade rapidly from the scene as soon as more pressing political issues surfaced. There was a widespread belief that the forces of bureaucratic inertia would soon emasculate it. The early achievements of the Efficiency Strategy have exceeded pessimistic forecasts because it gave a sharp edge to the politics of efficiency without overstretching the limited civil service capacity for managing change. Quick results established a measure of political credibility that earlier reform efforts lacked. Starting small, with narrowly focused scrutinies, increased the probability of success, and at the same time helped developed the confidence and competence needed to undertake more ambitious projects.

Looking to the future, there are some serious questions about whether the Efficiency Strategy is evolving in the right direction to rise to new and greater challenges. Judged by its own standards, some opportunities have already been missed. In 1986, in a report on the Efficiency Strategy, the Public Accounts Committee of the House of Commons criticized the record of implementation of scrutiny recommendations and the failure of departments to realize the savings foreseen. In addition, there have been occasions when potential savings and management reforms have been rejected by ministers for political reasons. One of the most unintelligent and persistent examples of this is the overriding priority given to reducing the number of civil servants, even when there is clear evidence that manpower cuts reduce effectiveness. In revenue departments the costs of additional staff in certain areas can be recouped many times over. But increasing revenue has proved less attractive politically than perpetuating the fiction that only reducing the civil service head count reduces public expenditure.

Winning early battles does not ensure winning the war. Nor does repeating initial successes guarantee long-term results. Instead, it may contain the seeds of its own destruction. In the business world cutting-back is often a prelude to a positive process of corporate renewal. Quantitative cuts are followed by qualitative regeneration to change the thinking of management and make strategic investments in improved organization. Applying this logic to government emphasizes the need to avoid a more-of-the-same approach and to develop a strategy that gives a clearer profile to the idea of lasting reforms. To some extent events have been moving in this direction, with the expansion of the programme of multi-departmental reviews and, most of all, the FMI. But these developments in the complexity of managing change within government have not been accompanied by changes in the politics of efficiency. The public presentation of the Efficiency Strategy has not kept track of its evolution on the ground. Whatever has been happening in practice, the politics of efficiency is struck in a groove. The public debate centres on costs and cuts. The public rationale of the Efficiency Strategy still gives priority to running a tight ship. A great deal of basic work which will produce long-term benefits is being done, but it lacks vigorous public advocacy and a renewed sense of coherence and purpose.

The Politics of Efficiency — a New Mandate for Reform
The initial reform package was successful because it combined several important elements. It brought external pressure to bear on the civil service and capitalized on internal self-doubt and dissatisfaction. It provided a clear direction for change and, in the Efficiency Unit, a mechanism and structure for implementation. To complete the management cycle, feedback and evaluation processes were established at the highest level to monitor departmental progress. The basic model remains valid, but the tasks have become more complex. Evolving from scrutinies to lasting reforms requires a new mandate which shifts the emphasis form short term savings and quantitative manpower reductions to a broader concern with qualitative improvements in management. Having established the need for greater cost consciousness, the Efficiency Strategy in the future should pay more attention to creating flexibility to enable government to respond promptly to change.

As the discussions of particular cases in earlier chapters indicated, there has been a growing tension within the Efficiency Strategy between the desire to continue with a relatively simple philosophy of reform and the increasing complexity of the problems that have to be resolved. There is more need to secure internal commitment and mobilize positive support to implement changes such as those envisaged in the FMI. While political clout remains essential — major changes require visible top-level commitment — cultural change, in the form of new concepts of management and new patterns of accountability, cannot be externally imposed. New ways of managing depend on understanding and acceptance, particularly when they require basic institutional changes that have long been regarded as beyond the pale by the civil service. The mythology of the British constitution stresses adaptability and flexibility as its cardinal virtues. The reality is different. The absence of authoritative written rules makes it more difficult, rather than easier, to break away from time honoured convention and established practice. The vagueness of an unwritten constitution makes it hard to differentiate between incremental and structural change and develop different approaches to them. In Whitehall parlance all cases are 'treated on their merits', a smokescreen phrase which reserves the right of ministers and their advisers to make decisions without explaining what principles are applied to judge the merits of particular cases.

The Management of Change

Adept playing of the political game got the scrutiny programme under way by circumventing opposition and minimizing the need for sophisticated skills in managing change. The more the Efficiency Strategy progresses the greater the need, not only to establish a new political mandate for reform, but also to increase capacities to manage large-scale structural change. Above all, this involves the willing consent and active cooperation of civil servants at every level. Commitment will not be easy to achieve. It will be hard to win support at middle management levels where the impact of cuts has been felt most heavily and where civil servants have first-hand experience of the effects of economies. More surprisingly, perhaps, there is still some way to go before senior civil servants are fully persuaded that there is a permanent change. Converts to the cause of good management were made quickly at senior levels, partly because it was prudent for them to respond to political expectations by playing the efficiency game. Adopting the language and terminology of management is one thing. Doing the right things takes much longer than saying the right things. It also requires much enhanced management capabilities.

In this respect, the Efficiency Strategy is still hampered by its cut-back associations. One symptom was the under-resourcing of the Efficiency Unit itself. This was attributed by one civil servant to the 'Calpurnia factor'. Like Caesar's wife, the Efficiency Unit should be above suspicion. It should not be seen as a generously funded organization requiring a degree of austerity of others that it does not apply to itself. The unfortunate consequence is that there is inadequate central capacity for thinking ahead to prepare the way for strategy development. If this avoids the situation where opponents can score easy political points, it is also congruent with a peculiar and ill-founded British penny-wise, pound-foolish belief that cheapness and value of money mean the same thing. Even British industry now appears to be latching on to the idea that quality matters.

In the management of change, it is more the case that organizations, public and private get what they are prepared to pay for. And they pay by investing their own time and effort in organizational renewal. In the last few years, business has moved away from seeing successive rounds of cuts as an adequate response to a rapidly changing environment. It now recognizes the importance of having a well-trained, adaptable and committed work force. Human resource management has become a high priority. This is not to suggest that there has been no progress since 1979. Real change has taken place, but the civil service has not crossed the threshold which ensures that change is a self sustaining part of the culture.

The emphasis on efficiency as cuts might be appropriate to a vision of government as a minimal organization presiding over a stable environment. But few serious contributors to the debate on these matters would project that as a likely future scenario. The pace of economic, technological, social and political change necessitates a state that has adaptive and learning capacities which will ensure responsiveness to this changing world. The management of change is becoming a permanent responsibility in government and civil servants will have to acquire skills in planning and managing change effectively. As we have already pointed out, the scrutiny programme deliberately minimized the need for sophisticated methods in order to produce quick results. Critics, and some advocates, would say that it was 'a quick and dirty' way of securing cuts and savings. What has become increasingly clear is that more deliberate and explicit use of available methods of managing change will produce better results and is becoming a critical factor in the process of improving public management. There are many ways of classifying methodologies and techniques of intervention and the following typology of strategies is only illustrative of a larger array. It is helpful in illustrating the choices that have to be made to ensure that the methods selected are appropriate to the task and likely to achieve desired results most efficiently (Blake and Mouton, 1978).

> *Prescriptive* — laying down new rules and procedures ex cathedra, relying on existing management to ensure implementation;
> *Catalytic* — adding further elements to an existing situation, to precipitate changes that were otherwise blocked;
> *Confrontation* — addressing the conflicts inherent in many change situations which the participants, individually, prefer to avoid;
> *Acceptant* — counselling participants in the change process to help them to come to terms with what is happening; adjustment to a changed situation;
> *Principles, methods and models* — diagnostic and developmental efforts to aid the acquisition of insight and build adaptive capacities into organizations; new concepts of management.

These options can be related to some of the cases discussed in earlier chapters, always recognizing that they are not mutually exclusive. Outwardly, the Efficiency Strategy has put the emphasis on a prescriptive approach. Scrutineers have to make their own firm recommendations to top management without giving much attention to implementation. Beyond that minimum requirement they are free to choose whatever other methods they think appropriate. The scrutiny of the Regional Development Grant administration discussed in Chapter 4 is an example of the successful use of a catalytic style of interventions. The scrutiny of the system for the payment of benefits to unemployed people considered in Chapter 5 required an effective means of confrontation at the interdepartmental level to expose departmental differences of interest and ensure a constructive process of conflict resolutions rather than a stalemate. Managing change at the intra- and interdepartmental levels will require combinations of the methods available.

Enriching the Concept of Public Management
Developing competences in the management of change is one part of a much needed process of enriching the concept of public management. Senior civil servants, on the whole, have seen management as a dull, routine, uncreative task, not really worthy of their talents. Their impoverished concept of management sprang out of a perception that management was what the lower, executive grades of the civil service did. It also sprang from a stereotyped and uninformed view of management in the private sector. A surprising number of civil servants believe that working within a market framework, and the requirement to make profit, somehow makes management tasks clear and simple. In Chapter 1 we defined the main features of the impoverished concept of management embedded in the culture of Whitehall. They are summarized below.

—Management as an executive function. Management presupposes the clear definition of objectives, policies and, if possible, quantitative performance measures.
—Management as an intra-organizational process. Management is what goes on within organizations; it is concerned with how work is done within organizations, with internal routines and procedures.
—Management as hierarchical control: coordination and control are achieved through well-defined hierarchies of responsibility and authority. Ideally, these are structured into distinct cost or responsibility centres.
—And finally the assumption that there are broad principles of management which apply with only minor adaptation to all organizations. This assumption is buttressed by the belief that many of these principles are already known from private business practice.

Improving public management involves moving away from this restricted concept. Lasting reforms requires an expansion of the meaning of management. Management is not just an executive process separate from policy-making: effective public management requires strong links between policy-making and implementation. In the real world, there is no clear division between management and politics.

Management is not just an intra-organizational process. Management means taking responsibility for the performance of a system. In public management, more often than not, systems are interorganizational. Central departments like the Department of the Environment or the Department of Education and Science work through networks of local authorities and non-departmental bodies. The management of public expenditure is an interdepartmental process. Effectiveness depends on managing the whole, including the relationships between component organizations, not just on tightening up internal systems.

Creating clearly defined hierarchies is not synonymous with management. Non-hierarchical forms of organization and accountability are needed for managing professionals and working in a market environment. Internal delegation and accountable management internally will not succeed unless external accountability arrangements support and reinforce them.

Public management requires innovation and fresh thinking rather than continued dependence on established practice and private sector models. There needs to be an array of models of management which reflect the circumstances of departments and the needs of programmes. Some can draw heavily on private sector experience. Some need development since they address problems which the private sector does not face. No single model of management comprehends the range of tasks and functions that government undertakes.

The Efficiency Strategy therefore had an uphill task in improving the practice of public management, partly because of the inherent difficulties and partly because the culture of Whitehall distorted and stereotyped what was being done. The task was not made easier by the pressure to highlight savings as the primary measure of success. Overemphasis on cost-cutting jeopardized the development of a richer concept of public management. Enriching the concept of management depends on developing some of the following themes.

1 Information

Information about organizational performance is a prerequisite of good management. MINIS has entered the mythology of the efficiency movement as the Department of the Environment prototype for later service-wide developments through the Financial Management Initiative. As information systems go, it was the equivalent of the blunderbuss — unrefined, blanket-coverage, unwieldly, unmanoeuvrable. It was a measure of the antiquated nature of the management process in government that MINIS could be regarded as a step forward. Progress has been made since the first round of MINIS, but information systems still have a long way to go to serve the needs of managers and policy-makers at all levels. Information systems are means of scanning the environment and formulating policies as well as monitoring current performance. The most important line of future development is into the realm of providing information for programme management as distinct from information about administrative costs. Information on the effectiveness of policy is still poorly developed. There has been slow progress in addressing the larger questions of managing programme expenditure effectively. Improving public management means providing value as well as saving money and it should not stop at the point where 'civil servants know the cost of everything, but the value of nothing' (Plowden, 1985). Some progress is being made: all new policy proposals before Cabinet, for instance, must have attached to them details of how the policy is to be evaluated (Joint Management Unit, 1985). What is required is a much stronger relationship between policy-making and policy implementation than the impoverished concept of management has assumed. Management information systems should link with policy analysis issues. Public managers will have to innovate and develop new kinds of management information systems.

2 Decentralization

Many aspects of civil service organization conspire to produce over-centralization — the constitutional convention of ministerial responsibility, the hierarchical metaphors that frame the relationships between different grades of civil servants, the negative bias of accountability processes which have defeated many attempts to increase decentralization. Part of the problem lies in seeing centralization and decentralization as contradictory principles of organization. The failure to recognize qualitative differences between first-, second-and third-order controls has meant over-reliance on detailed case-by-case examination and direct supervision, too little use of standardization and specialization and rudimentary development of strategic management frameworks. These criticisms apply with equal force in the different context of interdepartmental relations; if anything, strategic management is more important at that level than at the departmental level. Management shades off into institutional leadership (Selznick, 1957; Metcalfe, 1981).

Empowering budget-holders to make operational management decisions, with those at a more senior level setting the strategic framework within which operational management takes place, is a fundamental feature of the Financial Management Initiative. Making a reality of decentralization in the civil service, however, is a complicated, counter-cultural process. It involves not only improving the capacity of budget-holders to do their job, but developing new strategic management orientations among senior officials. It is useless to encourage middle-ranking civil servants to think of themselves as managers of budgets if the framework within which they operate militates against the capacity to fulfil that role.

3 Line Management

Better information and greater decentralization produce improved performance only if there is a clear pattern of line management responsibility. In government strengthening line management means bringing together responsibilities which previously have been divided among distinct departmental groups. The fragmentation of responsibility for policy, finance, establishments (personnel) and policy implementation has obstructed efforts to improve performance. The FMI has sought to reinforce the position of line management by establishing the general use of budgets as an integrating management tool throughout government.

This has come to be associated with the concept of accountable management which makes assumptions about loose-coupling that are often not justified in practice. The appealing simplicity of dividing government departments into self-contained units runs the risk of hardening into a dogma. Very often, effective public management depends on managing interdependence rather than independence.

Having said this, it is not the case that there is one best way of managing interdependence. Line management structures have to be developed to be flexible enough to take a full account of the problems of managing professionals and people working in a market framework, where they are providing services on repayment, charging the public for services and managing contracts. They will only work successfully if more compex internal management structures are devised.

4 Spend to Save

The changes discussed above are neither easy nor cheap to implement. The politics of efficiency and the management of change pull in opposite directions. In the long run more sophisticated management should produce substantial economies as well as achieve greater effectiveness, but in the short term it requires significant investment. Improving public management demands a 'spend-to-save' policy.

In substantive policy fields, the practice of appraisal to calculate the likely return on investment is well established: the costs and benefits of, for example, a road improvement are established, and when the project reaches the top of the list for investment it goes ahead. Similar techniques are applied to projects in the information technology field, although the potential returns are more difficult to judge. Investment in improved management is neither so well established nor so easy to evaluate. The rationalistic framework of economic calculation is not well suited to people management, where investment pay-offs are more difficult to prove. Marks and Spencer treat staff well, and attract and keep good staff, who make a significant contribution to high organizational performance. That causal relationship is established in the minds of management, but it would be hard to prove objectively. Such an act of faith does not come easily to the civil service, especially the Treasury, nor is it part of the belief system of politicians. Investing in reorganization is perceived as profligacy. Training and career development, along with other aspects of human resource management, have been starved of funds in the past. If there is a serious concern to improve performance, rather than just to cut costs, the investment block must be overcome.

5 Inter-organizational Management

Public management is getting things done through other organizations. One of the myths of administrative reform is that it is possible to create an organizational division of labour which virtually eliminates the need for coordination and negotiation across departmental boundaries. Just as there is a strong need for coordination and integration within departments, so at the interdepartmental level, are tasks and functions closely interconnected. Despite recurrent problems, this vital aspect of public management has been neglected. More effective means of policy coordination at the highest level, leading to familiar debates about the role of the Cabinet Office, or the Prime Minister's office, or some form of think-tank are familiar themes. But inter-organizational management goes much deeper. As well as high-level policy management, there is a great need to ensure that government departments and other organizations involved in delivering services to the same public should work closely and effectively together. The dilemma of, on the one hand, encouraging departmental independence in order to get departments to claim ownership of management change and, on the other hand, coming to grips with problems that span departmental boundaries has not yet been resolved. An enriched concept of public management must give a high priority to finding ways of resolving it which do justice to both.

6 Role of the Centre

Nowhere is the need for an inter-organizational perspective more evident than in discussing the role of the centre. This applies to the Treasury, with its responsibility for managing public expenditure, and it also applies to the Management and Personnel Office, with its central responsibility for non-financial aspects of management. Both departments have problems in resolving the conflicts between different responsibilities. The tension between the Treasury's responsibility for economic management and for expenditure control is familiar. In the past, conflicts have usually been resolved by subordinating value for money in the management of expenditure to the priorities of economic policy considerations. In addition, the Treasury has failed to understand how to increase decentralization without loss of control. It has dabbled too much in departmental concerns by carrying out detailed supervision, and has not done enough to establish systems or to define the strategic and cultural framework of management.

To an excessive degree, the centre has sought to control departments rather than to stimulate and reinforce departmental efforts to improve management and performance. Too much of the consultancy, inspection and review resources that should be at the disposal of line management have been deployed by the centre to monitor departmental compliance with centrally defined standards. The real challenge is to move beyond this role to develop ways of supporting and facilitating departmental management efforts to achieve year-on-year improvements in performance.

7 Accountability
These improvements in management depend upon redesigning the constitutional framework of public accountability. Thus far accountability has entered the picture primarily with reference to accountable management within the existing framework. As we have indicated above, there is a great deal of room for improvement, but there are also some under-recognized difficulties in establishing realistic and effective patterns of accountable management. At the same time public management does not operate in a political vacuum, and institutions and processes of public accountability should be designed to promote and enforce rising standards of performance. Just as there is considerable diversity in the functions of public organizations, so there should be corresponding diversity in the forms of accountability to which they are subject. Present arrangements impose too strong a pressure to conform to a uniform set of accountability requirements. Even if ministerial responsibility worked as constitutional theory supposes, it would not provide the stimulus to excellence that public management conspicuously lacks. A contingency approach is needed to match forms of accountability to organizational functions. Earlier chapters noted some of the practical issues that arise when civil servants are required to play professional roles or work in a market environment but accountability processes are not adjusted to confirm and reinforce these role definitions.

The concept of public management must be enriched by seeing

accountability as a component part of the management process rather than as something external to it. The doctrine of ministerial responsibility is the best alibi civil servants have for poor performance. The culture of Westminster goes hand in hand with the culture of Whitehall. Accountability to Parliament through ministers has not been conducive to effective managerial performance, but neither has it provided a public service that is responsive and accessible. The accountability processes that are supposed to make ministers answerable to members of Parliament actually lead to covering up and opacity. Although most civil servants would regard Parliament as a supreme irrelevance to good government, in fact their behaviour is fundamentally affected by parliamentary myths and rituals. Ultimately, better management in the civil service can come only from accountability processes which enhance managerial performance. The recognition by MPs that such changes would improve, rather than diminish, the real accountability of government is a vital step to take. Constitutional change is handicapped by the poorly developed state of constitutional law. As present discussion of the rights and duties of civil servants has shown, ministers have inherited much of the Crown's personal prerogative (House of Commons, 1986). Constitutional theory that distinguishes the person and the office of minister is required (Ridley, 1985), but Sir Robert Armstrong's pronouncements after the Westland affair have fused the two. Improving public management means a shift from personal service to ministers to professional service to publics.

8 Human Resource Management

The themes discussed above have major implications for human resource management in the civil service. In each area the development of policies for better management and the implementation of those policies depends on significant adaptations of personnel policies. Some of the needed changes are already being made in the review and revision of personnel policies and the more deliberate use of training to support modernization. Moves in this direction do not mean a wholesale transformation of the ethos and practice of civil service personnel management. But they do involve the incorporation of new values and expectations that formerly would have received short shrift from senior civil servants. It is not so long since the phrase 'a more professional and highly trained civil service' would have grated on the culture of Whitehall like the screech of chalk on a blackboard. There is now much wider acceptance of the need for professionalism in a managerial sense and for training to ensure improved performance and make effective use of limited resources.

Whatever may be said of the other Peters and Waterman principles, public management depends on productivity through people. Public managers at all levels will need enhanced capabilities for managing their staffs and ensuring that they are technically equipped and motivated to produce better results. They will also need to see that the organizational environment in which people work is flexible and adaptive in meeting change, as well as efficient in operational management.

The required developments in human resource management depend on changes in attitude and practice on two levels. The most important and difficult is cultural change in civil service concepts and values which have denigrated professionalism and discounted training. The tendency in all organizations for senior people to mould their juniors and successors in their own image means that these old habits will die hard. But the Efficiency Strategy reinforced by Prime Ministerial political clout has overcome some of the resistance to change and forced the senior civil service to rethink its role. As we have pointed out, the extent of change is limited because the politically preferred image of the public manager is the producer, working within a well-defined policy framework and committed to achieving better results with available resources. This value-for-money orientation is needed but in a changing environment public managers also need the skills of innovators willing to initiate strategic changes of direction and integrators who can design and implement the systems to make new policies work. Human resource management with these objectives in mind places a high priority on training to develop the requisite skills and organizational development to ensure their use. One without the other is a recipe for frustration and ineffectiveness.

It is worth noting that the civil service has begun to give a higher priority to training both to reinforce specific management initiatives like the FMI and to prepare officials for future management responsibilities at the top levels as well as in middle management. The Management and Personnel Office has the main central role in promoting improvements in human resource management. To have a long-term impact it will need to devise a strategy that attracts extensive support within the civil service in a way that the early phases of the Efficiency Strategy did not do. The emphasis was on cutting back and eradicating waste and the effects on the civil service, in combination with the government's tough industrial relations and pay stance, were demotivating.

But, as business, exposed to the quicker-acting sanctions of the market place discovered in the 1970s and early 1980s, cutting back is only the first painful phase of a difficult process of readjustment in which long-term success depends on securing whole-hearted commitment at all levels. If cuts follow cuts, the goodwill and enthusiasm necessary to set a new course and manage change evaporates. An atmos-

phere of mistrust, suspicion and defensiveness prevails and organizational renewal does not progress. Even if the right conditions are
created a considerable investment in human resources is vital to ensure
that the difficult challenges ahead can be met successfully. Government
has a very long way to go in this field before it reaches the standards that
business experience shows are necessary to ensure the flexibility to cope
with rapid and continuing change.

Management by Direction, or Management by Design

The previous section proposed themes for a new mandate for the
Efficiency Strategy. These themes not only draw on what has been done
but also map out directions for future development. Although each can
be considered in isolation, it is important to see that there are some close
links among them which are imperfectly reflected in what has been done
and which should be taken into account more systematically in the
future to create a new agenda for public management reform.

Not surprisingly, given the priorities of Thatcherism, what has been
attempted so far has given priority to increasing cost-consciousness.
Savings of money and manpower are widely used as appropriate and
sufficient criteria of success. Improvements are expected to show
themselves in cuts and eliminating waste, duplication and overlap.
Organizational changes and management reforms have been proposed
and implemented mainly with greater economy in mind. Looking to the
future, more attention needs to be given to increasing adaptability and
flexibility. Government faces an increasingly unpredictable future and a
rapidly changing environment. Cutting the costs of existing activities
and pruning administrative deadwood is only a preliminary stage in the
process of dealing with the problems of rapid and discontinuous change.
Public organizations, individually and collectively, will need
management processes that embody adequate learning capacity.

Criteria of success need to be pitched at a higher level to allow for
change in operational goals and policies. Organizational effectiveness
depends on accommodating to and even anticipating emerging
problems and smoothing processes of change rather than merely
minimizing costs in achieving current objectives. Effectiveness means
redirecting efforts and energies into new channels rather than
concentrating them in existing ones. Having begun to take management
seriously and to overcome some of its earlier scepticism, the civil service
will now have to broaden its approach and pay more attention to the
design of the cultural and institutional framework within which
operational management takes place.

> If government is to learn to solve new public problems, it must also learn to
> create the systems for doing so and to discard the structures and mechanisms
> grown up around old problems. The need is not merely to cope with a

particular set of new problems, or to discard the organizational vestiges of a particular form of governmental activity which happen at present to be particularly cumbersome. It is to design and bring into being the institutional processes through which new problems can continually be confronted and old structures continually discarded. (Schon, 1971)

As Chapter 9 pointed out, lasting reforms are an unending sequence of temporary solutions. Improved public management must take account of this evolutionary requirement and must reduce attachment to particular structures and systems as permanent solutions to government's management problems. At the very least, it is clear that the Efficiency Strategy has moved beyond mere cost-cutting to exert a real influence on the culture of Whitehall and the thinking of the civil service. However, it has not yet grasped the nettle of taking responsibility for improving public management. The concept of management that the Efficiency Strategy has implanted in the existing culture might be termed 'management by direction'. It emphasizes tightly organized systems with clearly assigned responsibilities for achieving precisely defined operational goals. Management by direction casts civil servants in the roles of producers of results or implementers of pre-ordained policies. It fits neatly with conviction politics. It is congruent with the role culture traits of the culture of Whitehall which require individuals to fit into organizational roles and order their behaviour according to stable patterns and procedures (Handy, 1981). Role cultures value compliance and conformity with the existing framework. Senior civil servants whose career progression has involved fitting into a variety of different roles are familiar with the process of moving from job to job in this way. They adjust quickly to new demands because their attitudes to successive responsibilities are largely reactive. Hence, the producer role links the old culture of Whitehall, with its ambivalence about management responsibility, with the much richer concept of public management that will be needed in the future. But it is only a halfway house. The flexibility required to cope with uncertainty and facilitate innovation involves a further cultural shift to stimulate the development of competences in managing by design, over and above competences in managing by direction.

Management by design is a continuing responsibility for cultural and institutional adaptation at the interface between operational management and the political and constitutional context. It is where major issues of public policy and public organization interact, neither being subordinate to the other. It casts public managers in innovator and integrator roles, developing new policy proposals and mobilizing the networks of support necessary for their adoption and implementation. Management by design involves creating flexibility through organizational learning and adaptation within existing structures and providing the leadership to transcend the limits of the established framework, to redefine the rules of the game.

Management by design is a pro-active, initiating management style rather than a compliant, reactive style. Moving from managing by direction to managing by design requires major changes of attitude and outlook, not least in relation to questions of accountability. The framework of organizational accountability which civil servants have thus far taken for granted in their efforts to improve public management itself becomes the subject of management attention. Taking responsibility for the performance of a system includes at least taking a share in designing the system. The innovator and integrator roles move public management into the higher-level issues of designing and managing changes in systems of accountability and the criteria of effectiveness against which performance is judged.

The Conditions of Progress

At present, the future of public management reform is finely balanced. On the surface the pace of improvement has slowed and there is a certain ambivalence about what has been done. The merits of cutting public spending — in the light of the failure to do so — seem less attractive than claiming credit for increasing expenditure in electorally sensitive areas. In addition, large scale reforms like the FMI take time to implement and do not produce immediate results. Incumbent governments are not in a position to make political capital out of waste and inefficiency which their opponents could blame them for.

On the part of the civil service there is a growing feeling that not much more can be accomplished. Under the prevailing assumptions about the scope of public management much of the remaining work appears as simply tidying-up and fine-tuning. Limited managerial concepts lead to limited aspirations. Even if this does not amount to a Whitehall counter-revolution and an attempt to return to the status quo, it is potentially a serious limitation. It may be reinforced if the Efficiency Strategy is perceived as simply one component of Thatcherism. At the political level, there are some signs of development of all-party support for continuing efforts to advance the cause of improving public management. How far this is based on a full understanding of the task involved is difficult to assess.

What is clear is that if the Efficiency Strategy stops at this point it will fail to achieve lasting reforms. There is an urgent need to broaden the strategic framework of reform; to move positively to embrace management by design; and to build public management capabilities to ensure flexibility as well as cost-consciousness. This requires a capacity for leadership, not only in the political sphere but also among senior civil servants. A whole generation of senior civil servants will have to revise fundamental assumptions about its role. This investment in improving public management has its costs, but they are trivial compared with the social and economic costs of failing to cope with change. 'Adapt or die' is the message of evolution.

11

The Next Steps

Introduction

In 1988, six months after this book was first published, the government announced that it had accepted a scrutiny report from the Efficiency Unit, entitled 'Improving Management in Government: the Next Steps'. The report became known as the Ibbs Report (Ibbs, 1988) after Sir Robin Ibbs, the then head of the unit, but was actually signed by the civil servants who wrote it — Kate Jenkins, Karen Caines and Andrew Jackson. The report was the culmination of a stocktaking operation on management reform in the civil service. This evaluation had begun in November 1986, but after completion, the report hung fire for almost a year, while it was debated inside government, and was then published. The purpose of this concluding chapter is to explain and assess the significance of 'Next Steps' in the progress of public management.

The core of the analysis was that the traditions of the civil service made it very hard to bring about delegated budgeting — the model on which the Financial Management Initiative was based — so progress in improving management had been patchy, and sometimes slow. One source of problems was the managerial inexperience of top civil servants: a scrutiny informant had used the memorable phrase — 'the golden route to the top is through policy not through management'. This has led top civil servants to focus on policy support to ministers in parliament, to the detriment of their managerial responsibilities. What pressure there was on departments to improve value for money tended to concentrate on the input/cost control side and neglect quality of service/outcome issues. In addition to this, despite the size and diversity of civil service operations, it had been governed by a single rule book of terms and conditions — 'structured to fit everything in general and nothing in particular'. And since the rules were centrally prescribed, the task of changing them was seen to be impossible for any one manager or even one department.

To overcome this administrative sclerosis, the report recommended three main priorities, to be pursued with vigour in service delivery, in the departments and in the central departments of Whitehall, the Treasury and the Cabinet Office.

1. 'The work of each department must be organised in a way which focuses on the job to be done; the systems and structures must enhance the effective delivery of policies and services.'

2. 'The management of each department must ensure that their staff

have the relevant experience and skills needed to do the tasks that are essential to effective government.'

3. 'There must be a real and sustained pressure on and within each department for continuous improvement in the value for money obtained in the delivery of policies and services.'

In order to focus on the job to be done, the scrutiny team recommended that 'agencies' should be established to carry out the executive functions of government within a policy and resources framework set by a department. The report did not specify whether the agencies should be within or outside the civil service. But, either way, they should have a well-defined framework, setting out the policy, budget, specific targets and results to be achieved. The main strategic control should lie with ministers and permanent secretaries, who set the policy objectives and budgets, but provided management operated within that strategic direction, they should be left as free as possible to manage. They should have the freedom to 'recruit, pay, grade and structure in the most effective way'.

The head of the agency should have personal responsibility for results, and should be accountable for their achievement, preferably direct to the Public Accounts Committee as Accounting Officer. The report remarked that this personal responsibility has implications for the doctrine of ministerial responsibility to parliament, but made no actual recommendations other than that legislation should be considered on this topic.

The task of the department in focusing on the job to be done should be to clarify the policy and resources framework, so that whether they are directly responsible for service delivery, or only able to influence it, they will no longer proceed by detailed prescription, but by a rigorous statement of strategic objectives and resource commitments. All of this should be tailored to the job to be done. This change, however, would fall apart unless 'the inevitable political crises are handled well'. It would be up to the department to safeguard the effectiveness of the agency while handling crises. In order to improve their capability to do their policy work with the precision about outcomes and resources that is required, departments would also need the same kind of flexibility on staffing as agencies.

It was further assumed that once these changes were in train, the role of the centre of government would change, to encompass the allocation of resources, the application of pressure on departments to improve value for money, the provision of an overview on change in the Civil Service, and the policing of essential rules on public service propriety. In other words, it would lose many of the detailed controls it has traditionally used.

One of the dilemmas of change is that though a shift in system requires the centre to relinquish the detail of control, it inevitably has a leading role in the strategy for implementation. The centre will only relinquish the constraints it holds if it has confidence that freedoms will be used responsibly. 'Centralise in order to decentralise': while other parties have a role to play in bringing in the new order — ministers, parliament, civil servants themselves — the report recognises the crucial role played by the central departments, and particularly the Treasury, in the development of this initiative. The dangers were apparent from what is known about the behind-the-scenes struggle which intervened between the report's production and publication almost a year later. The Treasury opposed its publication, and only with the greatest reluctance accepted the decision to go ahead with the Next Steps programme.

In order to make the most of the political clout which the Efficiency Unit team were able to muster behind the message of the report, they recommended that project management for implementation be done by someone at the highest level in the Civil Service, someone who, having made it to Permanent Secretary, would obviously know how to handle the Whitehall infighting that would take place as soon as the initiative proceeded beyond the generalities of broad principle.

The appointment of a Treasury official, Peter Kemp, as permanent secretary and project manager, was seen in some quarters as a clever move on the part of the Treasury — their Trojan horse who would in practice ensure that their power base remained intact. Experience has shown, however, that Mr Kemp does work for the devolution of detailed control, from the Treasury and within departments.

What Has Happened

A small Next Steps Unit was established in February 1988 in the Office of the Minister for the Civil Service, the department which had replaced the larger Management and Personnel Office. Under Peter Kemp as the project manager, the unit worked with organisations within government which had been identified in the Prime Minister's announcement about Next Steps as the first wave for consideration as agencies.

The initial work concentrated on the clear specification of the service requirement from the parent department to the agency, established in a contract-like document called a framework agreement. The framework agreement was only 'contract-like' because it was explicitly outside the remit of judicial review, being about administrative arrangements between two parts of a government department. In this respect, the Next Steps initiative differs markedly from the Swedish case, where agency status is underpinned by a framework of public law which backs up a genuinely contractual relationship. Without the prospect of judicial review, it is easier to fudge the specification and the measures of performance in the 'contract', but much of the Unit's energy has gone into establishing that framework as clearly as possible.

The first organisation to become an agency was the Vehicle Inspectorate, the Department of Transport's arm for testing heavy goods vehicles and for licensing garages which test cars for roadworthiness. The new agency was headed by Ron Oliver, who had also been in charge before agency status, but who now had the brand new title of Chief Executive to his name. The original Ibbs Report had not used the term at all, but at some stage in the development of the initiative some clever marketing brain had added this high profile label to the job of managing the agency. 'Chief Executive' carries with it connotations of independence and entrepreneurialism, and may have significantly affected the 'management of meaning' in the agency initiative.

The framework agreement spelled out as clearly as possible the relationship between the parent department and the agency. Attached to it was a business plan which set specific performance targets for the coming year, and a corporate plan which looked at the rather longer term future. Clarity of specification of performance measurement required that the potential agency's operational systems of cost control were robust enough to provide the right information. No organisation could become an agency without having done this spadework. The first few agencies were all, for one reason or another, well down this road. The Vehicle Inspectorate, for example, had earlier been on track for privatisation, and much systems development work was done in preparation for that. Her Majesty's Stationery Office, the third agency, had already been operating on a trading fund basis, a form of financial control based on quasi-commercial criteria.

Therefore, the early framework agreements did not involve much relaxation in the level of detailed controls. Delegations from the central departments to line departments, and from them to their agencies, remained much the same as they had been before agencies had been thought of. It seemed that specification had to come first, before greater delegation could be considered. As the initiative rolled on, battles were fought for particular freedoms. One example is the right to pay a small bonus based, not on individual performance, but on group performance, which the Vehicle Inspectorate had wanted. After many months of negotiation, incidentally diverting the energy and attention of senior management from their operational task, agreement was reached and at the time of writing — August 1990 — the first group bonus has just been paid.

Operational tasks range from the less-political to the highly politically sensitive. It is obviously easier to be specific about service requirements at the less-political end of the spectrum. Ambiguity is the stock in trade of politics, and being specific about politically sensitive services tests the agency model to its limits — and perhaps to destruction. As the process of setting up agencies rolled forward, it was clear that the easy apolitical targets were being picked off first. While no agency could ever be completely outside the realm of politics — inspecting for roadworthiness, for example, is done in the name of the public interest and carries costs and penalties for those being inspected — the early agencies presented relatively little political challenge to specification.

At the time of writing, 33 organizational units have become executive agencies. They range in size from several small agencies, such as the Queen Elizabeth II Conference Centre, and Veterinary Medicines Directorate, each with 50 staff, to the Employment Service with 35,000 and the Land Registry with 11,000. Their functions cover a range that includes regulatory activity, professional research services, commercial activities and various mixtures of the three. Table 1 lists the agencies which have been established, and indicates their size and their vesting day.

The most noteworthy of these agencies is clearly the Employment Service, not only because of its size, but also because of its political sensitivity. Constituents of every Member of Parliament use the services of this agency. Not only are they helped to find employment, they are also 'encouraged' to do so, and in certain cases, encouraged against their will. We are therefore in the heartland of the issues of individual rights that provides the raw material for parliamentary interest, and on which ministers are most reluctant to let go of the detail. The Employment Service achieved agency status rather later than was originally planned, which perhaps indicates the degree of difficulty with which a resolution of the framework agreement was reached.

The severest test of the agency concept is the Department of Social Security's Benefits Agency, which has the same direct impact on constituents as the Employment Service, but whose coverage is greater. Those who use the services of this planned agency include every citizen at one time or another in their life. Whereas the rights of the unemployed may be disregarded by an uncaring society, everyone's grandmother uses the Benefits Agency. Add to that two further factors — the Benefits Agency will have 70,000 staff, and be twice as big as any other agency, and the fact that the more it improves its quality of service, and therefore its take-up rate for benefits, the bigger the impact on public expenditure. These factors together make the Benefits Agency the case that will test the model to its utmost. Plans appear to be on target to take the service into an agency on 1 April 1991. It is likely that agency status will be achieved, but it remains to be seen whether the actual change in organisational process accords with the theology.

Agencies and Accountability

The parliamentary Select Committee on the Treasury and Civil Service continued to play a significant role in the process of management change.

TABLE 1: *Next Steps Executive Agencies Established as of 25 July 1990*

Executive Agencies	Date of Establishment	Staff numbers
Building Research Establishment	02.04.90	650
Central Office of Information	05.04.90	750
Central Veterinary Laboratory	02.04.90	550
Civil Service College	06.06.89	200
Companies House	03.10.88	1,150
Department of the Registers of Scotland	06.04.90	950
Driver and Vehicle Licensing Agency	02.04.90	5,250
Driving Standards Agency	02.04.90	2,000
Employment Service	02.04.90	35,000
Historic Royal Palaces	01.10.89	350
Her Majesty's Stationery Office	14.12.88	3,250
Hydrographic Office	06.04.90	900
Information Technology Service Agency	02.04.90	3,000
Insolvency Service	21.03.90	1,400
Intervention Board for Agricultural Produce	02.04.90	850
Laboratory of the Government Chemist	30.10.89	300
Land Registry	02.07.90	11,000
Meteorological Office	02.04.90	2,450
National Physical Laboratory	03.07.90	800
National Weights and Measures Laboratory	18.04.89	50
Natural Resources Institute	02.04.90	450
Occupational Health Service	02.04.90	100
Ordnance Survey	01.05.90	2,600
Patent Office	01.03.90	1,150
QEII Conference Centre	06.07.89	50
Radiocommunications Agency	02.04.90	450
Resettlement Agency	24.05.89	550
Royal Mint	02.04.90	950
Training & Employment Agency (NICS)	02.04.90	1,600
Vehicle Certification Agency	02.04.90	50
Vehicle Inspectorate	01.08.88	1,600
Veterinary Medicines Directorate	02.04.90	50
Warren Spring Laboratory	20.04.89	300
33 in number		80,750

It has produced three reports so far, each making different contributions
to the change. The first report (House of Commons, 1987/88) accepted
the principles behind the agency initiative, and allayed fears that the
formal distancing of ministers from the detail of the management of
services, even though only a recognition of the actual status quo, might
have so offended parliamentary *amour propre* that progress would have
been hampered. The report went further in recommending changes to the
system of accountability, so that as far as possible agency chief executives
should be the Accounting Officers, responsible to the Public Accounts

Committee of the House for the stewardship of public money in their operational control. Responsibility and accountability go hand in hand, so in strengthening accountability, the Committee were proposing to strengthen the chief executive's responsibility *vis à vis* the department.

The second report (House of Commons, 1988/89) established the principle that the Committee would take on a continuous monitoring role with regard to the initiative, and therefore not allow it to die a quiet death. The third report (House of Commons, 1989/90) put forward the notion that the agency approach was of itself politically neutral. The greater specification of strategic objectives and the measurement of their achievement were regarded as being about the modernisation of public management, rather than being umbilically tied to one particular ideology. The test of this idea will be when a different government comes to power, and the committee does not necessarily provide a representative view.

The issue which will most test the acceptability of agencies to a different government will be flexibility in staffing. The Treasury was opposed to the initiative from the beginning because they feared that it would involve a loss of control over public expenditure, particularly in the field of public sector pay which is the major area of expenditure. The Treasury appears to have shifted on this issue. It now believes that moving away from national pay bargaining and increasingly reflecting regional labour markets will reduce public expenditure. Carefully, but perceptibly, pay policy is changing. The public sector unions have made the same calculations, and do not like what they see: many of their members will lose, relatively speaking, by a move to flexible pay. Those who will gain, however, are unlikely to be willing to support a collective line opposing these developments. The position of the unions on agencies has moved as the fundamental economics of the situation have become clear. Whether they would be in a position with a new government to end pay flexibility is beyond the scope of this chapter to discuss.

One final development to note is the passage of the Agency Trading Fund Act, 1989. In extending the provisions of the 1973 Trading Fund Act, it created the legal framework for greater variation in financial regimes, allowing more flexibility in the use of funds. There were a number of additional delegations, in finance and personnel, which occurred without the need for legislation.

What Has Not Happened
We should not neglect some of the things that have not happened however. Familiarity with the Ibbs Report breeds myopia. Carefully re-reading it, two and a half years after its publication, reveals all sorts of surprises, including recommendations which have been quietly forgotten. The report was entitled 'Improving Management in Government', not just improving

the operational management aspect of government. Conspicuous by its absence is any sustained attempt to change the way that core departments do their own work. The challenge to their traditions is at least the equivalent of the challenge facing operational managers. Preparing the strategic specification of policy, and then negotiating its implementation calls for skills of a new order. No department seems to be taking a strong line on this, and the project manager's attention seems to be directed almost solely at the task of getting agencies into shape, and ticking them off on a list.

It is particularly important to enhance the capabilities in the policy divisions of core departments, since their responsibilities go well beyond intra-organisational concepts of good management. There is a danger that a mechanistic concentration on the creation of individual agencies will neglect the larger inter-organisational dimensions of public management.

Management Innovation, 'Managerialism' and Management Theories

The further development of public management reform requires creative thinking for two basic reasons. First, there is a well-established political science tradition of criticising from the touchline and offering *ex post* explanations of why things have gone wrong, without venturing into the more difficult and risky areas of prescribing how to make things go right. In particular, there is still quite deep-seated resistance to management ideas among academic commentators and researchers in political science and public administration to what is often disparagingly referred to as 'managerialism'. Managerialism confines management to the reduction of costs, the pursuit of economy and perhaps operational efficiency without venturing into the wider and more difficult domain of promoting effectiveness.

Up to a point, this is understandable. One function of academic work is to observe and criticize what has been done. But, especially in the field of public management, there is a wider function to perform in the development of new concepts and methods. Olympian detachment is not a real option, because all management theories are prescriptive. They relate how things are organized to some criteria of performance or policy objectives. 'Managerialist' critics are, explicitly, saying that things should be done differently even if they are diffident about publicly expressing the views they espouse.

The second reason is that the development of new concepts and methods in public management is especially important now, because we are probably reaching the limits of imitation of business management by government. There are good grounds for hypothesising that the Next Steps programme of agency development will be the final phase of public management reform which will be able to rely upon more or less accepted business management ideas. As we pointed out earlier in this chapter, it is already becoming apparent that many management problems in government fall outside the scope of the agency idea; the linkage between operational and strategic management; the impact of political sensitivity on managerial autonomy; the implications for public accountability and the role of the centre; these are some of the questions that are certain to demand clearer and more imaginative answers than the implementation of the Next Steps programme has so far produced.

In the future, public management will have to develop through innovation rather than imitation. Instead of looking no further than the application of currently available business management ideas it will have to construct new concepts that fit the diverse needs of government. Without fresh thought and critical evaluation of reforms that have been introduced it is very probable that development will slow to a halt. Running a business does not represent a universally applicable set of prescriptions and practices.

One of the most significant ways in which public management is not 'like a business' is in the importance and variety of forms of public accountability. Since, as we noted in Chapter 1, public accountability is the other side of the coin of management responsibility, efforts to delegate responsibility will exert pressures for change in the antiquated and, often, inappropriate mechanism of public accountability currently in operation. These pressures for change were partially but inadequately acknowledged in the Next Steps report. It is not enough to make marginal changes in current practice so that civil servants feel more directly exposed to Parliamentary scrutiny. Pouring new managerial wine into old accountability bottles may have explosive consequences. Part of the future agenda of public management will be designing accountability systems.

An important illustration of the problems can be drawn from the various attempts to improve the management of professionals and professional organizations in government. Getting the best out of professionals depends on designing organizations that are not hidebound by bureaucratic rules or dominated by business budgetary control systems. But such organizations should not be immune from management direction or accountability. In both respects, they should be subject to processes that reinforce rather than undermine professional commitment. A system of accountability that constantly overrides professional peer group criteria will produce poor results. Going against the grain of professional commitment will lead to demoralization and conflict between managers and professionals. Already there are clear signs of these problems arising across the whole of government, notably in education, the health service and the social services. Public management in the 1990s will need a wider set of models and a correspondingly wide set of forms of public accountability to assure effective and responsible performance.

Another large and important area in which public management must depend on innovation rather than imitation is in coping with the macro problems of steering networks of organizations. It is a serious limitation of the Next Steps programme that the concern with creating agencies has, once more, pushed the management of organizational interdependence into the background. Perhaps the distinguishing feature of public management is that good results depend on cooperation among many organizations with interdependent functions. Despite the current emphasis on introducing a business ethos, it is intensive and sustained interorganizational cooperation that is the hallmark of success in public management rather than the single-minded pursuit of individual organizational objectives. The importance of organizational coordination among ministries, services, levels of government rarely appears as a main priority or point of discussion about management reform. But it is rarely absent from stories of government failure or disasters which hit the headlines. Lack of coordination between the Ministries of Agriculture and Health lay behind the 'salmonella-in-eggs' scare. Agriculture and health along with food manufacturers and farmers are all implicated in the case of 'mad cow disease'. Any policy issue related to the European Community activates a network of organizational relationships within British government and beyond. Interorganizational coordination and the management of interdependence raise different issues from the effective management of individual organizations. Public interests and management problems often arise at the interface between organizations where different interests and priorities clash. Without effective management of these conflicts there is not an integrated framework for managing individual organizations.

This emphasis on macro problems and the management of interorganizational relations has important implications for the profile of the public manager of the future. Whereas the management-by-objectives tradition which underlies the agency concept portrays the public manager delivering the goods within a set framework, an interorganizational perspective places more emphasis on managing boundary transactions and adapting to the changing needs of the external environment. Public managers will require the more political managerial skills essential to adjust organizational activities to the larger political context.

As a final observation, it seems certain now that the idea of public management has come to stay. But, the Next Steps programme is certainly not the last word. The agency concept is a useful, rather than dramatic advance, relying as it does on imitating much that has gone before in the field of business management. The really interesting prospect is for a shift to innovation which will address the distinctive and difficult problems that contemporary governments face. Perhaps, in the 1990s, we will see the realization that it is government that has the difficult and interesting management problems and government will become the forcing-house of management innovation.

References

Ibbs, Sir Robin (1988) *Improving Management in Government: The Next Steps.* London: HMSO.

House of Commons Civil (1988) *Service Management Reform: The Next Steps.* 494, 1987/88.

House of Commons (1989) *Developments in the Next Steps Programme.* 348, 1988/89.

House of Commons (1990) *Progress in the Next Steps Initiative.* 481, 1989/90.

References

Abrahamson, Mark, (1967), *The Professional in the Organization*. Chicago: Rand McNally & Co.

Aldrich, Howard and David A. Whetten (1981) 'Organization Sets, Action Sets and Networks: Making the Most of Simplicity', in Nystrom and Starbuck (1981), Vol. 1, pp. 385−408.

Allen, David (1981) 'Raynerism: Strengthening Civil Service Management', *RIPA Report* 24 (Winter).

Allison, Graham, T. (1979) 'Public and Private Management: Are They Fundamentally Alike in all Unimportant Respects?', Public Management Research Conference, Brookings Institution, Washington, 1979; reprinted in James L. Perry and Kenneth L. Kraemer (1983) *Public Management: Public and Private Perspectives*, pp.72−92, Palo Alto, Cal.: Mayfield.

Ansoff, Igor, Roger Declerck and Robert Hayes (1976) *From Strategic Planning to Strategic Management*. New York: John Wiley.

Argyris, Chris (1970) *Intervention Theory and Method*. Reading, Mass.: Addison-Wesley.

Argyris, Chris and Donald A. Schon (1974) *Organizational Learning*. Reading, Mass.: Addison-Wesley.

Barker, Anthony (1982) *Quangos in Britain*. London: Macmillan.

Beckhard, Richard (1972) 'Optimizing Team Building Efforts', Journal of Contemporary Business 1 (3): 23−32.

Beckhard, Richard and Reuben T. Harris (1977) *Organization Transitions*. Reading Mass.: Addison-Wesley.

Berle, Adolf A. and Gardiner C. Meanes (1932) *The Modern Corporation and Private Property*. New York: Macmillan.

Berman, P. (1980) 'Thinking About Programmed and Adaptive Implementation: Matching Strategies to Situations', in Helen M. Ingram and Dean E. Mann (eds) *Why Policies Succeed or Fail*. London and Beverly Hills: Sage.

Berry, Dean and Christopher Lorenz (1983) 'Why Strategy Boutiques are Changing Tack', *Financial Times* (12 December).

Beyer, Janice M. (1981) 'Ideologies, Values and Decision-Making in Organizations', in Nystrom and Starbuck (1981), Vol. 2, pp. 166−202.

Blake, Robert R. and Jane S. Mouton (1978) 'Strategies of Consultation', in Robert T. Golembiewski and William Keddy (eds) *Organisational Development in Public Administration*. New York: Marcel Dekker.

Bozeman, Barry, and Jeffrey D. Straussman (1982) 'Shrinking Budgets and the Shrinkage of Budget Theory', *Public Administration Review* 42 (November-December 1982): 509−15.

Box, George E.P. and Norman R. Draper (1969) *Evolutionary Operation*. New York: John Wiley.

Bradley, David (1983) 'Management in Government: A Note on Some Recent Experience in the Department of the Environment', in Gray and Jenkins (1983): 37−45.

Cameron, Kim S. and David A. Whetten (eds) (1983) *Organizational Effectiveness: A Comparison of Multiple Models*. New York: Academic Press.

Chandler, Alfred D. (1962) *Strategy and Structure*. Cambridge, Mass.: MIT Press.

Chapman, Leslie (1978) *Your Disobedient Servant*. London: Chatto and Windus.

Chapman, Richard A. (1983) 'The Rise and Fall of CSD', *Policy and Politics* 2(1): 41–61.

Chapman, Richard A. (1984) 'Administrative Culture and Personnel Management: The British Civil Service in the 1980s', *Teaching Public Administration* IV 1: 1–41.

Christie, Campbell (1982) 'The Real Rayner Targets', *RIPA Report* 3(1).

Coates, Dudley (1985) 'Financial Management Development: A View from MAFF', paper given to PAC Conference on Issues in Policy and Administration, University of York.

Cooper, Sir Frank (1983) 'Freedom to Manage in Government', RIPA Winter Lecture Series, March.

Dahrendorf, Ralf (1982) *On Britain*. London: British Broadcasting Corporation.

Department of Employment, Department of Health and Social Security (1981) *Payment of Benefits to Unemployed People*. London: HMSO.

Department of the Environment (1979) *The Provision of Management Information to Ministers*. London: DoE.

Department of Industry (1980) *Administration of Regional Development Grants*. London: DOE.

Department of Trade and Industry (1985) *Burdens on Business: Report of a Scrutiny of Administrative and Legislative Requirements*. London: HMSO.

Deutsch, Karl W. (1966) *The Nerves of Government*. New York: Free Press.

Deutsch, Karl W. (1981) 'The Crisis of the State', *Government and Opposition* 16(3): 331–43.

Dror, Yehezkel (1984) 'Facing Momentous Choices', *International Review of Administrative Sciences* 2: 97–106.

Dror, Yehezkel (1985) 'Options for Increasing Innovativeness', paper given at a colloquium on Strengthening Innovativeness in Public Management, Maastricht (NL), European Institute of Public Administration.

Dunbar, Roger L.M. (1970) 'Budgeting for Control', *Administrative Science Quarterly* 16: 88–96.

Dunbar, Roger L.M. (1981) 'Designs for Organizational Control', in Nystrom and Starbuck (1981): 85–115.

Dunn, Edgar S. (1971) *Economic and Social Development*. Baltimore: Johns Hopkins University Press.

Dunsire, Andrew (1978) *Control in a Bureaucracy: The Execution Process*. Oxford: Martin Robertson.

Efficiency Unit (1985) *Making Things Happen: A report on the implementation of Government efficiency scrutinies*. London: HMSO.

Etzioni-Halevy, Eva (1985) *Bureaucracy and Democracy*. London: Routledge & Kegan Paul.

Flamholtz, Eric G., T.K. Das and Anne S. Tsui (1985) 'Towards an Integrative Framework of Organizational Control', *Accounting, Organizations and Society* 10(1): 35–50.

Flaxen, W. (1983) 'The Government Statistical Service and its management', *Management in Government* (1).

Forsyth, M. (1983) *The Myths of Privatization*. London: Adam Smith Institute.

Fry, Geoffrey K. (1981) *The Administrative 'Revolution' in Whitehall: A Study of the Politics of Administrative Change in British Central Government Since the 1950s*. London: Croom Helm.

Fulton, Lord (1968) *The Civil Service: Report of the Committee 1966-68*, Cmnd. 3638. London: HMSO.

Galbraith, Jay (1973) *Designing Complex Organizations*. Reading, Mass.: Addison Wesley.

Garrett, John (1981) *Managing the Civil Service*. London: Heinemann.

Goodman, Paul S. and J. M. Pennings (1977) *New Perspectives on Organizational Effectiveness*. San Francisco: Jossey Bass.

Gowler, Dan and Karen Legge (1983) 'The Meaning of Management and the Management of Meaning: A View from Social Anthropology', in Michael J. Earl (ed.) *Perspectives on Management*. Oxford: Oxford University Press.

Gray, Andrew and Bill Jenkins (eds) (1983) *Policy Analysis and Evaluation in British Government*. London: Royal Institute of Public Administration.

Gray, Andrew and Bill Jenkins (1985) *Administrative Politics in British Government*. Brighton: Harvester Press.

Griffiths, Sir Roy (1983) *NHS Management Inquiry Report to the Secretary of State, DHSS*. London: HMSO.

Gunn, Lewis A. (1985) 'From Public Policy to Public Management', paper presented to PAC Conference on Issues in Policy and Administration, University of York.

Hall, Richard H. and Robert E. Quinn (eds) (1983), *Organizational Theory and Public Policy*. Beverly Hills and London: Sage.

Handy, Charles (1981) *Understanding Organizations*. London: Penguin Books.

Hanf, K. and F.W. Scharpf (eds) (1978) *Interorganizational Policy-Making*. London: Sage.

Harrison, Roger (1972) 'Understanding Your Organization's Character', *Harvard Business Review* (May–June): 119–28.

Hartley, Keith (1984) 'Why contract Out?' in *Contracting Out in the Public Sector*. London: Royal Institute of Public Administration.

Heald, David (1983) *Public Expenditure*. Oxford: Martin Robertson.

Heclo, Hugh and Aaron Wildavsky (1981) *The Private Government of Public Money*. London: Macmillan.

Hedberg, Bo L.T. (1981) 'How Organizations Learn and Unlearn', in Nystrom and Starbuck (1981), Vol. 1, pp. 3–27.

Hedberg, Bo, L.T., Paul Nystrom and William H. Starbuck, (1976) 'Camping on Seesaws: Prescriptions for a Self-designing Organization', *Administrative Science Quarterly* 21: 41–65.

Hedberg, Bo and Sten Jonsson (1978), 'Designing Semi-confusing Information Systems for Organizations in Changing Environments', *Accounting, Organizations and Society* 3(1): 47–64.

Heseltine, Michael (1980) 'Ministers and Management in Whitehall', *Management Services in Government* 35: 61–8.

Hill, C.W.L. (1985) 'Oliver Williamson and the M-Form Firm: A Cultural Review', *Journal of Economic Issues* XIX (3): 731–51.

Hirschman, Albert O. (1979) *Exit, Voice and Loyalty*. Cambridge Mass.: Harvard University Press.

Hofstede, G.H. (1967) *The Game of Budget Control*. Assen, the Netherlands: Koninklijke Van Gorcum.

Hood, Christopher (1978) 'The Crown Agents' Affair', *Public Administration* 56: 297–303.

Hopwood, Anthony (1983) 'Accounting and the Pursuit of Efficiency', in Anthony Hopwood and Cyril Tomkins (eds), *Issues in Public Sector Accounting*. Oxford: Philip Allan.

Hoskyns, Sir John (1982) 'Westminster and Whitehall: An Outsider's View', Institute for Fiscal Studies, Annual Lecture.

House of Commons (1966) *Report of the Estimates Committee on the Government Statistical Service*. London: HMSO.

House of Commons (1982a) *Efficiency and Effectiveness in the Civil Service, Third Report of the Treasury and Civil Service Select Committee*, HC 236, 8 March. London: HMSO.

House of Commons (1982b) *Efficiency and Effectiveness in the Civil Service, Government Comments on the Third Report from the Treasury and Civil Service Select Committee*, 1981–82, Cmnd 8616, September. London: HMSO.

House of Commons (1986) *Civil Servants and Ministers: Duties and Responsibilities, Treasury and Civil Service Committee, Seventh Report*. London: HMSO.

Howells, David (1981) 'Marks and Spencer and the Civil Service: A Comparison of Culture and Methods', *Public Administration* 59 (Autumn).

Janis, Irving L. (1972) *Victims of Groupthink*. Boston: Houghton Mifflin.

Janis, Irving L. (1985) 'Sources of Error in Strategic Decision-Making', in Johannes Pennings (ed.) *Organization Strategy and Change*, pp. 157–97. San Francisco: Jossey Bass, pp. 157–197.

Jarratt, Sir Alex (1985) *Report of the Steering Committee for Efficiency Studies in Universities*. London: Committee of Vice Chancellors and Principals, March.

Jenkins, Kate, Brian Morris, Charlotte Caplan and Les Metcalfe (1984) *Consultancy Inspection and Review Capabilities in Government: Efficiency Unit Report to the Prime Minister*. London: HMSO.

Jennergren, L. Peter (1981) 'Decentralization in Organizations', in Nystrom and Starbuck (1981), Vol. 2, pp. 39–59.

Johnson, Nevil (1977) *In Search of the Constitution*. London: Methuen.

Johnson, Nevil (1982) 'A Triangular Affair: Quangos, Ministers and MPs', in A. Barker (ed.) *Quangos in Britain*, pp. 34–43. London: Macmillan.

Johnson, Nevil (1983) 'Management in Government', in Michael J. Earl (1982) *Perspectives on Management*. Oxford: Oxford University Press.

Joint Management Unit (1985) *Policy Work and the FMI*. London: HMSO.

Judge, David (1981) 'Specialists and Generalists in British Central Government: a political debate', *Public Administration* (Spring).

Kamens, David H. (1977) 'Legitimating Myths and Educational Organization: The Relationship Between Organizational Ideology and Formal Structure', *American Sociological Review* 42: 208–19.

Kanter, Rosabeth Moss (1984) *The Change Masters*. London: George Allen & Unwin.

Kay, John A. and Z. Aubrey Silberston (1984) 'The New Industrial Policy — Privatization and Competition', *Midland Bank Review* (Spring): 8–16.

Kay, John A. and D.J. Thompson (1986) 'Privatization: A Policy in Search of a Rationale', *Economic Journal* 96 (March): 18–32.

Kellner, Peter and Lord Crowther-Hunt (1980) *The Civil Servants: An Investigation into Britain's Ruling Class*. London: Macdonald Futura.

King, Anthony (1973) 'Ideas, Institutions and the Policies of Governments: A Comparative Analysis', *British Journal of Political Science* 3: 291–313.

Knipscheer, Jan (1985) 'Contracting Out to the Private Sector', in Jacques Pelkmans and Martijn van Nie (eds) *Privatization and Deregulation: The European Debate*, pp. 99–108. Maastricht (NL): European Institute of Public Administration.

Kuhn, Thomas S. (1962) *The Structure of Scientific Revolutions*. Chicago: University of Chicago Press.

Landau, Martin (1973) 'On the Concept of a Self-Correcting Organization', *Public*

Administration Review 33: 533–42.

Landau, Martin and Russel Stout Jr (1979) 'To Manage is Not to Control: Or the Folly of Type II Errors', *Public Administration Review* (March/April): 148–56.

Lawler, Edward E. (1976) 'Control Systems in Organizations', in Marvin D. Dunnette (ed) *Handbook of Industrial and Organizational Psychology*, pp. 1247–91. Chicago: Rand McNally.

Lawrence, Paul R. and Jay W. Lorsch (1967) *Organization and Environment*. Cambridge, Mass.: Graduate School of Business Administration, Harvard University.

Leavitt, Harold (1983) 'Management and Management Education in the West: What Right and What Wrong?', *London Business School Journal* VIII(1): 18–23.

Levitt, Malcolm and M. Joyce (1984) 'Public Expenditure, The Next Ten Years', NIESR Discussion Paper, 76. London: NIESR.

Lewis, David (1984) 'Improving Implementation', Ch. 12 in David Lewis and Helen Wallace (eds) *Policies into Practice: National and International Case Studies in Implementation*, pp. 203–26. London: Heinemann Educational Books.

Likierman, Andrew (1982) 'Management Information for Ministers: The MINIS System in the Department of the Environment', *Public Administration* 60: 127–42.

Likierman, Andrew and Susan Bloomfield (1986) 'Public Expenditure Control in the 1980s', London Business School, *Economic Outlook* (June): 23–36.

Lindblom, Charles E. (1965) *The Intelligence of Democracy*. New York: Free Press.

Mackenzie, W.J.M. (1978) *Political Identity*. Harmondsworth: Penguin.

Mackenzie, W.J.M. and J.W. Grove (1957) *Central Administration in Britain*. London: Longman.

Mackenzie, W.J.M. (1967) *Politics and Social Science*. Harmondsworth: Penguin Books.

March, James G. (1974) 'The Technology of Foolishness', in Harold Leavitt, Lawrence Pinfield and Eugene Webb (eds) *Organizations of the Future*. New York: Praeger.

March, James G. and Johan P. Olsen (1983) 'Organizing Political Life: What Administrative Reorganization Tells Us About Government', *American Political Science Review* 77: 281–96.

March, James G. and Johan P. Olsen (1984) 'The New Institutionalism: Organizational Factors in Political Life', *American Political Science Review* 78: 734–49.

Mayne, John F. (1982) 'Management Audit in the Ministry of Defence', *Management in Government* 373: 138–46.

McCann, Morgan W. (1977) 'Making Sense with Nonsense: Helping Frames of Reference Clash', in Paul C. Nystrom and William H. Starbuck (eds) *Prescriptive Models of Organizations*, pp. 111–23. Amsterdam: North Holland.

McCosh, Andrew M., Rahman Mawdudur and Michael J. Earl (1981) *Developing Managerial Information Systems*. London: Macmillan.

Melville, Sir Ronald and Sir Anthony Burney (1973) *The Use of Accountants in the Civil Service*. London: Civil Service Department.

Metcalfe, Les (1974) 'Systems Models, Economic Models and the Causal Texture of Organizational Environments: An Approach to Macro-organization Theory', *Human Relations* 27: 639–63.

Metcalfe, Les (1981) 'Designing Precarious Partnerships', in Nystrom and Starbuck (1981), Vol.1.

Metcalfe, Les (1982) 'Self-Regulation, Crisis Management and Preventive Medicine: The Evolution of UK Bank Supervision', *Journal of Management Studies* 19(1): 75–90.

Metcalfe, Les and Will McQuillan (1977) 'Managing Turbulence', in Nystrom and

Starbuck (eds), *Prescriptive Models of Organizations*, pp. 7–23. New York: North-Holland.

Metcalfe, Les and Sue Richards (1984a) 'Raynerism and Efficiency in Government', in Anthony Hopwood and Cyril Tomkins, *Issues in Public Sector Accounting*. Oxford: Philip Allen.

Metcalfe, Les and Sue Richards (1984b) 'The Impact of the Efficiency Strategy: Political Clout or Cultural Change?', *Public Administration* (Winter).

Metcalfe, Les and Sue Richards (1985) 'Evolving Public Management Cultures', paper presented at European Consortium for Political Research Joint Sessions, Barcelona.

Meyer, John W. and Brian Rowan (1977) 'Institutionalized Organizations: Formal Structure as Myth and Ceremony , *American Journal of Sociology* 83(2): 340–63.

Mintzberg, Henry (1973) *The Nature of Managerial Work*. New York: Harper and Row.

Mintzberg, Henry (1982) 'A Note on that Dirty Word "Efficiency", *Interfaces* 12: 101–5.

Mintzberg, Henry (1983) *Structure in Fives: Designing Effective Organizations*. Englewood Cliffs, NJ: Prentice-Hall.

Mitroff, Ian I. and Louis R. Pondy (1974) 'On the Organization of Inquiry: A Comparison of Some Radically Different Approaches to Policy Analysis', *Public Administration Review* (September/October): 471–79.

Mueller, Denis C. (1976) 'Public Choice: A Survey, *Journal of Economic Literature* 24(2).

Nash, Philip (1981) 'We Tried Before But Without the Clout', *Management Services in Government* 36(3): 137–44.

National Audit Office (1985) *Efficiency Scrutinies in DHSS*. London: HMSO.

Nelson, Richard (1974) 'Intellectualizing About the "Moon-Ghetto Metaphor"', *Policy Sciences* 5: 375–414.

Niskanen, W. (1973) *Bureaucracy: Servant or Master?* London: Institute of Economic Affairs.

Nystrom, Paul C. and William H. Starbuck (eds) (1981) *Handbook of Organizational Design*. Vol. 1, *Adapting Organizations to their Environments*; Vol. 2, *Remodelling Organizations and their Environments*. Oxford: Oxford University Press.

Nystrom, Paul C. and William H. Starbuck (1983) 'Pursuing Organizational Effectiveness that is Ambiguously Specified', in Kim S. Cameron and David A. Whetten (eds) *Organizational Effectiveness: A Comparison of Multiple Models*, pp.135–161. New York: Academic Press.

OECD (1982) *The Capacity to Budget: Adaptation of the Budget Process in OECD Countries*. Paris: Organization for Economic Cooperation and Development.

Payne, Alan (1982) 'The Review of R&D Support Services', *Management in Government* 37: 4.

Peacock, Alan (1983) 'Public X-inefficiency: Informational and Institutional Constraints', in Horst Hanuch (ed.), *Anatomy of Government Deficiencies*, pp. 125–38. Berlin: Springer Verlag.

Peat Marwick (1984) *Financial Management in the Public Sector*. London: Peat Marwick & Mitchell.

Perrow, Charles (1977) 'The Bureaucratic Paradox: The Efficient Organization Centralizes in order to Decentralize', *Organizational Dynamics* (Spring): 3–14.

Peters, Thomas J. and Robert H. Waterman (1982) *In Search of Excellence*. New York: Harper and Row.

Pliatzky, Sir Leo (1982) *Getting and Spending: Public Expenditure, Employment and*

Inflation. Oxford: Basil Blackwell.

Plowden, William (1981) 'Whate'er is Best Administered', *New Society* (9 April): 53–4.

Pollitt, Christopher (1984) *Manipulating the Machine*. London: George Allen and Unwin.

Pondy, Louis (1982) 'The Role of Metaphors and Myths in Organization and in the Facilitation of Change', in Louis R. Pondy, Peter J. Frost, Gareth Morgan and Thomas E. Dondridge (eds), *Organizational Symbolism*, pp. 157–66. Greenwich, Conn.: JAI Press.

Ponting, Clive (1985) *The Right to Know*. London: Sphere.

Public Money (1981) 'A Public Good?' (September).

Rayner, Sir Derek (1980) *Review of the Government Statistical Services: Report to the Prime Minister*. London: Efficiency Unit.

Rayner, Sir Derek (1982) *The Scrutiny Programme: A Note of Guidance by Sir Derek Rayner*. London: Management and Personnel Office.

Rayner, Lord (1983) The Business of Government, *The Administrator* (March): 3–6.

Richards, Sue (1985) 'Training for Policy Management' presented at a conference on policy analysis and training of public servants, EIPA, Maastricht.

Ridley, F.F. (1985) 'Political Neutrality and the British Civil Service: Sir Thomas More and Mr Clive Ponting v. Sir Robert Armstrong and the Vicar of Bray', in *Politics, Ethics and the Public Service*, pp. 31–42. London: RIPA.

Rogers, Everett M. and Joung-Im Kim (1985) 'Diffusion of Innovations in Public Organizations', in Richard L. Merritt and Anna J. Merritt (eds) *Innovation in the Public Sector*, pp. 85–108. Beverly Hills: Sage.

Rokeach, Milton (1960) *The Open and Closed Mind*. New York: Basic Books.

Ross, J.M. (1984) 'What Next Minister? Another Way of Looking at the Civil Service', *Studies in Public Policy* 127. Strathclyde: CSPP.

Russell, A.W. (1984) 'The Financial Management Unit of the Cabinet Office (MPO) and the Treasury', *Management in Government* 39: 2.

Schon, Donald (1963) 'Champions for Radical New Innovations', *Harvard Business Review* 41: 77–86.

Schon, Donald (1971) *Beyond the Stable State*. London: Maurice Temple Smith.

Schriesheim, Janet, Mary Ann Von Glinow and Steven Kerr (1977) 'Professionals in Bureaucracies: A Structural Alternative', in P.C. Nystrom and W.H. Starbuck (eds) *Prescriptive Models of Organizations*. Amsterdam: North-Holland.

Schumacher, Ernst Friedrich (1973) *Small is Beautiful*. New York: Harper and Row.

Scott, William G., Terence R. Mitchell and Newman S. Peery (1981) 'Organizational Governance', in Nystrom and Starbuck, Vol. 2, pp. 135–51.

Selznick, Philip (1957) *Leadership in Administration*. New York: Harper and Row.

Simmonds, Kenneth (1983) *The Fundamentals of Strategic Management Accounting*. Occasional Paper. London: JMCA.

Simon, Herbert A. (1957) *Administrative Behaviour* (2nd edn). New York: Macmillan.

Simon, Herbert A. (1961) *The New Science of Management Decision*. Englewood Cliffs, NJ: Prentice Hall.

Simon, Herbert A. (1962) 'The Architecture of Complexity', *Proceedings of the American Philosophical Society* 106: 467–82.

Simon, Herbert A. (1967) 'The Business School: A Problem in Organizational Design', *Journal of Management Studies* (February): 1–16.

Simon, Herbert A. (1973) 'Applying Information Technology to Organizational Design', *Public Administration Review* 3 (May-June): 268–78.

Sproull, Lee S. (1981) 'Beliefs in Organizations' in Nystrom and Starbuck (1981), Vol. II, pp. 203–24.

Starbuck, William H. (1965) 'Organizational Growth and Development', *Handbook of Organizations*, 451–533. Chicago: Rand McNally.

Starbuck, William H. (1975) 'Information Systems for Organizations of the Future', in E. Grochla and N. Szyperski (eds) *Information System and Organizational Structure*. Berlin: de Gruyter.

Staw, Barry (1977) 'The Experimenting Organization', *Organizational Dynamics* (Summer): 2–18.

Steel, David (1984) 'Government and the New Hybrids', in David Steel and David Heald (eds) *Privatizing Public Enterprises*, London: RIPA.

Stewart, Rosemary (1983) 'Managerial Behaviour: How Research Has Changed the Traditional Picture', in Michael J. Earl (ed.), *Perspectives on Management*, Oxford: Oxford University Press.

Strand, Torodd (1984) 'Public Management, Conceptual Issues and Research Suggestions', paper presented to a conference on Public Management in Europe. The Hague, The Netherlands.

Summerton, Neil (1980) 'A Mandarin's Duty', *Parliamentary Affairs* 33(4): 400–21.

Tarschys, Daniel (1985) 'Curbing Public Expenditure: Current Trends', *Journal of Public Policy* 5(1) 23–67.

Thomas, Ray (1984) 'The Critique of the Rayner Review of the Government Statistical Service', *Public Administration* 62(2).

Tricker, R.I. (1982) *Effective Information Management*. Oxford: Beaumont Executive Press.

Tricker, R.I. (1983) 'Perspectives in Corporate Governance', in Michael J. Earl (ed) *Perspectives in Management*, pp. 143–69. Oxford: Oxford University Press

Vickers, Sir Geoffrey (1970) *Value Systems and Social Process*. Harmondsworth: Penguin.

Wachter, Michael L. and Oliver E. Williamson (1978) 'Obligational Markets and the Mechanics of Inflation', *Bell Journal of Economics* 9(2): 549–71.

Weick, Karl E. (1976) 'Educational Organizations as Loosely Coupled Systems', *Administrative Science Quarterly* 21: 1–19.

Weick, Karl E. and Richard W. Daft (1983) 'The Effectiveness of Interpretation Systems' in Kim S. Cameron and David A. Whetten (eds) *Organizational Effectiveness: A Comparison of Multiple Models*. New York: Academic Press.

Wiener, Martin J. (1981) *English Culture and the Decline of the Industrial Spirit 1850–1980*. Cambridge: Cambridge University Press.

Wildavsky, Aaron (1972) 'The Self-Evaluating Organization', *Public Administration Review* (September-October): 509–520.

Wildavsky, Aaron (1975) *Budgeting: Comparative Theory of Budgetary Process*. Boston: Little Brown.

Wildavsky, Aaron (1978) 'Principles for a Graduate School of Public Policy', *Public Administration Bulletin* 26 (April): 12–31.

Wildavsky, Aaron (1979) 'Policy Analysis Is What Information Systems Are Not', in *The Art and Craft of Policy Analysis*, pp. 26–40. London: Macmillan.

Wilding, Richard (1982a) 'A Triangular Affair: Quangos, Ministers and MPs', in Barker (1982), pp. 34–43.

Wilding, Richard, (1982b), *Management Information and Control: The Role of the Centre*. London: RIPA.

Williams, Shirley (1980) 'The Decision-Makers', in *Policy and Practice: The Experience of Government*. London: RIPA.

Woodward, Joan (1965) *Industrial Organization: Theory and Practice*. Oxford:

Oxford University Press.

Wright, Maurice (1975) 'The Responsibility of the Civil Servant in Great Britain', *Public Administration* 23(4): 362–95.

Wright, Maurice (1980) *Public Spending Decisions: Growth and Restraint in the 1970s.* London: George Allen and Unwin.

Young, Stephen (1986) 'The Nature of Privatization in Britain 1979–1985', *West European Politics*, 9(2): 235–52.

Young, Hugo and Anne S. Sloman (1982) *No, Minister: An Inquiry into the Civil Service.* London: British Broadcasting Corporation.

Index

Index compiled by Peva Keane